000954

Hodgkiss Struthers

How To Get Out of This World Alive

The Introduction to Affective Realism

How To Get Out of This World Alive

The Introduction to Affective Realism

J. Hodgkiss Struthers

First Edition

MERRICONN BOOKS

How To Get Out of This World Alive
The Introduction to Affective Realism

J. Hodgkiss Struthers

Published by:

MERRICONN BOOKS, a division of MERRICONN GUIDANCE, INC.
Post Office Box 2713
Conroe, Texas 77305-2713 U.S.A.

Copyright © 1996 by J. Hodgkiss Struthers

Library of Congress Catalog Card Number: 96-94524
Struthers, J. Hodgkiss
    How to get out of this world alive: the introduction to affective realism / by J. Hodgkiss Struthers. — First Edition.
        p.   cm.
    Includes bibliographical references and index.
    ISBN 0-9652599-4-3 : $31.95

AHR 3432

Printed in the United States of America

Preface

If you were to ask me to describe the subject of this book in one sentence, it would have to be this: The subject of this book may very well be the greatest paradox that mankind has ever experienced. It's a case where man spent all of his days on this earth wondering about his existence; and then after a million or so years, he finds the answer staring him right in the face. Indeed, If man could get any closer to the paradoxical answer to his creation, he would have to step back and start searching again.

And too, there is a bit of irony concerning the subject of human existence. It lies in the way that young children will find it easier to understand the truth about human existence than it will be for many of the most intelligent adults in the human flock. One reason for this is that young children will have learned the truth about human existence before their social environments had a chance to contaminate their minds with the deluge of misconceptions which now stifle much of the adult human population on earth.

Most of the adult human minds on earth today are victims of misconception. In the advanced nations, many of the myths and invalid dogmas that were inherited from the past are now gone; but some slipped through the pages of time and are still with us today. One of these myths--the one which stands between us and our understanding of human existence--will be the major object of study in this book.

Acknowledgment

I have not attempted to cite all the sources and individuals that I have consulted in the preparation of this book. However, my indebtedness to scientists and other scholars who have gone before me will be clear to readers. One individual that is not so well known, but whom I have relied on heavily, is my wife of 50 years, Nell Struthers. Without her support, devotion, and encouragement, this book would have been much more difficult to complete. And finally, the diligence and effort of this book's editor, Gene Avery, is greatly appreciated. Thanks.

J. Hodgkiss Struthers

Table of Contents

Chapter One
Introduction To Affective Realism 9

Chapter Two
Some of Our Past 21

Chapter Three
The Mortal Domain 47

Chapter Four
The Trail of Reason 67

Chapter Five
The Table of Reason 135

Caboose 189

References 267

Index 271

WARNING / DISCLAIMER

Chapter One

Introduction To Affective Realism

OVERVIEW

You are going to find this book to be something like a train climbing a mountain. Each chapter likens to a boxcar in that it is filled with information that is essential to the trip, and at the end, you will find a section which we will be calling the caboose. From time to time, you will see numbers in brackets following words. These numbers are there to let you know that the caboose has further information about the subject which is being discussed on that line.

Perhaps you are wondering why the front cover of this book says, "For True Christians and Concrete Scientists." The reason for this is that one of the tracks leading up our intellectual mountain is for true Christians and the other is for concrete scientists. A true Christian is one who has made an authentic decision for Christ, and a concrete scientist is one who requires demonstrable causes and irrefutable facts. If you are a true

Christian, you may find that you have found out how to get out of this world alive when you get about half way through Chapter Four; if you are a concrete scientist, it may take a little longer; and if you are both a true Christian and a concrete scientist, it will probably be sooner. At any rate, by the time all of the readers have reached the end of the book, they will be moving on one track, which will be referred to as the Vector of Reason.

SECTION 1: WHAT PHILOSOPHIES ARE LIKE

It has been said that philosophy is the front line trench of science, suggesting that science does not stand paces behind philosophy, but is right there with it at the spot of inquiry. Behind the spot of inquiry lies the mass of scientific findings that have accumulated up to the present; in front of it lies the unknown. Whenever philosophy becomes the front line trench of science, it actually draws its substance and validation from the volumes of scientific information which lie behind, waiting to be expressed. This is an important understanding, because it shows that the philosophy which precedes a certain scientific effort is actually geared to it, and may not be just lifted out and moved to another location, for example, to some mystic persuasion. Like a rising balloon, the philosophy presented in this book--Affective Realism--will only work when it is accompanied by its scientific foundation.

Those of us who work in the sciences will sometimes stop to determine how well the ongoing investigation is fitting into the philosophical picture. Are the findings giving support to the philosophical premises; are they moving toward the philosophical goal? Or are they showing that the goal is unreal and out-of-reach, and that the entire philosophy may be nothing more than untenable nonsense? Is this construct [1] a real philosophy or is it just another fantasy? These are the questions which you the reader must ask as we move along.

There are numerous philosophy-science operations going

on all along the front line trench of science. Those that deal with matter and energy lie among the concrete sciences--such as biology, physics, chemistry, astronomy, and geology. Those that deal with human values will lie among the humanities--which include psychology, sociology, mathematics, philosophy, literature, and the English and foreign languages. Affective Realism draws its scientific information mainly from the concrete sciences, and to a lesser extent from the humanities.

SECTION 2: FIRST PERSON

While working thirteen years as a high school science teacher and eighteen years as a high school counselor, I came to rely on the first person form of expression (I, me, and we). It became one of my best tools for conveying constructs from my mind to the minds of the students. Using the first person in writing this book will also help me become more graphic when we come to the paradoxical understandings [2] which lie ahead.

SECTION 3: PHILOSOPHY AND RELIGION

The position taken in this book is that there are two ways of reaching actual truth. One way is through scientific investigation and the other is through religious worship. Each has done much to reveal the truth about human existence.

Plato and Aristotle. Imagine what the intellectual world was like back in the year 350 B.C. Aristotle (384-322 B.C.) was 34 years old and his teacher, Plato (427-347 B.C.), had three more years to live. In the mind of each of these men dwelled a compelling belief in a Supreme Being. In Plato's mind was a belief in a self-moved first cause; in Aristotle's mind was a reliance upon an unmoved-mover rather than a self-active first cause. There, three centuries back into the ancient world--that would be some 2350 years ago--the works of two of the world's most outstanding philosophers had begun. Two ancient philosophers, whose works spread across Greece and into the Roman Empire, and whose messages of a Supreme Being resounded throughout the intellectual world well before the time of Jesus--these same two philosophers were to have their works carry powerful influences into the new Western Civilization and the intellectual world which we know today. Not only did these influences fall upon the medieval Church, but in the case of Aristotle's work, the philosophy which was to become the front line trench of science began to fall into place. Scientific investigation had started to run its course.

However, Aristotle was preoccupied with deductive reason [3]. He had arrived at some general ideas which he thought to contain universal truths, and he regarded them as universals. From those universals, he derived ideas that became implicit in virtually every segment of Greco-roman society--in law, in science, in ethics, and in religion, to name a few. We can only marvel at how many of those ancient Aristotelian deductions [4] took hold and are still with us today, as with the syllogism used in our present judge and jury systems of justice.

Most scientists regard Aristotle as being the father of science. He initiated almost everything it takes to have a scientific procedure--methodical investigation, sensed data, cause and effect [5], and an evolving Natural world [184]. But he neglected to add two things that make concrete science work.

If you were to buy a new car, and then find that they had put kerosene in instead of gasoline and that it had no brakes, you would probably be disappointed with its performance. Aristotelian science was like that: it looked good but it would hardly run. Something was missing. And 1900 years would pass before scientists learned what it was. It seems that Aristotle was calling for deductive reason as the method of science when it should have been inductive reason. He became satisfied with the deduction of causes and demonstration of their effects, when he should have insisted upon the demonstration of both the causes and their effects.

At around the turn of the 17th Century, Francis Bacon

(1561-1626) set things straight, and while mathematics became the language of science, induction became its method of reason. It was then that demonstrable cause and effect [6] became the first principle of scientific investigation; concrete science had been born; and the deductive sciences were left to the humanities and some of the religious persuasions.

To find the influences which Plato and Aristotle had on the medieval Church, one should examine the works of Thomas Aquinas (1225?-1274). It was Aquinas who masterminded the integration between Aristotelian philosophy and Catholic theology. This integration led to the formation of the Church movement known as Scholasticism: it also became a basis for nearly all of modern Catholic theology.

A Plato-Aristotle Difference in View. Plato's works had some influence on the medieval Church, but not as much as Aristotle's. Plato's works had some influence on the development of Modern Education, but not as much as Aristotle's. Western Civilization became what it is largely because of these Plato-Aristotle influences. With this in mind, let us consider the difference in view which existed between Plato and Aristotle.

Plato placed great weight on the existence of ideas. He believed that ideas were permanent things that "stuck around" during mortal life and became involved in helping to create a new world--a world of ideas. He referred to that new world as "Reality," and the study of it as "realism." Aristotle, on the other hand, believed that ideas were fleeting things. He maintained that knowledge was the important thing to consider, because it could be deduced from the universals. Plato died in 347 B.C.--leaving twenty-five years for Aristotle to further his knowledge-centered line of reasoning, before dying himself.

Today, those of us who reside in Western Civilization can look around and see what this great development produced. One thing that seems to stand out is that a greater value is being placed on the knowledge which enters our minds than is being placed on the manner in which it gets there. Only today are we beginning to comprehend the role which an idea plays in the communication and retention of knowledge. Plato's manner of reason, which involves the generation of ideas, is a hand that has yet to be fully played. This brings us to a point where one can see what Affective Realism is all about: it is a philosophy which is attempting to play Plato's hand out.

Could It Be?   There was a period of about 350 years between the start of Aristotle's teaching and the birth of Jesus of Nazareth. There was a period of about 350 years between the writings of Francis Bacon and the arrival of plastics, television, and computers. I have often wondered how our advanced intellectual world would receive the teachings of Jesus, and how advanced his intellectual world would have been, had Aristotle put inductive reason into his science. Could it be that we are 2000 years late in playing Plato's hand? Could it be that it was the hand which Jesus was playing?

SECTION 4: THE THREE ELEMENTS OF HUMAN PERSONALITY

The three major elements of human personality have become the central considerations in three prominent lines of psychological investigation.   One of these lines is Psychoanalysis, where the elements are referred to as the *ego*, the *superego*, and the *id*.   The second line is Rogerian Psychotherapy, where the word meanings remain the same, but the names change, so that the ego becomes *cognition*, the superego becomes *affect*, and the id becomes *organismic*. And in similar fashion, the third line, Transactional Analysis, changes the ego to *adult*, the superego to *parent*, and the id to *child*. However, this third line moves rather quickly away from the study of individual behavior and into the study of the interpersonal relationship and group process. It is mentioned here only forasmuch as it addresses the actual elements of human personality.

Sigmund Freud (1856-1939) was the father of Psychoanalysis, and towards the end of his life, his studies moved in the direction of group process. If he had lived longer, he might have developed the basis upon which Transactional Analysis stands today. Eric Berne (1910-1970) fathered Transactional Analysis and Carl Rogers (1902-1987) began Rogerian Psychotherapy.

Human Feelings. The following table indicates some of the feelings-to-act that are produced when one of the three elements of human personality is dominating the mind.

FEELINGS-TO-ACT

State of Mind	Feelings Produced	
Psychoanalytical Approach		
ego state --	I was doing that.	I am doing this.
superego state --	I should do that.	I must do this.
id state --	I want that.	I want to do this.
Rogerian Psychotherapy		
cognitive state --	I was doing that.	I am doing this.
affective state --	I should do that.	I must do this.
organismic state --	I want that.	I want to do this.
Transactional Analysis		
adult state --	I was doing that.	I am doing this.
parent state --	I should do that.	I must do this.
child state --	I want that.	I want to do this

You will note that these three lines of investigation are all referring to the same elements of personality and the feelings which they produce. What we are doing in this study is to take the name of the original line of investigation or the one which students of human personality refer to most, and let it be the name of the overall approach to that aspect. In this case, where we are considering the lines that investigate the elements of personality, Sigmund Freud was the original investigator and Psychoanalysis was the name that he gave to it. So we will be using the term "Psychoanalysis" to represent all of the lines of investigation that are aimed at the three elements of personality. Thus you will understand what I mean when I say that this study has arrived at seven unique aspects of human personality and seven intellectual approaches to them, Psychoanalysis being one.

Eclectic View. Sometimes an investigator will work along two or more approaches at the same time and come up with a common intellectual ground from which to view human personality. This is referred to as an eclectic view. This study has noted that four of the approaches to human personality are viewing its configuration, hence we refer to them as being the four structural approaches. The other three approaches are viewing the functions of human personality, and they will be referred to as the functional approaches. We will be attempting to bring all seven of the approaches in to eclectic view, and in so-doing, be able to achieve a conceptualization of human personality. That will be referred to as the *eclectic display*.

SECTION 5: THE SEVEN APPROACHES TO HUMAN PERSONALITY

There are hundreds if not thousands of lines of investigation that pursue human personality. What we are holding to here is that each of them falls into one of the following seven approaches if its main criterion is demonstrable cause and effect:

Structural Approaches

1. Psychoanalytical
2. Biophysical
3. Existential
4. Phenomenological

Functional Approaches

5. Gestalt
6. Humanistic
7. Behavioral

The position taken in this study is that any line of investigation whose conceptual ground leads to demonstrable causes and effects will fall into one of these approaches. In other words, because we are working at the philosophical level, we don't have to deal with demonstrable causes and effects: we only need to have lines of reason which points to them. This is the value in having philosophy as a front line trench of science: it gives the concrete scientists a pretty good idea of where to look next. Affective Realism is a philosophy that gears to concrete science.

Acknowledgment.   These seven approaches to human personality are going to be our guideposts as we climb what will be referred to as the Trail of Reason. Grateful acknowledgment is given to the numerous students of human personality who have preceded us in blazing this trail; for had they not developed these seven approaches to guide us, the top of the "hill" and the eclectic view of human personality--the eclectic display--might still be beyond our grasp.

SECTION 6: SOME FINAL NOTES OF INTRODUCTION

Myths and Dogmas. It took me thirty-seven years to train my mind to ignore wrong myths and dogmas that were somehow picked up during childhood and when I was a young adult. Then, after working through most of those untruths, I was pleasantly surprised to find that what was taking me so long to master the subject matter in this book was not the matter itself, but it was those doggone myths and dogmas. What I found was that once I got past some of the myths and dogmas that people like Aristotle laid upon my forefathers [7], the subject matter in Affective Realism became very easy to comprehend.

The first principle of personal counseling is to listen and avoid probing. I am not here with you to listen to your reactions as you read this book. Therefore, I have no way of knowing whether the words in this book are probing into a part of your thinking that had better be left alone. This is something that you the reader must be alert to. If while reading this book, or even when you are thinking about reading it, you get nervous or anxious, then stop and discuss your feelings with others. And they don't have to be professional students of human personality. That might become necessary when one fails to heed nervous or anxious warning signals; but if the problem is that this book is threatening some myths and dogmas that are holding your world up, then discuss the situation with those who share such myths and dogmas with you, and either adjust to the truth of things or stand firm against it as part of a group; for it is better to endure a world of nonbeing with members to support you than it is to suffer such naked folly alone.

In this day and time, it is essential that those who stand with truth stand together, and that those who stand with invalid myths and dogmas stand responsible for the delusions they create. This is the time when the upholders of truth will make the intellectual call to the Fold of Reality.

Mental Health. Roughly fifty percent of the American adult population have either had mental health problems or are having them now. This book has been developed for use by people who are operating in the normal-range of mental health; so it is important that it not be thrust upon unsettled minds unless it is part of a therapeutic program which is overseen by a licensed professional student of human personality [8].

For True Christians and Concrete Scientists. My knowledge of Middle Eastern, Eastern, and Oriental religions is practically nothing. The same goes for all of the new persuasions that are emerging today. Concerning the reading of this book, I could not advise the members of those orders, except to say that if they are not interested in pursuing the teachings of Jesus Christ, then they should consider following the concrete science track. Either way, they will arrive at the truth of human existence.

The reason this book is specified for true Christians and concrete scientists is that those are the ones who appear to have freed themselves of most of the nonbeing myths and dogmas concerning humanity and what it is all about. If there are other religions that meet this specification, then their consolidation with true Christianity is certainly inevitable.

Three Jobs to Do. I have three jobs to do in writing this book. The first job is to reaffirm the real existence of Almighty God and Christ. The second job is to provide a God-oriented philosophy that will help bolster the existing front line trench philosophy of concrete science. And the third job is to call all mankind to the Fold of Reality. What I have come to see in writing this book is how the thing called human personality exists in the Universe, and will continue to exist in the Grand Scheme of Things. With these things in mind, I ask that you come with me along this book's pathway of reason and join in giving call to the Fold of Reality.

All reasoning humans will get out of this world alive. The question is, what will they be free to do after that happens?

Chapter Two

Some of Our Past

SECTION 1: EVENTS LEADING TO THE BIRTH OF HUMANISM

Scholasticism began in the 9th century and declined in the 16th century. Plato's philosophy was somewhat involved during the early part of the Scholastic Movement, but Aristotle's philosophy became more and more turned to as the centuries passed. Upon the arrival of the 13th century, Scholasticism had come under the full control of a rationale based upon Aristotelian philosophy and Catholic theology. As the 16th century approached, the rationale came under attack, and Scholasticism began its decline.

Scholasticism declined but it has yet to go completely away. During the Middle Ages, it reached its high point in spreading Aristotelian logic and Church theology to every place where Catholic influence was in effect. That included most of Europe.

Doctors, university people, and Church personnel gathered into an intellectual higher circle from which the Scholastic rationale would rain down and into the lives of the people. There it took hold, making deduction its method of reason and Christian ideals and principles its system of universals. These universals became implanted in the mind of the individual and accounted for much of his or her superego. To a large extent, Aristotelian logic became the cognitive system [9] for bringing the individual's superego into harmony with his or her id. This is what Scholasticism was doing: it was controlling the interplay between the three major elements of human personality.

It is hard to think that there in the distant past the members of Scholasticism would have the same understanding of human personality that we have today. We can only imagine them looking at the people in the street and saying....Hey! Everything's going down the drain. The people have lost their morality. They have lost their ability to tell right from wrong and good from bad. They have no goals, no principled behavior, no ideals to guide them. They are suffering from a dangerous reduction in superego strength. If we don't turn to the works of Plato and Aristotle and get some help in implanting Christian ideals and principles to raise their superego strength, their superegos will disappear completely, and they will not be able to live responsible lives. If this happens we will again become prey for the barbarians.

As it turned out, the Scholastics did turn to the works of Plato and Aristotle. They developed a rationale which was valid enough to bring the Church and Western Civilization up and out of the Dark Ages. And serving as the political counterpart, the Holy Roman Empire joined in the action.

During the 16th century, an army of scholars noted that after lengthy education, students were being graduated with good ability in reading, in arithmetic, in singing, in spelling, in writing, in the recall of knowledge, and in reciting the works of others; but they lacked the ability to generate original ideas. What happened? What was missing? The scholars pondered. Then one of them, Francois Rabelais (1483?-1553), wrote about a mythical graduate called Gargantua.

The army of scholars began to attack Scholasticism, charging that it had serious errors in its curriculum and teaching methods. This garnered sentiment among many Catholics, and eventually fueled them with enough nerve to leave the Church. The developments which led to the Thirty Years' War (1618-1648) were on the make.

Concerning this inability to generate original ideas, it took the rest of the 16th century and part of the 17th before possible answers began to arrive. Rene Descartes (1596-1650) was among the first in modern times to place importance on human ideas. To many, he stepped out on a weak limb when he maintained that ideas arrive innately. Nevertheless, the very fact that he considered ideas, together with his mathematical and philosophical contributions, earned him the title, Father of the Modern Era.

The Birth of Humanism. Remember those cold, hard winters and the first days of spring which would always seem to follow? Remember when you would walk onto the lawn and feel the warm sun on your back and hear the birds singing; and see the trees in bud, the crocuses in bloom, the grass starting up all over again? Remember how revived you felt on those spring days? If you do, then you know how some 16th century Christians felt when they broke free from the Catholic Church's "shackles" and moved out from under the dark cloud of authority that lurked behind, ready to pounce. What they were experiencing was not the feeling of revival, as you had, but rather it was a feeling which was entirely new to them. It was the feeling of being a free human for the first time, a feeling of being free to begin life anew.

This new feeling of spiritual freedom quickly spread; and before long, the Lutheran Church became the first Protestant Denomination. It was first not only in worship by self-actualizing [10] humans, but first to lend praise and rejoice in the new-felt Humanism--free to sing in the vernacular, free to understand their song. And while all of this was going on in religion, a similar socialization was taking place in the secular lives of Protestants and those who were just happy to be free from bad religious experiences. Back then in the first half of the 16th century the secular form of Humanism was also under way. Bolstered by that army of scholars whose spirit and vigor made it soon to become a movement, and then a philosophy, Humanism was to become the philosophy which laid much of the foundation for the works of Francis Bacon, Michael Eyguem, Lord of Montaigne (1533-1592), John Amos Comenius (1592-1671), and Jean Jacques Rousseau (1712-1778) [11]. In that it reflects from what it is actually like to be human, Humanism has revealed a unique dimension for psychologists to consider, and because of this, it has become recognized as one of the several approaches to human personality.

The roots of Humanism extend back into the 15th century when, in Italy, it was devised by the upper class as an approach to patrician [12] education. However, the main thrust of the Humanistic Movement came when the army of scholars launched their attacks against the Church in the 16th century. That was when people left the Church in droves and joined the Protestant Reformation, and when others turned to classical literature and art. That was also the time when the Renaissance (14th-17th centuries) came in to full bloom and when the period of New Learning got under way.

The New Learning. Back during the first half of the 16th century, the army of scholars had become agreed on one definition of Humanism--that it is the study of unmolested human nature [13]. What happened was that they saw three different ways in which this study could be carried out. When seen as one, the three different ways was called the *New Learning*. Yet in practice, the army of scholars divided into three different groups.

Each group in the New Learning was composed of students of human nature who had similar beliefs as to how the New Learning should be carried out. One group believed that the

New Learning should be based on Scripture and the teachings of Jesus Christ. This group of humanists became associated with the Protestant Reformation; and in England, its curriculum became known as the doctrines of the Reformation. The second group in the New Learning consisted of humanists who were still clinging to the belief that all true knowledge and art should come from the ancient Greek and Roman cultures. This group of humanists--let us call them the back-looking humanists--gave rise to the 16th century Renaissance, when the revival of ancient literature and art was abundant yet faced with the discovery of the New World in the Americas. The third group in the New Learning was comprised of humanists who believed that some of the ancient past was worth considering, but certainly not enough to become justified as an educational system in itself. This group--the front-looking humanists--began to consider such things as individuality, pragmatic behavior, and man's relationship with Nature. This was the branch of the New Learning that laid the foundation for the 17th and 18th century philosophers who we mentioned earlier.

Martin Luther (1483-1546) and Peter Ramus (1515-1572). Martin Luther's fame may seem to have come from the fact that he reacted to the sale of indulgences by the Catholic Church and to some of the absurdities that were being uncovered in Scholasticism's curriculum, teaching methods, rituals, and needless authority. Reacting to these things may seem to be the cause of his great fame, but put yourself back there along with him and many of the other 16th century Christians. They were viewing the works of Aristotle as being the mountain of intellect and the Catholic Church as the mere bridge connecting it to the Christian ideals and principles. When Luther called Aristotle an accursed heathen, a damnable heathen, and denounced him completely, he was hitting at the giant whose name Catholics held in awe. This was the action which brought him the greatest fame back then, and to some, even today.

Peter Ramus was perhaps the most fiery of the army of scholars. He was always lashing out at the Catholic Church and

Scholasticism...so much so, in fact, that he drew wrath from both the Church and the King of France. Nevertheless, he awakened to the idea of the individual being free from the shackles, free to explore the Universe, free to live love and to think truth as he or she knew it. It was around the time of this awakening that the front-looking Humanism fell into place, and if I had to call someone its father, it would no doubt be Peter Ramus. He had completely severed all ties to the Church and Aristotle and was intellectually free to help chart the future for front-looking Humanism. In his masters thesis, Ramus insisted that everything that Aristotle said is untrue.

There were some misconceptions back during the first half of the 16th century. One was when Martin Luther called Aristotle a damnable heathen. Both of my dictionaries give the religious definition of a heathen as being a Godless person, and they give the secular definition of a heathen as being an uncultured person. Well, Aristotle was certainly no religious heathen. How could he be, when he was involving God as the First Cause of every bit of matter with form in the Universe? And as for Aristotle being a secular heathen, he was one of the leaders of a respectable Greek culture--a culture which draws respect even today.

It appears clear that Martin Luther's departure from the Catholic Church was justifiable, but his condemnation of Aristotle was understandably obtuse. By that I mean that while Luther's exiting from the Catholic Church was understandable, his condemnation of Aristotle was only partly correct. Aristotle was wrong on many things, but not on the Law of Cause and Effect [14] and placing importance on sense data. Next to putting deductive reason in as the method of reason in the biological and physical sciences, Aristotle's biggest mistake was to cling to the *colossal myth*--which holds that Actuality and Reality are the same thing. And of course not even Martin Luther thought to condemn that; except possibly on spiritual ground.

As for Peter Ramus saying that everything Aristotle said is untrue, I can only imagine. He was living in a mostly Catholic country--France. He attended college in Paris. Later, he attended and taught at the University of Paris; and he wrote grammars in Latin, Greek, and French. He had at his disposal everything it took to evaluate copies of the original works of Aristotle, thus we may assume that he did just that.

One cannot argue the possibility that Ramus found numerous errors in Aristotle's work. I am neither a student of history nor of philosophy, and yet I know of some errors that Aristotle made. The very fact that Ramus was using Aristotelian errors as his master's thesis at the most prestigious University in a Catholic country speaks well for the possibility that Aristotle made irrefutable errors. If Ramus hadn't made a good case in his master's thesis, you and I might not be reading about him today. But as things turned out, he was allowed to teach college in France for at least thirty years before being murdered in his study.

SECTION 2: BACKING UP INTO THE ANCIENT WORLD

Miletus Thales (640-546 B.C.) has been viewed as the founder of Greek astronomy and philosophy. His undertaking was frequently a matter of denying or confirming ideas that were brought down from the past, for example, that the stars are holes in the sky that were pierced by great archers, or that the sailors should not go out too far else they fall off. Some of those absurd ideas were filtered away by Thales and others who came after him, but some stayed on as part of popular belief. For instance, the belief that sailors would fall off if they went out too far lasted clear into the Middle Ages, when, in 1492, Columbus proved otherwise.

Socrates (469-399 B.C.) was a market square teacher and philosopher who walked about, giving people explanations of things they were interested in--mainly, things about religion and politics. A bald and chubby man in old clothes, whose own interests were in the "why's" of human existence--Socrates explained things as he saw them, and that put him into "hot water." Many of the citizens of Athens got the notion that he was telling things that were contrary to popular belief; so for fear that he would spread such outrageous nonsense and contaminate the minds of youth, they took action against him. He was arrested, convicted of impiety and innovation, and placed in prison. There, he was made to drink the hemlock juice which ended his life. However, much of his insight was carried on by one of his students--Plato.

Plato (427-347 B.C.) and Aristotle (384-322 B.C.) made up another teacher-student team. In 350 B.C., Plato was seventy-seven (77) years old and Aristotle was thirty-four (34) years old. Plato was to live three more years. With this background in mind, let us try a supposition. Let us suppose that Plato called Aristotle into his office and after they had become seated, Plato said:

Concerning the Validity of Reason

Aristotle, I have called you in here because there is an extremely important matter for us to discuss. Your intellectual ability is outstanding, and I am sure it will show in your writings. I am confident that your thinking will be carried on through many centuries of human progress. However, there is one aspect of your philosophy which I consider to be an immense blunder, and if you do not take steps to correct it right now, the more enlightened people of the future will drop your work like a hot leg of lamb.

Here is where I think your blunder lies. It is in the way you propose doing science. Much of your science is valid. You provide for experimentation, you make use of the senses to verify facts, and you are making use of the two universals which Socrates and I have considered irrefutable--the Law of Cause and Effect and an evolution wherein that which survives is good. Your blunder is not in these things, but in the way you handle these and other things in all of your writings. Allow me to explain.

In my hand is one of your science essays. In it, you say that flies are produced by garbage pails. If you look out the window, you will see a garbage pail on the other side of the street. Let's walk out there and examine that garbage pail.

Here we are. The owners of this garbage pail have gone to the mountains for the summer, so I took the opportunity to test your scientific conclusion that garbage pails produce houseflies. Looking at all of the flies around, it certainly appears that your conclusion is valid. However, perhaps we should not jump to conclusions before exploring other possibilities.

Look down at the bottom of the pail. You will note that there is only one housefly on the bottom and that there are no others flying around inside the pail. Watch that fly. There! It just dropped something. No, it's not that. This is a different color. Let's let the fly escape, and then fasten this wax paper over the top, so that other things can't get in. Now we will wait three days. [Three days pass.]

Well I'll be darned! That little speck turned into a tiny worm. [Three more days pass.]

Now the worm has turned into something with a scab around it. [And three more days pass.]

So what do you see? It's a housefly. You have just witnessed the metamorphic system of reproduction.

That garbage pail didn't produce the new housefly. The old fly did. And I think that if you will examine closer, you will find that only females drop that kind of speck.

Aside from developing the idea of metamorphosis of the housefly, what else did we learn from this experiment? One thing that you learned, Aristotle, is that you can't always trust your deductions. Your deduction that garbage pails produce houseflies is completely wrong, and yet you had it already written up and were prepared to send it out to the people as being a statement of actual truth. How many other erroneous deductions have you made?

This brings us to the blunder which I think you are making. It has nothing to do with your deductive method of reasoning. Your system of deduction from such valid universals as the Law of Cause and Effect and the good-bearing evolution is itself valid, providing you do not allow human error to creep into the picture. For instance, you wrongly assumed that the garbage pail did something which it was incapable of doing. In concrete science, one must not assume anything in his or her concluding thoughts: there, the assessments must always be predicated upon demonstrable facts. What you did was to make deductive reasoning the method in all of the sciences. When you did that, you removed yourself from the practice of concrete science and entered into a line of investigation which does not require the demonstration of cause and effect. Deductive science fits that bill, and although it might be useful in the social studies, it has no place in the biological and physical sciences. They require a method which first demonstrates a cause and its effect, and then goes on to generalize about it. That is what concrete science is all about: it reasons from the particular thing to the general idea in a method known as inductive reason. That is your blunder. You have the wrong kind of reasoning in the sciences which require demonstrated cause and effect.

We used inductive reason in discovering the metamorphic reproduction of the housefly. As a result, we not only found your garbage pail deduction to be an error, but in finding the principle of metamorphosis we moved human progress noticeably ahead. Just imagine what an impact it would have on human progress if you were to use inductive reason to evaluate all of your biological and physical science deductions, and maybe some of your social science deductions as well.

Concerning Philosophy

For as much as our philosophies concern human personality, the core of my philosophy centers upon ideas, whereas the core of your philosophy centers upon knowledge. What it will amount to in the centuries which lie ahead is that my philosophy may turn a few heads, but it will not become meaningful to large groups of people until your science has gone before and revealed most of the principles and Laws of Nature. After that is done, then what I have to say concerning the paradoxical nature of human ideas will be easy to comprehend. Therefore, I urge you to place inductive reason into your science and evaluate as many of your deductions as possible. If you do not do this, then your works will fall, and they may drag mine down with them.

Concerning Predictions

As I see it, there are two predictions which can be made at this time. The first one is that if you make the corrections of which I speak, then your great deductive ability will provide the people with meaningful knowledge in such social areas as politics, logic, and ethics. Furthermore, your science will reveal most of the principles and Laws of Nature. And after that is done, then my philosophy may be brought to bear. All things considered, from start to finish, this process would take about 350 years. You and I would not be around; so we must do our very best to make our works error-free.

The second prediction is that if you do not make

the corrections of which I speak, then your great deductive ability will help the people to become good and orderly citizens for a while. This would last for about two hundred years. But then, the people's grasp of the universals and the First Cause would wane--due to your erroneous deductions and lack of inductive science--and they would be reduced to a gathering which centers on gladiators and pagan gods. This too would take about 350 years to happen.

Concerning the Jewish Movement

Recall our discussions on Abraham (1996-1821? B.C.)--progenitor of the Jews? He began a movement in which all of the members recognized the one real God. This is much like what you and I have: we both believe in the one real First Cause, although we differ somewhat on what we think It or He is and can do. But when you come right down to it, you and I and the Jews are all believing in the same thing if we can agree that God Almighty is the one Real God.

Recall also what the Jews have been saying about some member of the Tribe of Judah arriving to help human progress along if need be? I think that the entire Jewish movement has been created to act as a fail-safe in the event that our works are not successful. And so, to continue my prediction, that is exactly what would happen if our works were to fall. The fail-safe would place the entire thrust of Jewish history into a religious movement designed to guide mankind to its Maker. Realizing the need for reason, the members of this new religion would turn to your works, and mine; however, they would not possess enough concrete knowledge to handle my message regarding the paradoxical nature of ideas. Hence, for the most part, they would be dealing with your works.

Even if your works were to fall in 350 years,

they would still be the dominant influence upon those who remain intellectually inclined. This would be because your thinking cornered the intellectual market, if you will, and the new Real God-oriented religion would have no other place to turn to for reason. At the same time, I can understand how the providers of this new religion--the Jews--would turn away from your works as a source of reason and wait until something better comes along; for after all, your works would have already failed once. Nevertheless, if the Jews should decide to disregard your error-ridden and blunderous works as a resource for reason and elect to wait for something better to come along; furthermore, if the social conditions along the Mediterranean rim should decline to a level which threatens the survival of humanity, let alone its progress, then it seems entirely probable that the Supreme Being will intervene and provide something to put humanity back on track.

So you see, you and I are left in a quandary. If in about 350 years your works should fall, then the Jews would have to go in one of two ways. The problem right now is to determine which of these two ways my prediction should go. Should it follow along with the Jews, assuming that they will gear to your works and, as they go, correct your works' blunder and errors while pursuing the one Real God; or should it follow along with the intervening actions by our one Real God. What it will boil down to is whether or not the Jews will realize that religion without reason is to leave Reality's pathway to God.

The Jewish history shows them to have been a wholesome lot whose dedication to God has been outstanding. The question is, when are they going to awaken to the need for reason? At this very instant, they are living a little over 200 miles across the Sea in Canaan, yet they have done little to gear to our reasoning in Athens. But we cannot blame that on them: we must blame it on you; for you have not corrected your errors and made your work irresistible to them. So as for which way my prediction should travel, it will go with the intervention which the Supreme Being will make if you do not correct the errors in your works.

I am sure that if humanity is made to follow this new way, it will be one which involves worship, reason, the true Reality, and Almighty God. There would be no room for pagans and self-serving agents of God.

Permit me to conclude this prediction with an allegory whose symbols will become grounded as history unfolds.

SECTION 3: AN ALLEGORY SUPPOSEDLY WRITTEN BY PLATO

THE RUN OF ALL RUNS

Think, if you will, of a chariot whose right horse[1] was blind. This would mean that the left horse[2] had to see where the team [15] was going.

The chariot driver started the run[3], not knowing that the right horse was unable to see[4]. And to his great dismay, he further learned that the horse on the right was not only blind, but that it had arthritis and a damaged hoof [5] as well.

As the run progressed, these ills affected the harmony of the team, and when the chariot approached the halfway point, its pace was near to a halt. This infuriated some of the passengers[6]--so much so, in fact, that they jumped off and ran onto the field[7]. It happened then, that one[8] of them stopped to ponder and several others[9] grouped to ponder as well.

Thinking things through, the first ponderer built his own chariot[10], hooked it up to a team of fresh, young horses, and started running down the track[11]. The group of ponderers divided into three lots. The first lot[12]--eyeing the first ponderer's chariot--started to run after it and went aboard; the second lot[13] looked back to see where they were coming from, and they stayed; and the third lot[14] looked ahead to see where they should go, and they pondered.

Meanwhile, the driver of the original chariot began to doctor the blind horse--taking great care to eliminate some of its arthritis, but doing little to help the damaged hoof. Then, guiding the chariot back onto the track, he resumed the run.

Noting that two chariots were on the track, others[15] began to build, and soon there were many chariots in the run. As the speeding chariots disappeared ahead, the third lot began to walk after them; but for the dust[16] they hung well onto the field. Then they came upon a sign saying, "Think Up!"[17] This startled them, and after pondering a while, they started back to walking. But then they came upon another sign saying, "Think Up!" I say, "Think Up!" Upon this, they pondered again, and finally decided to try thinking up. That was what they did; and thereafter the side-watchers[18] called them the field-thinkers[19].

At first, the field-thinker manner was to look down at the earth[20] and think; and then, thinking all the while, they would turn their heads to the sky and think harder. But nothing happened.

Finally, it dawned on the field-thinkers that they were doing something wrong; so they experimented; and in almost no time, they learned how to think. It was to look down at the earth thinking, and, grabbing handfuls of earth, thrust them to the sky, thinking even harder. With this came flashes of light, and to their joy, the earth in each hand turned to good; and on each good[21] was a label saying, "Now you have it.

Run with it." To this they responded by gathering a large pile[22] of goods. Indeed, it was so large that once again they felt need to ponder.

The field-thinkers reasoned, and it soon became clear that in order to carry a pile of goods that size, they would have to build a landcraft with a sail[23], and they did. Loading the pile onto the landcraft, they began to push, but that was too draining and slow; and it happened that, while they were sitting almost in doze[24], one of them incidentally created a good; and he marveled at how, when the flash came, a puff of wind[25] did as well--even to move his hand. This brought all of them to quick thinking, and, yes, they pondered.

Thus it became known to all around that by turning handfuls of earth to the sky a wind would move against the sail, and as handfuls came faster the wind would also blow harder. Hence, by working at high vigor, the field-thinkers were able to bring so many flashes that the landcraft sped at top maximum and night turned into day[26].

Upon learning of these wonders--speed, power, light, and seemingly an infinite number of other goods-- the side-watchers hooted and danced with joy. Some of them jumped aboard the fieldcraft, while others had reveries on how they could use these things and become money-grabbers and game-makers and dol- lar-women and leeches upon mankind. The remain- ing few became teaching field-thinkers, and they traveled to all other tracks and fields on earth and taught at how to be a field-thinker.

And it came to pass, that because all pieces of good give word as to where a track should be headed[27], many other tracks on earth turned toward the field- thinkers.

Meanwhile, the landcraft was zooming along, but neared to a halt when ahead stood the driver of the original chariot hailing for help. One field-thinker asked, "Is something wrong?" "Yes," replied the driver, "the blind horse is too down to go on. He has two bad eyes and one bad hoof." "No problem, no problem at all," said the field-thinker. Leaning back to the pile, he picked out two horse eye goods and one horse hoof good, and took them over to the blind horse. But just as he was about to apply the horse eye goods, he stopped to say, "There is no wrong in this horse's eyes. Its problem is that wrongs' from the rest of its body have covered and blocked its vision." And for the taking off of the wrongs[28], the horse turned to the field-thinker and whinnied an abounding horse-felt thanks[29].

Then the field-thinker started to apply the horse hoof good to the bad hoof; but there again, he found no wrong with the hoof, except that someone had put the shoe on backward. After putting the shoe on the hoof correctly[30], the field-thinker asked if anything else was wrong. "Yes," the driver responded, "this horse has arthritis." "No problem, no problem at all," said the field-thinker; and he leaned back for a horse arthritis good. And once again, upon approaching the horse, it became evident that it did not have arthritis, but that its entire body was covered with skin wrongs. "Here!" he called to the driver, "help me take these things off." When it was done, the driver gave thanks, leaped aboard the original chariot, and whisked away to resume the run.

Churning Earth as never before, the field-thinkers and the fieldcraft finally caught up to the now-swift original chariot, and onward they sped in pursuit of the other chariots. Soon the overtake was complete, and all acted pleased to be abreast. It was at this point that one of the drivers yelled out, "The bridge! The bridge[31]!" And not only were they all pleased, but they became thankful as well.

The yell brought everyone up to quick-thinking--including those in doze and those in slumber[32]. Then one of the drivers spoke out, "The bridge is so close and tight[33], and the track even now is narrowing upon it[34]." This gave great concern to all of the passengers and to all of the drivers and to all of the field-thinkers; and as they pondered, the side-watchers winked[35] as if to ask, "What are you going to do now, good-getters[36]?"

The good-getters went on pondering, until a passenger on the right remarked, "We have company." Then a passenger on the left said the same; and soon, there were thousands of chariots approaching upon a score of different tracks; and each new passenger and each new driver declared himself and herself a good-getter. Now, the problem had become so big that not even pondering could say as to which chariot should go first across the bridge and on to the finish line.

This prompted one of the field-thinkers to rise and head for the bridge--to see what it would take to solve the problem. And as he was walking, the driver of the original chariot stood up before the throng and with a loud, deep voice said, "I never met the Man[37]. He was taken about forty years before we started to build this original chariot. But I did see the Wise Man[38], and he had this to say about our problem, 'The Man is building a track for you to follow straight to the bridge; and it is good that you will have it to use; for you will be passing low side-watchers who will be much the same as those you see around you here--money-grabbers and game-makers and dollar-women and leeches upon mankind. Hold to the words of the Man and your trip will succeed.

    Your biggest problem will not be here, or along the way, but at the end, when you must decide which chariot will go first across the bridge and on to the finish line.

What I suggest is that you build a chariot which is more narrow than the bridge, but as long as need be to hold all of the passengers[39]--who will then be known as good-getters. This way, when you arrive at the bridge, all you will have to do is unlock the gate, pass over the bridge, travel the short distance to the finish line, and enter into the Greater Reality[40] and eternal life. All will be first: none will be last.'"

Hearing this message from the Wise Man, the entire throng became exuberant and entered into fellowship and likeness of reason; and they began to tear down the old chariots and build the one which would carry them across.

It was then that the field-thinker returned from checking the bridge. "The bridge looks fine," he said, "but it has a locked gate[41] and it must be unlocked before we can get across. And too, this poster was fastened to the gate. Allow me to read it to you: 'Welcome good-getters. You finally made it. But before you may cross, you must produce the key[42] which will unlock the gate. We gather that you have brought with you a pile of goods, and that from it the field-thinkers will develop the key. We suggest that they start by taking two key goods from the pile: one will be labeled *down vision*[43] and the other will be labeled *forward vision*[44.] Then take them to the center throng, set them on the Earth[45], and wait.'" And they did.

The field-thinker continued to read: "Now all who are good-getters must approach and touch[46] the down vision good with the right hand and the forward vision good with the left; and as they walk away, they will be carrying one of each the same." They did and it happened.

The field-thinker read further: "Now the good-getters should place their down vision goods on the Earth before them and observe the true Earth below. What they will see is the Earth as it is today[47]; and they will note that it looks like a sea shore, where land comes upon beach and beach comes upon water. However, they may be surprised when they learn that by its nature the down vision good is made to focus upon human intelligence rather than land, upon human philosophy rather than beach, and upon the unknown rather than water." At this, the good-getters marveled and the side-watchers smirked with smiles of displeasure.

"There are two more things to cover," the message continued, "one is that the field-thinkers must now grasp the yo-yo rings atop their forward vision goods and lower[48] them into the philosophy below; but first, they must write a short note requesting that a key be made to unlock the bridge gate. Then slip the note into the side-pouch and lower away." And they did.

The field-thinker returned to his reading of the poster, "The second thing to cover has to do with the red glow[49] in the distance. That glow is caused by side-watchers who trained to be field-thinkers, but somehow went astray. Their thinking has become warped, and instead of creating goods, they are creating bads[50]; instead of working with the way of the Earth, they are working against it; hence, when they dip into the Earth, they bring up bads--whose nature is not to do service, but to destroy, and whose contribution is nothing but to fizzle into a puff of red smoke[51]. You who are not working the down-to-philosophy goods should go over there and see for yourself. You will find them lifting normal, healthy babies out of the wombs and making them to lie in piles until they are almost dead, and then out of certain parts they produce new babies. Those quacksters[52] will argue that the mothers didn't want the babies and that all they were doing was to take from unwanted babies and build babies that others would want. But in doing this, their callousness has presumed upon the Maker and His Earth's Process and Way; and although their rewards may now be counted in money, their end net will be to lie in their warpness and enjoy the doom which they have just begun. Counsel those quackster imposters; bring them from warpness to reason and into the range of decency. And to convince them of their folly, you should inform them that you have yourself been to the bridge, and that the gate is locked; and even now, the field-thinkers are developing the key. Explain that they too may become good-getters, but only after coming to reason and decency and respect for the Earth's Process and Way. Tell them that if they do this, they may then go to the center of the throng, touch the two goods, then join you in sending this message in note to their counterparts below. And then tell them to go to all other red glows on the horizon and do as you will have just done. If you all do these things, then the end of humanity on earth may be delayed for as much as a thousand years; and even then, if reason and decency prevail, and if the Maker wills, it could be longer than that."

Then during the quiet which followed, a passenger turned to the returning field-thinker and asked, "The poster began by giving welcome to us--the good-getters--and then it went on to give a message. Is there no more message on the other side?" The field-thinker turned the other side and held it high. It said, "Welcome Plato."

END

THE RUN OF ALL RUNS LEGEND

1.	chariot	Catholic Church
	right horse	Aristotle's works
2.	left horse	Christian ideals, principles, and goals
3.	driver	Catholic theology
	run	Christian religion
4.	see	Aristotelian universals concealed
5.	arthritis	lack of internal harmony
	damaged hoof	ineffective scientific method
6.	passengers	Catholic Christians
7.	field	Reality
8.	one	Martin Luther
9.	others	roots of Humanism
10.	chariot	Lutheran Church
11.	track	Christianity, Christian direction, or way
12.	first lot	first Protestants, first Lutherans
13.	second lot	Renaissance leaders, back-looking humanists
14.	third lot	Modern Humanism, front-looking humanists
15.	others	Protestant Denominations
16.	dust	Supernatural Dogmas, disregard for Nature
17.	Think-Up!	Use inductive reason!
18.	side-watches	unreligous citizens
19.	field-thinkers	concrete scientists
20.	earth	Nature
21.	handfuls	actual use of inductive reason
	to the sky	bring particular ideas up for evaluation
	flashes	awakening
	light	enlightenment
	good	irrefutable truth, scientific fact
22.	large pile	accumulation of scientific information
23.	landcraft	organized science, an approach to truth
	sail	readiness for support
24.	doze	waiting for new scientific frontiers
25.	wind	technology
26.	top maximum	beginning of modern science
	day	beginning of the Enlightenment
27.	be headed	Natural procession, romance with Nature
28.	wrongs	Aristotelian errors
29.	thanks	valid parts of Aristotle's works shown
30.	correctly	putting inductive reason into science
31.	bridge	Actuality-Reality Interface
32.	slumber	inactive students of science or religion
33.	close and	requiring highly specialized science and
	tight	technology

34.	narrowing upon it	religious anticipation of scientific progress
35.	winked	reflecting oblivion to what was happening
36.	good-getters	anyone who accepts truth and Actuality
37.	Man	Jesus of Nazareth
38.	Wise Man	Apostle Paul
39.	passengers	all who have accepted truth and Actuality
40.	finish line Greater Reality	realization of self Greater Reality
41.	locked gate	beyond the usual understanding of Reality
42.	key	paradoxical understanding of Reality
43.	down vision	grounding down to actualization
44.	forward vision	seeing what to do next
45.	Earth	allegorical symbol for Nature
46.	touch right left	psychological suggestion to act specifically toward one good specifically toward the other good
47.	today	the day one reads this line
48.	lower	suggestion to return to actualization
49.	red glow	alarm
50.	bads	unnatural circumstances
51.	red smoke	unnatural deeds
52.	quacksters	physicians violating the hippocratic oath

This marks the end of the section dealing with the relationship between philosophy and religion. It is important for you to understand, however, that this book contains no quotations from Plato or his works. Every reference which this book makes to Plato is mostly a product of my imagination, and follows upon the supposition of what I think he might have to say if he knew how crucial inductive reason is to valid philosophy and concrete science.

SECTION 4: SUMMARY OF HISTORICAL OVERVIEW

1. We have covered three of the seven approaches to human personality: Psychoanalysis, Humanism, and Gestalt. You should have experienced the third one, Gestalt, if you had a

smile or two while reading the preceding allegory. The moment you smiled was when you were enjoying a Gestalt. When you found yourself trying to find out what the allegory was talking about was when you became the needful figure; when you made contact with the appropriate historical event, you made contact with the benevolent ground; and the Gestalt climax occurred when you smiled. Positive Gestalts are climaxing whenever you find yourself smiling or laughing. Negative Gestalt occurs whenever the climax is not reached--the result being crying or some other expression of displeasure.

2. The allegory provided here was made to have familiar symbols which, like a carpet in a domed stadium, would pass over the historical ground. The truth of the matter is that the allegory is an imagined platform whereupon one can perform Gestalts with the ground--which in this case is memory. If you find it easy to acquire Gestalt climaxes in this kind of situation, then you may be sure that you have developed the ability to think in a construct whose ground is made up of philosophical, religious, historical, scientific, and Natural events. If you feel that another allegory would better fit your personality, then go ahead and build it; but if you have been raised in Western Civilization, and if you intend to keep the same goals as we have here, then you must keep the ground close to what we have laid out here. Reason?...because that's the way it all happened. This subject will be covered in more detail later.

3. Perhaps you have been wondering as to where this book is heading. What is it driving at? What is its main objective? The objective is stated in item #42 of the allegory's legend--where the key is defined as being the paradoxical understanding of Reality. That is what this book is heading for. As for the purpose of this book, it is to help develop a philosophy which will point out attainable scientific objectives for the long-awaited years ahead.

4. Aristotle was a famous Athenian, but he didn't get that way

by doing everything himself. No, he had a staff of assistants and pupils who went out and gathered information; then he would look things over and, after classifying them, come up with a rule that would cover all of them. He applied this system in the study of astronomy, zoology, botany, and mechanics: he also applied it in such areas of the humanities as psychology, rhetoric, poetry, oratory, politics, and art. In that system, he was actually going through the motions of inductive reason; however, he chose to use those motions only as a means of confirming deductions which he had derived from the universals. You see, the matter of first cause of any material thing was already resolved by the universals, so why would he have to dig deeper than the formed object itself? Aristotle's genius involved an intellectual system whose flow of reason was mainly from the universals to the particular thing, and, while that system worked quite well in dealing with social matters, it rarely if even pursued cause beyond the physical object itself; and because of this, science became stalled for almost two thousand years.

Juan Luis Vives (1492-1540) is credited for providing the medieval forerunners of the philosophy of Realism. He was intensely interested in using inductive reason in helping science to produce things useful in everyday life, and surely if he had changed this idea of using science as a useful tool to the idea of using science as a means of human progress, Francis Bacon would have had fewer new things to say. Vives had been a friend of the elderly Erasmus; he was Catholic, although he thought well of Humanism; he contributed many firsts in the fields of education and psychology...being the first medieval scholar to realize the importance of sense data and the need of correct use of the mother tongue; and it appears that the only thing that made him keep distance from the army of Humanists was the fact that he still favored Aristotle.

Certainly there is nothing that you and I can do to correct the happenings of the past. However, a little hindsight here in the present might help us to keep those costly errors from happening again. Juan Luis Vives was 48 years old when he died:

his home was in the Netherlands. If he could have lived twenty-seven more years, he would have died the very year that the religious wars began; and that was in his homeland. If during those extra years of living, he could have counseled the Catholic leadership to get inductive reason into its Aristotelian science, then all of those resources that went to the preparation for war could have been diverted to inductive science and the discovery of Natural treasures that would provide the level of human progress which we know today. But that didn't happen. Instead, Germany lost one-half of its population, while countless other lives were lost elsewhere in Europe.

5. All this study will be addressing are things that are happening here in the present and may happen in the future. Moreover, it will be dealing only with human personality--meaning that our concern here will be with the structures and functions of a human personality. You might say that this book is providing for an interpersonal relationship between you the reader and me the writer. However, I have no desire to know of any myths and dogmas that you might be harboring, nor do I have desire to condemn them, if they exist. Aside from reaffirming the Real Existence of Almighty God and trying to provide some information to the front line trench philosophy of concrete science, my job is to call as many humans to the Fold of Reality as possible. I hope that you will follow the Trail of Reason which is presented in this book, see what the Fold of Reality is, and then join me in making the call.

True Christians try not to make value judgements except when they are founded in practical bearing and demonstrable fact.

Chapter Three

The Mortal Domain

SECTION 1: WHAT IS THE MORTAL DOMAIN?

The Population Explosion. The almanac estimates that in 1650 A.D. the world population was 470,000,000; in 1950 A.D. it was 2,510,000,000; and at the present time it is 5,500,000,000. What these numbers are telling us is that during the 300 years between 1650 and 1950 the world population grew by two billion people, and that during the forty years from 1950 to 1990 it grew by almost three billion people. Combining this human expansion rate with the constant fact that people can live comfortably on about one-fourth (¼) of the earth's surface, you will see how the possibility becomes increasingly evident that given the current trend mankind is going to reproduce itself out of existence.

This trend is nothing new. I had just graduated from college in 1950 and it was an alarming topic even then. However, what makes it even more compelling to me now is the realization that the human expansion rate is increasing by a measure that I never thought possible. Back during the 1950's, most of the educators who I knew joined me in thinking that the human population explosion was certainly coming, but that it would not become a pressing concern for at least 200 years. How wrong we were! The explosion is already upon us.

Another factor to consider is life expectancy. In 1850, the American life expectancy was 39.4 years; in 1950 it was 68.2 years; and at the present time it is 75.7 years. As for life expectancy in foreign nations, the world almanac makes it clear that the length of human life varies directly with cultural advancement. For example, the average life-span in European nations is about the same as ours, while life-span in most South American, Asian, and African nations tends to average about twenty years lower than ours. Especially since World War II, the high life-span nations have been helping the low life-span nations to advance culturally. Such assistance is certainly commendable, although the fact cannot be ignored that this type of action is promoting the population explosion and that, in so-doing, it is helping to bring the long-foreseen chaos out of the distant future and making it a Reality which we must contend with here and now.

An exploding population of five and one-half billion humans with rising life expectancy is almost the shortest way to define the Mortal Domain. I say "almost" because we are not factoring in the most important truth about human existence-- which is that not one of the five and one-half billion people knows exactly what he or she is. Therefore, one definition of the Mortal Domain is that it is the five and one-half billion earth-bound humans whose exploding population and rising life expectancy are compounding a possible misfortune in the light of their wonderment as to what they are.

SECTION 2: CONCRETE SCIENCE---A REVEALER

For the past 350 years, concrete science has been working like a bulldozer in pushing the unknown back and away from humanity while at the same time uprooting myths that stand in the way. Here, we are going to discuss some of the truths and myths that concrete science has revealed. We should be clear on one fact, however: concrete science is not the revealer of truth; it is one of the revealers of truth. We must not overlook the part that the Christian religion has played in leading the individual to pragmatic experience and the readiness for truth through practical bearing.

What the Mortal Domain has become is a giant playing field, where two leagues are actively engaged in the game of humanity. One league is called the Being League, because its members are committed to actual things, events, and/or conditions. The other league is called the Nonbeing League, because its members are committed to apparent things, events, and/or conditions. What should be interesting to you and me is the fact that we are active players in this game. It's still going on, not as a social play, but as a psychological happening in your mind, and in mine. These Leagues do not exist outside a human mind. The game of humanity is being played in all of our minds; and the way the game ends will depend upon which League is dominating in your mind, in my mind, and in the minds of the other members of the Mortal Domain.

The Being League is the one which I try to play in--the reason being that it is the source of irrefutable facts. For example, after taking courses in embryology, histology, and cytogenetics [16], I came to know for a fact that the fertilized human egg is as much a member of the human race as the greatest one amongst us. I am comfortable working with the understanding that the fertilized human egg has 100% of the Natural human potential which he or she will unfold throughout child and adult living. While it is true that this potential can be adversely affected by such things as drugs and physical damages during prenatal and postnatal development, and that it will best unfold through optimum nutrition, there is only one way that the nurturing environment can change it; and that is for someone to go into the genetic makeup of the individual and alter, remove, or replace the gene or genes which provide for a predetermined human potential and its expression.

The Capsular Theory. Most of the things that we will be discussing in this section are directly related to truth and Actuality; that is to say, in our discussion of human reproduction, we will be telling some of the truths as to how it actually occurs. These understandings came as a result of scientific investigations that were made between the start of the American Civil War and the start of World War II. The following is a brief review of that period of time.

Before 1859, there was a widely accepted theory that the father's body created the new individual, placed it in a tiny capsule, and then inserted it into the womb during intercourse. Since the dawn of humanity, this capsular theory made very good sense; for it was obvious that if the new child came only as a result of sexual intercourse, then where other than the father could it have possibly come from? Over thousands of years of socialization this capsular theory became woven into much of the social fabric of Western Civilization. It was particularly evident as an influence in the setting of family values [17]; where, for longer than recorded history will say, the father was situated as being the central family figure; where the children saw themselves as being extensions from his loins; and where in full agreement the mother would serve as helpmate. In these families, the capsular theory became one of the earliest influences in the setting of family values within the child's mind, and because it was so completely accepted by members of the family and community, it became the basis upon which the rest of his or her [18] values would develop, and then go on to give the paternalistic "ring" to the family and community.

As you scan back over the early development of Western Civilization, you will note that there was enough cultural inertia to carry forward the absurd myths that the pagan and more advanced cultures had generated. Many of those myths became part of the fabric in early Western culture. Christianity was just getting under way at that time and one of the first actions its membership took was to distance the new Christian culture from the gladiator-pagan past. But the capsular theory made just too much sense to be left behind. By saying this, I do not mean to imply that the capsular theory had a big influence in bringing about Catholic Church paternalism. Being neither a theologian nor a Catholic, I know little if anything about the Catholic Church's founding rationale; and this applies to my grasp of the Middle Eastern, Eastern, and Oriental faiths as well.

Cell Theory. For 1665 years, Western Civilization was allowed to develop without anyone having knowledge of the cellular nature of living things. For 1665 years, then, the capsular theory was free to influence Western values without any serious threat to its good sense logic. Then finally, in 1665, Robert Hooke (1635-1703) built a compound microscope--perhaps the first one--and discovered the cellular nature of cork. After that, came numerous studies of microscopic life--the most notable ones being Schleiden's study of plant cells and Schwann's study of animal cells. In 1838, Schleiden [19] presented the first outline of what has come to be known as the Cell Theory; yet it was not until 1858 that Rudolf Virchow (1821-1902) revealed that cells arise only from preexisting cells. Thus while Robert Hooke fathered the field of cytology, and Schleiden and Schwann introduced the Cell Theory, it was not until Rudolf Virchow's Theory of Cell Lineage came along that the Cell Theory became complete.

Responses to Discoveries in 19th Century Concrete Science. After 1859, the basic nature of the family began to change from paternalism to dualism, that is, from a father-oriented family to a family that was more often mother and father oriented. The reason that such a change came in 1859 was because that was the year when Charles R. Darwin (1809-1882) published his work *On the Origin of Species by Means of Natural Selection.* Darwin did not himself put an end to the capsular theory of inheritance, but he did manage to open the door through which its slayers would pass. Allow me to structure this a bit further.

The 19th century was a period when the intellectual community gave great response to a philosophy developed by Jean Jacques Rousseau (1712-1778). Called *Romanticism*, this philosophy brought about a tremendous positive regard for Nature. It has been said that in bringing people to have romance with Nature, Rousseau influenced more humans than any one else on earth except Jesus of Nazareth. Also, the first half of the 19th century was a time when the scientific community was taking renewed interest in Aristotle's conception of evolution, which, as you will recall, he had discovered at the philosophical level some 2200 years earlier. Such was the setting when Darwin came out with the idea of survival through protoplasmic development. He opened the door to a new frontier of science-- organic evolution--and in their quest for earlier causes, members from every branch of biology flooded through, including the slayers [20] of the capsular theory.

As might be expected, however, the discarding of the old capsular theory of inheritance came fast in the scientific community but to varying degrees slower in the humanities, theologies, and lay public. This change moved swiftly throughout the scientific community because its members wanted actual truth. They found it easy to cast myth and dogma aside and follow the premise that every effect is caused. They followed Nature's Law of Cause and Effect; and once they had the microscope and the understanding that actual causes of offspring--in this case, babies--had yet to become known, they started searching for them. Before the end of the 19th century, they had revealed the process of fertilization and were swiftly bringing embryology in as one of the fields of biology. At the turn of this century, Gregor Mendel (1822-1884) finally became recognized for his discovery of the Laws of Inheritance, thus bringing genetics in as another field of biology. The line of reason which clearly establishes the human as being a Natural phenomenon was becoming stronger by the day, and like hounds upon the scent, scientists followed it right to the end.

DNA and RNA. During the period which extended from the late 1800's to the start of World War II, cytology began to integrate with embryology, genetics, chemistry, and physics. During that period the Chromosome Theory was developed and the processes of mitotic (non-sexual) and meiotic (sexual) cell division became understood. And during the period which extended from the start of World War II to the early 1960's, that same group set out to discover the chemical make up of non-sexual and sexual cells. It was during the latter period that DNA (deoxyribonucleic acid) and RNA (ribonucleic acid) became identified, although the exact contents and shapes of their giant molecules did not become fully understood until after 1961.

The year 1961 stands out in my mind because that was when I took cytogenetics--where, on the first day of class, the professor walked over to a three-foot model of the DNA molecule and pointed to a baseball-size hole in the middle of it. He said that the first one to name the atoms which belong in that hole will receive a million dollar reward. We pondered to no avail; but a year or so later, someone did identify the correct atoms, and I suppose the finder received the million dollars. The important thing is that finally the atomic content and shape of the DNA molecule had become known.

Referred to as the building blocks of the genes, the DNA molecules are currently being studied for the parts they play in the unfolding of human and non-human potential. In addition, this research has already provided the lay public with tools to help solve such crimes as rape and murder by tying the criminal to the scene of his or her crime, and in helping to resolve paternity suits and conflicts arising from the inadvertent exchange of babies. This shows about how far our understanding of DNA has come; and as for our understanding of RNA, we are swiftly learning its role in such body functions as immunity and tissue development. But mark my word, twenty years from now, these findings will be viewed as beginnings of an entirely new frontier for concrete science--the study of human affect.

Genetic Engineering. This new field for gene repair, removal, and replacement will do many wonderful things for mankind. Think of how helpful it would be to those of us who possess inheritable links to cancer, Parkinson's disease, or Alzheimer's disease if the responsible genes were removed. This would certainly increase life expectancy and hasten the population explosion that much more, but I am sure you will agree that because such advancement comes under the heading of human progress it is acceptable. You may also agree that the axiom for genetic engineering should be to do whatever is necessary to increase the length and/or quality of human life, but not through unwelcome expense to the donor individuals, whether they be living, executed, or Naturally dead.

Responses to Discoveries in 20th Century Concrete Science. Certainly there were some members of the humanities, the theologies, and the lay public who joined the scientists in making a fast withdrawal from the capsular theory; however, many of them tended to resist such a change--where an idea assumed as fact had to be realized as myth. By now, 135 years later, the vast majority of people in Western Civilization have adjusted to the truth of how Nature provides for human fertilization. Still, judging from the last presidential election, and from some of the recent Supreme Court decisions, it appears that many, if not most, American adults do not yet fully comprehend the human reproductive process. In fact, the human reproductive process seems to be plagued by a whole series of myths. It seems that we just get rid of one myth concerning human reproduction, and then we come upon another, and then another.

This next myth is being revealed much closer to our time: it is therefore more apt to have been passed on to us as children and remain prominent in the system which we refer to as modern values. It now lies at the cutting edge of human progress. It is the mythical *apparent* human body.

The Actual and Apparent Human Bodies. To some, this may be one of the most perplexing subjects. How can there be a difference between the actual human body and the apparent, or seemingly whole, human body? As a means of answering this question, let us suppose that we bought a copy of Gray's Anatomy and hired an artist and a female model. We would then hand the anatomy book to the artist and ask him or her to make two nude sketches: one was to be a sketch of the model's apparent body and the other was to be a sketch of her actual body.

After finishing the sketches, the artist would no doubt report that the apparent sketch was easy to do, for all that had to be done was to sketch the image which his or her sense data provided. But in sketching the actual body of the model, the artist would have had to refer to the anatomy book, so as to find out exactly where the model's body left off and where the external world began.

The sketch of the actual body would show little resemblance to the sketch of the apparent body because the artist would have arrived at some deep inroads made by the external world and, in one place, it would have to show a hole passing from top to bottom through the body. Known as the alimentary canal, this hole opens to the external world at the mouth cavity and continues through the cavities of the esophagus, the stomach, the small intestines, the large intestine, the rectum, and then through the anus as a continuance of the external world.

The model's body dumps enzyme into the mouth cavity; it dumps enzyme into the stomach cavity; it opens and closes the sphincter valve as a means of controlling canal flow; it deposits bile and enzyme into the cavity of the small intestine, and there absorbs food and other material into the blood stream; and in the large intestine, it absorbs water. The only way that a substance in the alimentary canal can become a part of the human body is for it to be absorbed by the walls of the canal--as through the villi of the small intestine--and be deposited into the blood stream. The point to be made here is that materials traveling along the model's alimentary canal can only become part of her body when they are absorbed into her blood stream;

otherwise, they lie outside her body and are part of the external world.

As for the inroads which bring the external world deep inside the model's body, there are five main ones. One is where the outer ears funnel the external world in to the ear drums, and where the auditory tubes bring the external world from the mouth cavity to the inner side of the ear drums. This way, the body is able to keep atmospheric pressure the same on each side of the ear drums, and at the same time be able to pick up on vocal cord vibrations.

The second main inroad into the model's body is that which leads to the lungs. Beginning near the rear of the mouth cavity, the trachea carries the external world past the vocal cords and then branches into two bronchial tubes. These bronchial tubes branch into smaller and smaller ones until they are able to effect the exchange of gases between the model's blood stream and the external world--oxygen into the blood stream and carbon dioxide out of it. Through breathing, carbon dioxide laden air is moved away from the model's body and the oxygen laden air is brought in to proximity with it. The point to be made here is that at no place in this respiratory process does air--which is seventy-eight percent nitrogen--ever leave the external world and enter the model's body: if this were to happen, she could die within minutes. This is the main reason why nurses hold the syringe up and expel any gas that might otherwise be passed into the blood stream during an injection.

The third main inroad into the model's body is where the external world extends through her nostrils and into her nasal cavity and sinuses. This is where air is filtered and cooled or warmed before entering the mouth cavity, the trachea, and the lungs. Here again, although it may appear that the external world stops at the nostrils, in Actuality, it continues on through the nasal cavity and into the lungs; and there are always tissues present to separate it from the model's blood stream and other body parts.

The fourth main inroad into the model's body is her urinary tract. This is where the external world extends from the vaginal area through the urethra to the urinary bladder, the ureters, and the renal tubules of the kidneys. When urine is discharged from the kidneys into the renal tubules--that is the time when urine leaves the actual body. When urine is discharged from the urethra in the vaginal area--that is the time when urine leaves the apparent body. So you see, we have two standards to go by. If we made the actual body our basis for judgement, we would have to say that urine is brought in to being in the kidneys and discharged into the renal tubules, thus starting the flow down the external world inroad through the ureters, the bladder, the urethra, and be deposited at a place distant from the body. But if we made the apparent body our basis for judgement, we would tend to say that urine is brought in to being in the body, discharged by the urethra in the vaginal area, and deposited at a place distant from the body. What we should be clear on is that each of these standards of judgement are telling the truth, except that while the actual body judgement is telling the complete truth about urine production, the apparent body judgement is leaving room for misconceptions about urine production: for example, the notion that urine is brought in to being in the urinary bladder is a myth; but in Actuality, it is brought in to being, that is, born, in the kidneys.

The fifth main inroad by the external world into the model's body is her reproductive tract. This is where the external world moves between the model's labia, past her hymen--which will be moved aside as a result of accident or intercourse--then through the vaginal orifice, the cervix, the uterine cavity, and on to the upper end of the Fallopian tubes, or oviducts. It is sometimes in one of these tubes that the male sperm and the female egg join, thus bringing a new human individual in to being.

Apparent Body Judgement. This is where many people will tend to generate differences, depending on whether they develop their human values with actual body judgement or with apparent body judgement. If you are one of those who develop their human value-systems by using apparent body judgement, then the chances are that one of your values is the belief that the model would have the right to flush out any foreign object that begins to develop in her reproductive tract, and that local, state, and federal governments should protect that right. This manner of thinking argues that if the model doesn't want a human individual growing in her reproductive tract, then she has just as much right to flush it out as she does to remove urine or feces or a tapeworm.

If you hold to the apparent body value judgement which was just described, then you must feel very comfortable in knowing that most of the esteemed leaders in American government and probably most of the American adults believe exactly as you do.

What was your feeling of commitment as you read the last subsection? Did you find yourself agreeing that a woman has the right to flush her child from her body before the optimum time of delivery? If you agreed, you were operating in the *Nonbeing League*: if you disagreed, you were operating in the *Being League*. And this is the way it happens in the making of all human value judgements: either you commit to Actuality and operate in the Being League, or you commit to the apparent and run the risk of operating in the Nonbeing League. The Nonbeing League is the one whose members subscribe to apparent (nonexistent) things, events, and/or conditions.

Abortion. During the winter of 1993, one of our leaders said on television that he did not approve of abortion, but that he also upheld the right of a woman to determine what happens in her own body. I agreed with that when he said it, and I still do. A woman has the right to determine what may stay and what must go from her body. However, when the leader went on to conclude that a woman has a legal right to have an abortion, I immediately found myself on the other side of the fence; for it became clear that he was reflecting from laws that were conceived through apparent body judgement. Allow me to explain human prenatal development from the actual body judgement point of view.

Human Fertilization and Embryonic Development. When an egg leaves the ovary, it is funneled by a fine tissue to the upper end of one of the two Fallopian tubes. On very rare occasions, this fine tissue is missing, or out of place, and the egg comes to rest in the mother's abdominal cavity. When this happens, the upper end of one of the Fallopian tubes may be left uncovered, thus allowing sperm-loaded semen to move into the abdominal cavity and effect a fertilization of that egg. This is the only possible way that normal human life can come in to being within the mother's actual body. However, because a maternal placenta would not be there to provide full nurture, the individual would fail to develop. I have read about other cases where an egg would begin to develop in an ovary and be discharged directly into the abdomen with an umbilical-like cord connecting it to the ovary. These abnormal developments have been known to grow as large as grapefruit and require surgical removal. Certainly any abnormal development which is found growing in or in relation to the human reproductive system is in need of surgical intervention. What I react to is the removal of a normally developing human individual from the reproductive tract before the optimum or life-saving time of delivery has arrived.

After an egg is released by one of the ovaries, it is ushered a short distance and deposited in the upper end of one of the Fallopian tubes. This depositing action is the exact time and place that the egg is discharged from the mother's actual body. The egg is then lying in one of the Fallopian tube cavities, whose lining is an epithelium which extends in a continuous manner down to the uterine cavity and lines it as well. The thing that we must become clear on is that the uterine cavity and the cavities within the Fallopian tubes are outside the actual female body, and because the canal of the cervix and the vaginal cavity also lie outside the actual female body, the entire reproductive tract is technically nothing more than a pouch whose opening to the outside becomes set during embryonic development.

Some may say that the hymen seals off the reproductive

tract and thus makes it a part of the actual female body; but the fact is that the hymen is mucous membrane which covers only part of the vaginal orifice. Perhaps the best indication of this is where some women have lived several or many years as adults without having their hymens ruptured, either by accident or by intercourse, and yet they were able to discharge menstrual fluids in a normal manner. Other than on extremely rare occasions, when an abnormal development of tissue might seal off the vaginal orifice or the canal of the cervix and make the reproductive tract a part of the actual female body, the cavities of the reproductive tract are continuations of the external world, and to reason otherwise would be to generate misconceptions which occur in what we refer to as the League of Nonbeing--where reasoning is based upon things imagined or apparent, but not shown to be actually so.

Blood Relationships. There is an idea going around on the street--that is to say, in everyday life--that children share their mother's blood during prenatal development. Playing this idea out, the believers contend that all biological brothers and sisters are blood relatives because they carry their mother's blood. The fact is, however, that all normally developing prenatal children manufacture their own blood and keep it entirely separate from their mother's. Therefore, the idea that two people are blood related because they share their mother's blood is a myth. On the other hand, it would be wrong for us to discard the blood relative idea simply because some people fail to grasp the actual truth. The actual truth is that biological brothers and sisters are blood relatives in the sense that they each contain blood which derives from at least one of their biological parents. Here is one further indication that during prenatal development the child is existing outside the mother's actual body, but inside her apparent one. No one dies as a result of the blood relative myth, but look out for this next one: it's the killer of all killers.

The Birth Myth. Both of my large dictionaries say that a human is born when he or she is delivered from the womb; and yet one of them also states that a thing is born when it is brought in to being. Which is the correct explanation of human existence? Does a human first exist when he or she slips from the vagina, or is it when a human egg becomes fertilized by a sperm in one of the Fallopian tubes or in the uterine cavity? The chances are good--some will say very good--that a sperm will fertilize the egg before it reaches the uterine cavity; assuming, of course, that intercourse had just occurred.

When viewed under the microscope, human sperm look like polliwogs (tadpoles) swimming around. The first one to break through the egg's wall will shed its tail and head for the egg's nucleus. The moment it unites with the nucleus is the time when the diploid number [21] of chromosomes will have been reached, when a new human individual will have been brought in to being, when 100 percent of his or her human potential will be in place, and when such potential begins its unfolding through cellular division. All of these events will have happened outside the mother's actual body but inside her apparent body. The question is, what do you want to base human judgement upon? Do you want to base it upon the actual case or upon the apparent case?

Hopefully you will agree that the most dependent of all human life is that boy or girl who is developing in his or her own space which extends from the external world and becomes the cavity of the mother's reproductive pouch. The mother controls the pouch because it is part of her body; however, God, Nature, and humanity control the space inside that pouch because it is part of the external world. What is happening today is that under permissive circumstances a woman lies as an animal, opens the front door of her reproductive pouch to a rush of sperm, and then claims the right to destroy any human individual who is born out of that play. What has also happened is that top leaders of the American government have presumed women to have the right to destroy human life which grows in their reproductive pouches. I submit that the legal profession should review those points of law which are now being derived from the apparent human body and consider the fact that valid laws are always derived from things, conditions, and events that are actual--in this case, the actual human body. I further submit that, as with the arrival of Christian and democratic values, the greatest lessons taught by our forefathers were those that showed how human progress occurs when humanity pulls with God and Nature, and how human decline [22] occurs when it pulls against them--as it was in the days of pagandom and self-serving monarchies.

As I understand it, a boy or girl who is in prenatal development can be legally destroyed if he or she is less than ninety-one days old. Does this mean that at the age of ninety-one days the child has finally become a citizen and is entitled to survival rights? Could this standard be raised to 100 days next year and 120 days the year after and 130 days the year after that? Or might we expect that the American leadership will awaken to the fact that citizenship begins at actual birth, possibly in one of the mother's Fallopian tubes, but no later than in the uterine cavity?

Being Values are Imperative in This Study. It may seem that I am writing this section as part of a crusade against human abortion, but that would not be entirely correct. The truth is that while I am strongly opposed to the abortion of healthy children from healthy mothers, I am using the subject of abortion in an effort to save some readers a great deal of discomfort. The subject of this book deals only with Actuality: it is not suitable for those who favor apparent values. Saying this another way, I am using the subject of abortion as a way of distinguishing between the human mind whose judgements are based upon actual things, events, and conditions and the human mind whose judgements are based upon imagined or apparent things, events, and conditions. Judgements which are made upon actual things, events, and conditions are produced by members of the Being League, while judgements which are made upon imagined apparent things, events, and conditions are produced by members of the Nonbeing League.

In order to reach our main objective, we are going to be following a very narrow Trail of Reason. The only values we will be able to use are those founded in the Being League. Here lies the key which was mentioned in Chapter Two. It will be to push aside the Nonbeing League in our minds and consider only actual things, actual events, and actual conditions. Then, after we have climbed to the uppermost view and found what human existence is all about, we will be able to return to the streets of everyday life and report our findings.

SECTION 3: ALMIGHTY GOD AND CHRIST ARE AS REAL AS YOU AND I

Out of the five and one-half billion people who inhabit this planet, there is not one of them who knows what he or she is. Since the dawn of humanity, this has been the unknown which our forefathers had to come to grip with, and the way they dealt with it was to acknowledge themselves as being children of God and become a society upon that basis. This turned out to be the trick of things; for by pursuing the Father through reason and worship, they were able to bring their God-oriented society to where it is today. Today, humanity is found to flourish in a number of such societies. Each has a unique approach to God, as in the Western Societies, the Middle Eastern Societies, the Eastern Societies, and the Oriental Societies. Yet all of them consist of members of the human race and the brotherhood of mankind. Most members of every society are searching for Almighty God. If the members of one society find light at the end of the proverbial tunnel, then it is their responsibility to let the other societies know. This is the spirit in which this book is written; for in the sight of God we are all members of the same flock. The report here is that Almighty God is Real.

The Case of Western Civilization. While the roots of Western Civilization go as far back into the ancient world as Abraham, Socrates, Plato, and Aristotle, its true beginning was when Jesus of Nazareth went throughout Palestine and urged the people to reason their way to self-understanding and receive lasting life as a result. He also advised them that if they could not reason their way, then they should follow the way in spirit, and receive the same self-understanding and lasting life after their bodies had died. Here, today, two thousand years later, we look out over the Western human flock to see how well it did.

Here, today, two thousand years after the beginning of Western Civilization, we find that two great human camps have developed along the Way of Reason. One is a secular camp, whose members consider actual things, events, and conditions through reason: it is known as concrete science. The other is a religious camp, whose members consider actual things, events, and conditions through worship, and it is known as Christianity. What you and I must agree upon is that both the concrete sciences and the Christian denominations serve the Real Almighty God and follow the same Real Christ--the main difference being that concrete science serves and follows through reason, while Christianity serves and follows through faith and worship. One way of explaining what has happened in the making of Western Civilization is to say that if Christianity is the backbone of Western Civilization, then the concrete sciences are the arms and legs that help it work. One supports the other.

This Book is a Central Undertaking [23]. In Chapter Two, this book came close to religion when it reviewed some of the history of Western Civilization, and it is coming close to religion in this section; but from here on its reference to religion will be little if any. I want to mention this here because we will soon be getting on the Trail of Reason, and the only intellectual values we will be using are those of concrete science and the seven philosophical approaches to human personality which mark the way.

Another thing that we must become agreed to is that we will not be harboring desires to reform any of the Christian religions; nor will we be taking issue [24] with any religion concerning such things as religious dogmas and ideals. The position we will be taking is that religious dogmas and ideals that are founded in actual truth will still be around after human existence is revealed, and those that are not so-founded will melt like icebergs when humanity hits the "warmer waters" of human progress. Having said this, I urge all true Christians and concrete scientists to move with me to the top of the Trail and see for themselves what the uppermost view is like. All they will need to do is press the Nonbeing League aside and keep our Real Almighty God in mind; for if they do, they will receive some help along the way. And of course this message stands as an invitation to the members of all other religions on earth, if they are truly aligned with our Real Almighty God.

God and Christ are as real as you and I.

WARNING
This book is written for true Christians and
concrete scientists. If you feel nervous or
anxious before or while reading this book,
stop reading and discuss your feelings with
others. These are indications that you may
need to move slowly into this subject matter.

Chapter Four

The Trail of Reason

SECTION 1: TOOLS FOR THE CLIMB

The main objective [25] of this book is to provide the reader with a line of reason which ends with an understanding of how we humans survive death. Good and bad, old and young, intelligent and obtuse--all humans survive mortal death. And only Almighty God can make it turn out any different. Here, we will be considering the essential tools for reaching this understanding.

Six Essential Tools. We will be using many tools as we climb, but six of them seem to be most involved in this study. These are:

1. Perception. This term is used in many different fields of endeavor and has a specific meaning in each one. In this study, perception will be defined as the process of realizing mental images and/or feelings from sense data that originate in reactions between the human sense organs and objects in the body or environment. A *percept* is a product of perception where only one sense-datum is realized.

2. Idea. An idea is the basic unit of reason: a unit of information whose unique quality remains fixed and beyond change. Ideas are the unique products of conception: they are the building blocks of Reality. In this regard, ideas are to Reality what atoms are to Actuality. Because ideas are real in nature, they can not be destroyed or affected by any force in Actuality.

3. Conception. Conception is the process of creating meaningful ideas from sense data and affect; for example, taking information from such perceivable objects as word symbols, photographs, and designs, and joining such data with established real data (affect)--the product being ideas and clusters of ideas. *Reason* is orderly and logical conception. A *concept* is a cluster of ideas: the product of conception: a mental image abstracted from perceptions, percepts, and/or reflections from affect (past experience): it is a building block section of Reality, where the blocks are ideas.

4. Reality Construct. Every living human being is engaged in the process of building his or her own Reality. Concepts are clusters of ideas (clusters of building blocks) that become sections in the construction of an individual's Reality construct [26].

5. Projection of Self. Contrary to what many now think, projection of self does not cast away from one's body and toward objects in the environment; it only appears to happen that way. Actually, it is a projection which begins in the thalamic area, that is, the central part of the brain, and comes to rest at meaningful points in the Reality construct of the individual. Insofar as projection of self occurs at or soon after delivery and continues as being the sole or primary mental facility for interacting new and old human experiences with the environment, it may be said that one's Reality construct is a part of his or her own self, and that in this respect, projection of self is self-realization.

6. Self-Actualization. Self-actualization is the mental facility where the self uses only being values, and where by having an absence of nonbeing values to "muddy its waters" of conception, it is able to reconstruct the external world as it actually is and view humanity as it actually occurs.

Unfortunately, humanity is a phenomenon whose entire membership has displayed nonbeing values to varying degrees. In fact, aside from Jesus of Nazareth, who many of us view as having operated with perfect self-actualization, there have been relatively few who even came close to such performance. Speaking only of the ancient Mediterranean world and Western Civilization, I would say that the following people came close to operating with perfect self-actualization: Abraham, Aristotle, Albert Einstein, Abraham Lincoln, Moses, Plato, Will Rogers, Rousseau, Socrates, Paul of Tarsus, and Juan Luis Vives.   Understand, however, that these are names which I would place on a list of close performers and that they by no means comprise a completed list.

It was mentioned in the last chapter that something would become available to help you climb the Trail of Reason [27]. It is something that you may already be aware of, but in case you are not, we should examine it here. This study is an intellectual effort which is being performed at the philosophical level of reason; subsequently, as would be expected, it contains premises and objectives. If we were to take all of these premises and objectives and determine the one thing that they are aiming for, we would then know the goal of this philosophical endeavor. The name of this philosophical endeavor is Affective Realism and its goal is the understanding of how a human being will survive death, or to say it a bit more graphically, how to get out of this world alive. What I have found is that when I perform this study with close to perfect self-actualization, my tear ducts respond whenever I reach a new understanding of the goal, thus bringing me closer to it. This slight wetting of the eyes has been my Staff during the past thirty-nine years. It can also be your Staff while making the climb ahead. It is not a mental facility which is given to us in some mystic way; rather, it is one that we have had as part of our personalities all along, and which we may now use as a tool for the climb. The caboose goes into greater detail on this subject, but what we should agree upon here is that there is nothing mystic going on, and that whatever else it may be, for us, it is an intellectual manifestation of crying.

Definitions of a Reality Construct. The definition of Reality construct which concrete scientists generally subscribe to is that it is a conceptualization of Reality. The definition of Reality construct which the philosophy of Affective Realism [28] adheres to is stated below.

> A Reality construct is a Natural phenomenon that is produced by and attached to a living human body. Throughout mortal life it builds from and upon concepts, perceptions, percepts, affects, and psychological feelings that the producing body experiences in life. It constitutes a medium which is both different from and coexisting with Actuality.

Structure of a Reality Construct. At the philosophical level of reason, we can explain some of the structure of a Reality construct. It has at least seven dimensions--length, width, height, time, being, nonbeing, and incidence of effect. Although the last four occur internally, they are dimensions because like the others they are unique in nature and provide both quantitative and qualitative values to the whole structure. As for the properties of a Reality construct, it appears to have no measurable mass: however, because we humans are able to recognize it, to project ourselves into it, and to explore it, its existence is evident. One aim of this study will be to provide a philosophical explanation of these real aspects of human personality.

This is the chapter where you and I will be working as a team to reach the top of the Trail of Reason. It will be where I feed information to your senses, where your mind perceives the incoming sense data, where in your cognitive state (level of reason) you reconstruct the experiences that I was having while developing this new information, and where in a process known as concept development, you will be bringing this flow of newly reconstructed human experiences into your own construction of Reality. I think that if we can keep our minds zeroed in on Actuality, we can reach the top of the Trail in about seventy pages of writing and reading.

The teamwork which we will be experiencing during the climb is going to require the use of most of our mental facilities, and certainly each one of them will have an influence on our performance; for example, our ids and superegos will be constantly feeding need energy into our cognitive arenas and interact to form our ego states. But although most of our mental facilities are vital to our powers of reason, we will be making special use of only the six tools which were just discussed.

SECTION 2: AFFECTIVE REALISM

Affective Realism is the philosophical study of the origin, formation, maintenance, and characteristics of the human Affective Reality in its Natural state.

What is an Affective Reality? The answer to this question is what our study is aiming to provide. Not only are you going to find that answer, but you are in store for a number of paradoxical understandings concerning human existence--past, present, and future. If we were to tell what our Affective Realities are at this point in the study, we would have to say that they are our Reality constructs getting ready to enter the final stage of mortal development. This may be confusing, so let me say it another way. If you were to die this minute, your self would sever its tie with your physical body and join your Reality construct in becoming your Affective Reality. Your physical body would be dead, but you would be "floating around" in your Affective Reality, thus becoming free to matriculate with the Greater Reality. However, this would happen only if you died. If you were to keep on living, then your Reality construct would continue its mortal stage of development and you would eventually be able to view your Affective Reality while it is still in tie with your living body. Helping others to reach this viewpoint is what Affective Realism is aiming to do. In the understanding that goes with this view, one will realize how human survival of death did, does, and will inevitably occur.

The Risk of Dogmatic Science. If you are a concrete scientist, you may be thinking that I have abandoned you, that I have lost hold of the Laws of Nature, and that what we are doing here is just another case of chasing impossible dreams. If you have such a feeling, let me remind you of the people in ancient Athens who believed stars to be holes in the sky that were pierced by great archers, and how Socrates was made to drink hemlock for teaching to the contrary and about understandings that led to our knowledge of the Universe; of how Copernicus explained the solar system three years before his death, but in fear of the Church he refused to publish; of how the rounded shape of the earth was not demonstrated until the 15th century; or of how certain red-faced lobbyists in Washington evaporated on that day in 1957 when Sputnik went up. The story of human progress is a tale of broken myths and new Realities.

The Founding Value. If you are a concrete scientist, you may also be thinking that the story of human progress is a tale of broken myths and new Realities because man's native desire for truth made it unfold that way and that a century and a half ago concrete science came along to help it unfold faster. Being a concrete scientist myself, I couldn't agree more; but being an affective realist, I have to say that I agree almost more. What I am saying is that as a concrete scientist I too am allegiant to the

Law of Cause and Effect, Natural Selection, and the need for demonstrable facts. However, as an affective realist I find that my own self has been assuming something as fact when in Reality it may turn out to be the biggest nonbeing value of them all. It seems to be the one human value that stands as foundation for most other human values. It is our apparent Reality. Let us call it the *founding value* [29]. Working our way past the founding value is what we will be doing as we climb the Trail of Reason. So if you are a concrete scientist, I ask that you not label this study until after its points are made; for although the values of science might appear to be correct in every way, they too bear varying degrees of rooting in the founding value and must change so as to root fully in Actuality. Otherwise their concreteness may be lessened.

If you are a Christian who has little training in concrete science, you should have no difficulty in making the climb. However, there is one thing you should bear in mind: Affective Realism joins the concrete sciences in opposing any thought of final causes or predetermined designs in Nature--a system of thinking known as teleology [30]. The position here is the same as that which is taken by most Natural scientists--that in the fabric of life to which humanity belongs, and in the sight of God, all life forms are determined through the process of Natural development and exist as a result of Natural Selection. Teleology is to concrete science much as the devil is to Christianity: it is an obtuse system of thought whose existence is created, but only in reckless human imagination.

We have what can be a tough climb to make. I say "can" because climbing the Trail of Reason can be hard or it can be easy. In fact, the whole philosophy of Affective Realism can be hard or it can be easy. Which it will be is entirely up to you. What it amounts to is that the closer you can come to realizing your self's existence from your being dimension the less you will have to root your intellectual values in what only appears to be Reality and the more you will be able to gear them to the actual things, events, and/or conditions that become the objects of your study. This is the easy way to climb the Trail of Reason.

The hard way is to keep your intellectual values rooted in the founding value (the apparent Reality) and try to climb. Some students of human personality who have been climbing along the Biophysical Approach have been doing it the hard way. They need to stop to consider the possibility that they have been searching for truth within a make-believe Reality. Both the Biophysical Approach to human personality and Affective Realism must gear to Actuality. This is the only way that all of the other six approaches can join them eclectically.

AFFECTIVE REALISM: GOAL, PREMISES, AND OBJECTIVES

Goal: The understanding of how human survival of death did, does, and will inevitably occur.

Premises:

1. God is Real
2. The real human will survive death.
3. The real human can comprehend his or her existence.
4. Mortal Reality is a human creation.
5. Man is a product of Natural development and selection.
6. Both real and actual components of human personality are geared to the Laws of Nature.
7. Man is the eternal fruit of Nature.
8. The eternal fruit of Nature is ready for harvest.

Objectives:

1. To provide a line of reason which leads to one's realization of self as an Affective Reality.
2. To express the difference between Reality and Actuality.
3. To summarize Natural history enough to show that man both emerged and developed as a Natural phenomenon.
4. To present evidence that a medium interface exists

between Actuality and Reality.

5. To explain how one can become mobile within his or her personal Reality.

SECTION 3: THE SEVEN APPROACHES TO HUMAN PERSONALITY

While operating at the philosophical level of reason, we will be forging into an intellectual arena where many theologians and philosophers have already been. It is the arena where the human self is the object of study and where its explanation is the game. But we will be entering with gear that only the latest stages of human progress have provided. Granted, as it was for those who came before us, we will have all of our mental facilities to help us, particularly those that were discussed earlier as being tools for the climb; we will have Nature and the physical realms which it provides; and we will have all that our forefathers developed and came to be known as the Wisdom of the Ages. In addition, we will have access to that giant storehouse of knowledge which concrete science has built, and we will have the seven approaches to human personality which have only lately begun to converge upon the one valid understanding of the human self. Although we will not have concrete science to pave the way, we will have the necessary tools and knowledge to work with and a stand of impeccable principles to light our way. That is what the climb will be like--nothing concrete, nothing proved--only a Trail of Reason based upon Nature's way, flowered with newborn knowledge, and lit by glimmering principles from out of the past.

What We Will Be Using from the Seven Approaches to Personality. If you are a professional student of human personality, you know of the approaches to personality. You also know that those who follow them sometimes dwell on possible aspects of human personality that have little if anything to do with our goal, for example, mental telepathy and out-of-body experiences. If such things are actually true, then concrete science will eventually confirm them. Until that time, they are of little concern to us here. What we will be doing is to take from each approach the principles that help us to reach the top understanding and place us within reach of our goal.

Looking back, it seems that I have circled human personality close to a thousand times, and each time around, I could count only seven approaches to the top understanding--wherein all seven approaches would "jive" eclectically into one view. I would not say that there are only seven approaches to human personality. I am merely saying that in my experience there were seven approaches to the top, and when any one of them was ignored, or set aside, then the top understanding could not be realized. I therefore submit to you that the seven approaches listed below are the essential ones.

Seven Approaches to Human Personality

Approach	See Page
1. Psychoanalytic	14
2. Humanistic	23
3. Gestalt	43
4. Existential	57
5. Biophysical	59
6. Behavioral	93
7. Phenomenological	113

Five of these approaches have already been used in this study. You will find that they are listed above in much the same order as when they were first used. We will be arriving at approach number six shortly. Approach number seven will not come in to use until we near the top of the trail. We will be bringing all seven approaches closer together as we go along. Then we will reach a point where we can visualize an eclectic display of human personality.

SECTION 4: THE FOUNDING VALUE

We have reached the point in this text where the Trail of Reason begins. However, before starting the climb, we should stop and take note of where that will be. Although we already have much of the information which tells us this, it might be wise for us to review it and add a term or two. This way, the Trail's starting place will come into sharp focus.

In earlier discussion, there was caution made so as to not lead the reader into thinking that the founding value is bad for man. On the whole, the founding value has been good for man. It has been the psychological foundation for most of his religious pursuits, most of his philosophical pursuits, most of his scientific pursuits, most of his endeavors in the arts, and virtually all of his everyday living. But we should also take note of how the founding value has been the psychological foundation for untenable monarchies and socialistic schemes, for outrageous wealth and self-service, and for crime in general. Yet, everything considered, the founding value has been good for mankind.

What Is the Founding Value? The founding value is and has been a mythical Reality which was first ascribed to by the earliest of mankind a million or so years ago. It is a mythical Reality which has appeared so convincingly true down through the Ages that, as near as I can tell, the only ones who questioned its validity were Plato, Jesus of Nazareth, some of the prophets, some of the philosophers, and some of the mathematical physicists here in modern times.

Our first paradoxical understanding comes in regard to the nature of the founding value. There can be no question as to whether or not the founding value exists. It does exist, but not in the way people think. You see, the founding value exists only in human minds, or to be more precise, in human Reality constructs: it does not exist outside our bodies and "all over the place". For as long as human biology stays as it is, the founding value will be the basis for Reality which is created as a result of human perception and conception, and extends as a plane [31] between the being and nonbeing dimensions of the Reality construct. In fact, its presence is what gives essence to those dimensions. Do not be surprised if when the day comes you find that your founding value is the idea that became your Reality's first building block. It is the idea which is expressed by the feeling of omnipotence--where what you see, what you hear, what you smell, what you feel, and what you taste is you, all a part of you.

In passing, let me say that every time my mind entertains the thought of the founding value, I am reminded of what Ralph Waldo Emerson wrote about the kitten chasing paper upon the stage of life. Man, the omnipotent self playing humanity upon the apparent stage of life--such is the story of mankind.

The Founding Value and Actuality. The nature of the founding value may become clearer if we bring Actuality into the picture. Actuality is everything that the human senses can perceive. It includes everything that our senses can immediately perceive; it includes everything that our technology can uncover and bring to perception and/or conception; and it includes all man-made symbols, most notably, words, photographs, and designs. From this, one might gather that the concise way to define Actuality is to say that it includes everything in the Universe except the human selves and their respective Reality constructs.

If a human could live life and experience only perceptions and conceptions that deal directly with Actuality, then he or she would have developed a founding value which is a mirror image of Actuality. This means that the individual's Reality construct would contain only being values, and that because there are no nonbeing values, there would be no nonbeing dimension. That person would be experiencing perfect self-actualization. Unfortunately, humanity has not had people like that. Many of us think that one human did come along and experience perfect self-actualization, but other than that, only a relatively few have even come close.

If all of the people in American society, and for that matter, all human societies, were carrying on perfect self-actualization, then everyone would be able to handle this book with complete ease. There would be no nonbeing values to get in the way and impede the climb. But as it happens, we all have nonbeing values to contend with. In response to this possible "road block," it is recommended that the reader be realizing his or her self as close to the being dimension as possible. Otherwise the state of denial [32] will be pressed upon the self by the existing nonbeing values, and the climb will be abandoned in the belief that it is an impossible ploy. You will know what I mean as we move into the next section. If your personality is anything like mine, you are going to find yourself fighting to stay with truth and Actuality. If at the first try you are unable to "climb," do not allow yourself to become discouraged, but regroup by counseling your nonbeing values to "lay off" and let you move still close to the being dimension. One thing to look forward to is that once you have been able to start the climb, the hard part will be over, the Trail will have become set, and you will have an interesting climb to the top.

SECTION 5: THE ISOLATED SELF

The most threatening experience in my life came about five years ago when I realized that my self stood completely alone in the Universe. Before that time, I saw myself as being a family member and a Christian and an American and a man and a host of other things. I was "chugging" through life with a complete list of things that I could claim to be. But it was not until that day about five years ago when I confronted myself and asked about me: What am I? It was then that I had to face Reality and realize that it, Reality, was not "all over the place" but inside me, and that what I call "I" is as alone in the Universe as any star in the sky. The shock was brief, however, and I soon found myself awakening to some aspects of Reality that American education somehow neglected to mention. We will be discussing them as we climb.

If at this point I were asked to tell in a few lines of poetry what would take many pages of prose to say, it would be to tell how five and one-half billion objects twinkle in the Universe, bringing the light of Reality to the heavens--true and working objects called man. Man's main problem has been that he works behind a veil of nonbeing, not always realizing his duty in Reality to God and his proper role to play upon the stage of life.

SECTION 6: EXPLANATION OF TERMS

In this study, there are four terms which are so closely related that they may appear to mean the same thing. In some studies, these terms might be considered synonyms and be used interchangeably throughout the text. However, we are following a very narrow trail that requires precise meanings in each paragraph. It may be helpful for you to know the following meanings as their wordings appear in our text.

1. Actuality. Actuality includes every thing, event, and condition that exists in the Universe other than the human selves and their respective Reality constructs.

2. Nature. Nature is that part of Actuality which is in a dynamic state of motion. It includes the human selves for as much as they introject Natural values.

3. Physical Realm. The physical realm is that part of Actuality which is conceived to be in the static state for the purpose of study and the formulation of hypothesis: one of the base factors in cognition: a framework from which to reason.

4. Reality. Reality is a human creation: except for its nonbeing values, it is the developing counterpart of Actuality: a medium which is different from but coexisting with Actuality.

SECTION 7: ACTUAL TIME: A PROPERTY OF MOTION

On March 14, 1879, in the town of Donau, Germany, one of the greatest mathematical physicists was born. As a child, his mathematical genius carried him so far into the world of mathematical physics that his teachers could not keep up with his thinking, and he was regarded as being somewhat retarded. Then it happened that some noted mathematicians got word of his thinking and began to take his theories seriously--one of them being the theory of relativity. With Hitler's rise to power, he came to the United States and in 1933 he accepted membership in the Institute for Advanced Study at Princeton, New Jersey. He became an American citizen in 1940 and died here in 1955. His name was Albert Einstein (1879-1955).

Einstein's theory of relativity became recognized by mathematicians soon after the turn of this century: it brought him much acclaim, and gradually the entire field of physics began to change from being based upon the wave theory of motion to being based upon the quantum theory of motion. This new quantum theory explained how energy, matter, and the velocity of that matter are related and how this can be proved through mathematical equations.

Not long after the start of World War II, Einstein sent President Roosevelt a letter reporting the possibility that small amounts of heavy matter can be converted into immense amounts of energy. Almost immediately the Manhattan Project was begun at the University of Chicago; testing was done in the American desert; and in August of 1945, the first atomic bomb was dropped on Japan.

The theory of relativity provided mankind with the necessary insight to build an atomic bomb. It also provided other insights into Nature: one enabled scientists to comprehend the truth about Nature as a whole, and thus provide the mathematical basis for applying the quantum theory across the entire field of physics. This allowed physics to become one continuous mathematical derivation from mechanics to electronics, to nuclear physics, and to matters covered by Affective Realism.

Another insight led mankind to the understanding of how, in Nature, time is a property of motion. What the theory of relativity says is that whenever an object is placed in motion, time becomes a property of that motion. If the object is stopped, then it would have no motion, hence no time to display; but if it were given sufficient motion to raise its speed to the absolute velocity, that is, somewhere at or in advance of the speed of light, then motion would cease to exist and again there would be no time to display.

Still another insight that Einstein's theory of relativity provides is that, in Nature, there are no straight lines, but that the circle is the measure of distance. In addition, it points out that, in Nature, there is no closure--meaning that before two objects can meet, there will be a reissue of matter and/or form, and possibly an energy change as well.

Bertrand Russell (1872-1970). Albert Einstein's approach to relativity was done almost entirely at the mathematical level of reason. It was deep math, very deep math. In fact, as a boy in the 1930's, I recall it being said that there were only five or six people on earth who could understand what Einstein was proposing. In 1925, Bertrand Russell wrote a small book entitled "ABC of Relativity" [33]. In it, he gave a verbal explanation of how the theory of relativity explains Natural events. The matters discussed in this small book leave the reader amazed if not shocked, and possibly with some of the frustrating conclusions that Russell had--one being that the laws of physics may not be as reliable as we think.

If you are a mathematical physicist, you may be able to say whether or not Bertrand Russell was expressing the theory of relativity in a valid manner. As a biologist, I found myself unable to say whether or not he really knew what he was talking about, although I must admit that his little book left me both startled and wondering. However, as an affective realist, I found myself not only startled and wondering, but curious as to the possibility that Russell might have been reasoning upon an unclear basis. It appeared that he was assuming that Actuality and Reality were the same thing [34], which of course was not true. This does not mean that the ideas he came up with are necessarily wrong. It only means that his basis for reasoning must be unscrambled, that is to say, Actuality and Reality must be viewed separately, before his ideas can fall into valid perspective. What is the case in Actuality, what is the case in Reality, and what is the perspective which views the distinction between the two? In bringing the case in Actuality into focus, we have gained one-half of that perspective and can say that in Actuality--whose moving part we call Nature--time is a property of motion and should be called *actual time*.

SECTION 8: REAL TIME: A FRAMEWORK FOR REASON

We attempted to bring actual time into perspective in the previous section. Now, we will attempt to bring *real time* into that same perspective and note the distinction between the two.

Real time is a human creation; it is the framework of reason which we use in most all of our intellectual endeavors. Only in our mathematics and technical devices--for example, the Wilson cloud chamber--have we easily moved beyond this framework and explored the insensible workings of Nature. Yet, as it manifests in all human episodes of life, real time becomes the chain which links a human's past to his or her future; it is the duration of and between perceived and/or conceived events; it is tictoc time, measuring in seconds, minutes, hours, days, weeks, months, years, and on to eternity; and it is the fourth dimension of human Reality.

If you are still not clear on the distinction between Actuality and Reality, and actual time and real time, then consider the fact that actual time is a property of moving matter, while real time exists in the absence of matter. What the perspective is showing is that there are at least two spatial mediums in the Universe where things exist: one is occupied by matter, energy, and actual time; the other is occupied by matterless values, energy, and real time.

SECTION 9: THE ACTUALITY-REALITY INTERFACE

The term "interface" has several different meanings. Its meaning in this study will be that it is a common boundary between two different spatial mediums--Actuality and Reality.

The Actuality-Reality Interface [35]. It might be helpful if we reviewed each of these spatial mediums. Actuality includes every thing, event, and condition that exists in the Universe other than the human selves and their respective Reality constructs. Reality is a human creation which, except for its inadvertent accumulation of nonbeing values, is a developing counterpart of Actuality.

When these two mediums come together in common boundary, the Actuality-Reality Interface exists. Where the Actuality-Reality Interface exists first is always in the thalamic area of the human brain: from there, it continues as the common boundary between Actuality and the individual's Reality construct. If there are five and one-half billion living human brains on earth, there are that many Actuality-Reality Interfaces there as well. Let us call them the A-R Interfaces.

It is important that we take note of how an A-R Interface is a common boundary between two mediums, and should not be mistaken for the presence of bilateral symmetry in the human body, where recognition is given to such things as right and left cerebral hemispheres, right and left kidneys, and right and left lungs. Bilateral symmetry occurs in that part of the human body which exists on the Actuality side of the A-R Interface, and though it may have its own interface, and come under much scrutiny by us later on, it has little if anything to do with the interface which we are talking about here. What we are distinguishing is the interface which exists between two spatial mediums in the Universe--Actuality and Reality.

Certainly the most outstanding feature of the A-R Interface is the way in which it intersects the cognitive arena of a human personality. On the Actuality side enter the animal need impulses that many refer to collectively as the id; on the Reality side enter the intellectual need impulses that many refer to collectively as the superego; and in the middle of it lies the ego whose function is to determine how to meet the needs that are expressed by nervous impulses which enter the arena on either side. The following section gives some explanation of the terms we have been and will be using.

SECTION 10: EXPLANATION OF TERMS

1. The Fold of Reality. The Fold of Reality is that point in human mentality where the values of Actuality and Reality are in exact agreement at the A-R Interface: it is the intellectual point where the Vector of Reason emerges.

2. Thalamus. The thalamic area is where impulses reporting felt pleasures and pains throughout the body are brought in to awareness; it is where the cognitive arena and most if not all of the id and superego components are located. The thalamus is like a flying bird in the lower center of a human skull: the bird's body is like the thalamus itself and its wings are like the thalamic radiations which wing upward into the two cerebral hemispheres.   The thalamus is the crossroads and point of synapse for all sense data except that of smell.

3. Cognition.   The process of gaining knowledge through mental experience: the action of knowing.

4. Conscious.   The conscious level of cognition is where the full state of awareness exists; it is the location of the ego; it is the level at which some perceptions and all conceptions are scrutinized by the ego and found to either reconcile or conflict with existing id and superego impulses.

5. Cognitive Arena.   The cognitive arena is where all conscious, subconscious, and unconscious behaviors and affects manifest in or near the thalamus of a living human brain.

6. Subconscious.   The subconscious is the level of cognition which lies just below the conscious level; it is the cognitive level which affects thought, feeling, and behavior without entering consciousness; it is the level of partial awareness where many perceptions are received and responded to unnoticed.

7. Unconscious.   The unconscious is the level of cognition which lies below the subconscious level; it is that part of the psyche where all prior experience is recorded; its expression in awareness is extremely rare--often being referred to as a Freudian slip.

8. Id.   Being of more primitive origin, the id reacts on a pleasure-pain level; it is the seat of psychic energy; it is the origin of psychic differentiation into the superego and ego; it is the central nervous system's vehicle for expressing animal needs in the cognitive arena--including the phylogenetic [36] needs which are felt through sexual want and intuition, and the ontogenetic [37] needs which are felt through such wantings as hunger, thirst, and the desire for warm shelter; it produces the feeling of "I want." The id operates primarily in the thalamic area; it is functionally geared to the thalamus and hypothalamus, and on very rare occasions, will allow impulses from the reticular and other formations in the old brain to "slip" through. The old brain has sometimes been described as the knob of the spinal cord.

9. Ego. One's ego is his or her self, or soul; it is the component of cognition where value judgements are made and where responsibility for them becomes felt; it is the seat of reason; it is usually expressed by the words "I" and "me"; and it produces the feeling of "I am."

10. Superego. The superego is often referred to as man's inner policeman and conscience: it is the psychic component which brings forward the attitudes gained from past experience and enters them in the cognitive arena as guides to deliberation in the present: such attitudes include principles, ideals, and other values which were gained through long-standing experience in family, church, school, and other relationships in society and Nature: it produces the feeling of "I should."

11. Affect. Human affect includes the qualitative results of psychological experiences which occur as response to sensory, superego, and/or id stimuli during acts of cognition and become recorded in the subconscious and/or unconscious states. Such experiences usually occur at the conscious level.

12. Unconscious State. The unconscious state includes two of the components of human personality--the *biological format* [38] and the *Reality construct*. Aside from such things as Freudian slips and hypnosis, impulses coming from these two components enter the ego state via the id and/or superego, and become expressed at the conscious or subconscious levels.

13. Intellectual. Human intellectual behaviors are those that arise during the superego's influence upon deliberation; they occur when influences from the past become the logistics for reasoning in the present: if the id is man's animal side, then the superego is his intellectual side. One's intellect is his or her ability to bring controlled emotion, structure, logic and order into the process of concept development.

14. Emotion. Human emotion emerges during the anticipation of threat to or collapse of the intellect or body in general: it is expressed after the fact as grief: it is a physiological departure from *homeostasis* during acts of will, accident, and moments of disease; and is a functional factor in cognition.

15. Reason. Human reason is the cognitive process which makes facts intelligible; it is the intellectual act of pursuing truth; it is a line of thought which supports a valid judgement or belief; it explains a fact or validates a course of action. Deductive reasoning is when one reasons from a general rule or universal to a particular thing or fact. Inductive reasoning is when one reasons from a particular thing or fact to a general rule or universal. Reason is orderly and logical conception.

16. Biophysical Approach to Human Personality. This approach deals with all components of human personality that are biological, physical, and/or chemical in nature: dealing with components of human personality that are actual in nature. We are fortunate in that our study, Affective Realism, does not require the reader to have advanced learning in the Biophysical Approach to human personality. Some insight is essential; but if you are not a concrete scientist, then mastery of the terms which were discussed in this section should be sufficient to bring your Affective Reality in to view. Of course this is not to suggest that biophysics is no longer necessary as an approach to human personality: on the contrary, it will always be a way of understanding the vital workings of human personality, to apply scientific method, and to bring what we now see at the philo-sophical level down to the level of concrete science and irrefutable understanding.

A Note to True Christians. You may have already allowed your Affective Reality to come in to view. When you made your decision for Christ, you automatically set nonbeing values aside and began the process of self-actualization. In other words, you began to operate at or very near to the Fold of Reality. All you had to do was to acquire enough intellectual information to convince your self that Actuality and Reality are different. If the first view of your Affective Reality [39] was like mine, you experienced a flash of light followed by a clear view of your Reality. Then, located in your frontal lobes, the view may have waned back and become a useful and permanent reference to the past.

If your Reality has not yet come in to view, then keep reading. It will happen when you have acquired enough convincing intellectual information.

SECTION 11: COEXISTING UNIVERSES

This study recognizes two coexisting Universes. One is made up of Actuality, which includes every thing, event, and condition other than the human selves and their respective Reality constructs. Consisting of moving matter, energy, and space, this is the Universe which we think of as being ours. It is the one we regard as the Measurable Universe, the Macro-Universe, or simply the Universe. The other Universe is or contains what this study refers to as the Greater Reality. In concrete science, this may be what has been referred to as the Anti-Universe, because it has been found to contain low or no mass particles. In religion, it may be the long-regarded Promised Land, or Heaven. In this study, the Anti-Universe and Heaven will be considered to be the same thing, and will be referred to as the Greater Reality.

Man's introduction to the Anti-Universe came during the late 1950's and early 1960's when some nuclear physicists developed devices--the Wilson cloud chamber being one--which could detect low or no mass subatomic particles coming to earth from the sun. Having little or no measurable mass and very little magnetic moment [40], these tiny particles were found to be able to pass all the way through our earth with only a relatively few of them being absorbed--the neutrino being perhaps the best example. With this understanding, concrete science has arrived at a basis for reasoning that an Anti-Universe not only exists, but that it may very well coexist with our Macro-Universe and the Actuality of matter and energy which fills it. During the last three decades, nuclear physicists have carried this reasoning further and found that there may be more to the Anti-Universe than having low or no mass antiparticles moving away from the stars, as with neutrinos moving from the sun to earth. There also appear to be low or no mass antiparticles which are counterparts to many if not all of our Universe's subatomic particles with mass.

Could it be that while the folks in religion have been looking up for Heaven the folks in nuclear physics are finding it by looking around? Could it be that by reaching this subatomic threshold between the Macro-Universe and the Anti-Universe, concrete science has found the Interface which exists between Actuality and Reality? The position taken in this study is that it has. The threshold between the Macro-Universe (Actuality) and the Anti-Universe (Reality) [185] will be referred to as the *A-R Interface.*

The Super Collider. At the beginning of this decade, our nuclear scientists were well on their way toward completing the Super Collider near Waxahachie, Texas. It was looked upon as being one of mankind's best ways of investigating the threshold between the two Universes. But regrettably the American Congress didn't see it that way, and in 1993 the project was cancelled. Today, for as much as American nuclear physics is involved, the latest frontier on the road to human destiny lies very nearly "dead in the water."

SECTION 12: VIEWING THE ACTUAL HUMAN BODY

The correct way of viewing the actual human body is to see it as a Natural phenomenon which is in company with all of the other Natural phenomena on earth. Upon viewing all of these creations together, it is noted that they are living within a medium which consists of moving matter, energy, and space; that humanity is the most advanced Natural movement in the lot; and that there must be more to human destiny than a mere earthly demise. After much deliberation and progress, we humans find ourselves so advanced that we seemingly understand most of the things that are going on inside this medium which we call Actuality. Yet there are two main questions left unanswered, What are we? and, How can we get out of here alive? When we look into mirrors, we see our actual human bodies. Now we must look beyond those mirrors and consider what Nature has done to help us answer these two questions.

SECTION 13: VIEWING THE REAL HUMAN BODY

Man has been existing on this planet for over a million years [41]. During that time, he has lived according to the Natural Laws of Cause and Effect and Natural Selection, and gradually over that long period of time, his central nervous system has developed to such a degree that it can gear him to a medium into which he can go to realize higher values of living, and at the same time, escape death. All he had to do was to live and survive through reason, and Nature would do the job of making him able to enter this medium. He began to reason, he entered, and he found the Reality which we all now enjoy.

In case you are thinking that Nature lacks the wherewithal to help man commence life in one medium, live there for a while, and then change in a way that will permit him to live in another medium, think also of the Insect Class where many of its members spend the egg and larva stages in water and then metamorphose into the adult stage which can survive in air. Or think of the Amphibian Class of the Vertebrate Subphylum where most of its members spend part of their lives in one medium, water, and then metamorphose into an adult stage that can survive in another medium, air, as with the salamanders and frogs.

Also, you may be thinking that for Nature to produce organisms which can metamorphose so as to live part of their lives in a water medium and another part in an air medium is one thing, but to produce an organism which can live part of its life in a moving matter medium, Actuality, and then metamorphose so as to be able to live in a low or no matter medium, Reality, is something else. If we were living back before the turn of this century, I would agree with you. As a concrete scientist, I would think that such a change is impossible. However, early in this century, Albert Einstein came out with the theory of relativity which shows beyond a doubt that matter and energy are not only related, but that they can be the same when their velocities are adjusted. So today, I have to say that such a metamorphic condition does lie within the realm of possibility and is very much a worthwhile subject for concrete science to investigate; although we may have to wait for the mathematical physicists to explain it in terms that will give the whole story.

Coexistence. This is what may be the most vital of the paradoxical understandings--the understanding that a human's actual body and real body coexist. When you stand before a mirror, you view your actual body. People have been doing that since the dawn of mankind--gazing at their images in smooth water, then at their images in silvered glass mirrors, and now at images upon X-ray screens. All of those viewings, and rarely if ever has anyone been able to see his or her real body. Of course we understand why this is. It is because our animal senses can only respond to things which consist of matter and energy. This is how life operates on the Actuality side of the A-R Interface. What we must do now is to apply our methods of concrete science to the Interface between the actual and real human bodies and discover a way to view through it; although I am sure that aside from resolving such things as crime and leadership capacity, the individual's right to privacy would be protected.

SECTION 14: ENVIRONMENTAL INFLUENCE

Feral Children [42]. Early in this century, a great deal of attention was given to a report coming out of the Far East. The report described how a pack of wolves had found a small human baby along a train track, how a female member took charge and carried the baby off to her den, and how, after about four years, some hunters found the small boy running with the pack of wolves. Because he was displaying wolf culture, this feral child became known as the wolf boy. He was brought to America for study and controlled exposure to human culture. Years later, it was reported that he responded positively and was for the most part living a normal human life.

Later in this century, another feral child was found living in a chicken coop in one of America's small midwestern towns. It happened that the mother wanted a baby girl, and when the new child turned out to be a boy, she literally cast him to the chickens. About three years later, some workmen found him hopping after garbage with the chickens. Known as the chicken boy, he too reacted positively to human culture and went on to live a near normal life. There have been several other cases of feral children reported, and in most of them the individuals went on to live close to normal human lives. Here we have some rather strong indications that a developing human child is to some degree a product of his or her environment.

This reminds me of something said in 1970 by a learning theory professor on the first day of class at the University of Houston. He said that he could care less about what goes on inside the human head, and that all he wanted to know about was the overt behavior of the individual; for by providing positive and negative reinforcements to that behavior, he could guide the individual into becoming geared to the moldings of society. Today, we can see how that professor's obsession with the Behavioral Approach prevented him from bringing it into eclectic overview with one or more of the other six approaches, and thereby move psychology closer to a full understanding of human personality.

During the remainder [43] of this chapter, we will be considering those conditions in human personality that will enable us to bring all seven of the Approaches together into one eclectic view of what personality really is. There are some conditions that we will not be considering, for example, the hormonal and physiological conditions. But although our view may be incomplete, it should be enough to enable you to enjoy the sights of Affective Realism.

SECTION 15: MAJOR BIOPHYSICAL FACTORS IN HUMAN PERSONALITY

Biophysical Emotional Reactions. Our senses react to things in the environment by creating meaningful sense data and sending them through nerve fibers to places in the body where the type and degree of response is decided upon. Also, internal organs of the body will send meaningful data to the same or similar places, and the type and degree of response will be decided upon. If the nervous and/or chemical condition in these places is in balance, the individual will be experiencing comfort, because there are no distress signals coming in to disturb the balance; but when a distress signal arrives via a connecting nerve fiber [44], the nervous and/or chemical condition will fall into imbalance. In many cases, the imbalance will itself be the deciding mechanism for initiating response. Balance will be regained if the response is successful; but if it is unsuccessful, the distress signal will be passed on to the cerebral cortex, where symptoms of the emotional imbalance will be initiated as a new kind of response. If this response--for example, a pain-- is not dealt with below the conscious level, its persistence will eventually send signals to the conscious level [45]. In cases where balance of a nervous and/or chemical condition is maintained by itself being the deciding factor, a *nonaffective emotional reaction* [46] is said to exist. The place where many if not most of these reactions occur is the hypothalamus, and during the times when all of its reactions are in balance, the state of homeostasis exists.

Our study does not require us to pursue nonaffective emotional reactions any further than this; nor does it require us to give more than passing notice to other nonaffective nervous reactions, for instance, spinal cord reflexes and proprioceptors [47] throughout the body. Still, we should not overlook the way in which nonaffective emotional reactions influence human thinking, as in mood swings. This is a subject we will cover in a later section. What our study does require at this point is that we examine those emotional reactions that are involved in conscious and subconscious experiences. These are what we will be calling *affective emotional reactions* and have as main objects of study for the rest of this chapter.

The major difference between nonaffective emotional reactions and affective emotional reactions lies in the way that nonaffective emotional reactions retain balance by reducing organismic need impulses coming in from places all over the body. On the other hand, affective emotional reactions retain balance by reducing affective need impulses which come in from the senses and/or the unconscious (eg, the Superego) and become met at the subconscious level, or, if not resolved, drive on up to the conscious level and become realized as interest in or hunger for the sense data that will indicate a rewarding response and thereby balance the reaction involved.

Because affective emotional reactions are involved with prior human experience, it may be correct to assume that the environment of the individual and sense data become major variants in continuing nervous processes [48] where such reactions work to provide a human mental state, e.g., the conscious state [49]. The contention here is that the place where most if not all of these reactions occur is the thalamus.

Research in biophysics has shown that the thalamus is the junction where all the sensory fiber tracts (except the olfactory) synapse before continuing on to the cerebral cortex. Research has also indicated that most of the information coming from the environment and one's physical body will pass through the thalamus before going on to the cerebral cortex.

The Thalamic Area. Located in the lower center of the skull, the thalamic area is the juncture in the new brain where emotional reactions are used to maintain homeostasis and to direct the body's interaction with environment. It includes all of the nervous formations that Nature has provided to achieve these ends, primarily, the thalamus and the hypothalamus.

As was stated earlier, most of the nervous and/or chemical conditions [50] found in nonaffective emotional reactions occur in the hypothalamus and most of the conditions found in affective emotional reactions occur in the thalamus. This means that most emotional reactions occur in the area which includes both the thalamus and the hypothalamus; hence we call it the *thalamic area* and say that it is the control center because it is where most emotional decisions-to-act occur. It should be added, however, that research is still under way on this matter, and that the thalamic area may be found to contain still other essential nervous tissue formations.

The Control Center. Some of the early Greeks believed that the control center, or soul, in human personality was located in the blood. Later, some of them had the idea that it was located in the heart. Here in this study, it is considered to be located in the thalamic area.

Transcendence Of New Values. You should find it interesting that what we have just been considering from the Biophysical Approach and calling the thalamic area is almost the same thing as that which we will soon be viewing from the Psychoanalytic Approach [51] and calling the *id*. The only difference between them is that in man, and to a much lesser extent in some other higher mammals, the id begins the process wherein values transcend from the biophysical state of existence to the psychological state of existence.

SECTION 16: MAJOR PSYCHOLOGICAL FACTORS IN HUMAN PERSONALITY

The Id. An explanation of the id was provided in Section 10. However, perhaps we should review it before going further.

Being of more primitive origin [52], the id reacts on a pleasure-pain level; it is the seat of psychic energy; it is the origin of psychic differentiation into the superego and ego; it is the central nervous system's vehicle for expressing animal needs in the cognitive arena --including the phylogenetic needs which are felt through sexual want and intuition, and the ontogenetic needs which are felt through such wantings as hunger, thirst, and the desire for warm shelter; it produces the feeling of "I want." The id operates primarily in the thalamic area; it is functionally geared to the thalamus and hypothalamus and on some occasions will allow impulses from the reticular formation in the medulla [53] to slip through. The medulla connects the forebrain and cerebrum with the spinal cord.

Function of the Id. In this study, the id is seen as playing an extremely important role in helping biophysical nervous energy to transform into or generate psychic energy and bring need information up to the subconscious and/or conscious levels of awareness. Although concrete science is only now getting to the explanation of the biophysics in this process, it appears likely that much of it may be happening in the laminated tissues of the thalamus.

It should be emphasized that the connection which we make between the id and the thalamic area has to do only with the need information and sense data that enter the thalamic area from the senses and other organs of the body. What we are going to do in this study is to focus on need impulses which enter the id at the bottom and sense data impulses which enter it at or near the top and envision the psychological phenomenon which occurs as they interact.

The Cognitive Arena. The cognitive arena [54] is the zone of transition between the biological and psychological states. It is where all conscious, subconscious, and unconscious behaviors and affects manifest in or near the thalamus of a living human brain. The unconscious level blends in to become the upper-most attachment to the id; the subconscious level blends in much the same manner with the unconscious level; the conscious level blends the same with the subconscious level; and as for that which lies atop, the ego, the following is a review made in section 10.

The Ego. One's ego is his or her self, or soul; it is the component of cognition where value judgments are made and where responsibility for them becomes felt; it is the seat of reason and where ideas first occur; it is usually expressed by the words "I" and "me"; and it produces the feeling of "I am."

A Brief Overview of Nonaffective, Affective, and Cognitive Emotional Reactions. Nonaffective emotional reactions lie low in or below the id; their stimulus impulses originate in body organs; their response impulses deal with the causes of these stimulus impulses; and their reaction balance is maintained through direct or indirect [55] dealings outside the cognitive arena. Affective emotional reactions lie high in or above the id and follow much the same program, except that the originations of their stimulus impulses are affect and the senses rather than body organs; their response impulses [56] are issued below the conscious level [57] of awareness; and in cases where learning had not preceded the event, the stimulus impulses are passed on up to the conscious level and enter into *cognitive emotional* *reactions* which manifest as the elements of cognition. These cognitive emotional reactions produce the response impulses which constitute the emotional fabric of reason and the feelings of "I," "me," and "I am."

Ontogenetic Need Impulses. These are need impulses [58] that are relayed low in the id and passed up to the conscious level where they effect such individual want feelings as hunger, thirst, elimination, and the desire for physical comfort.

Phylogenetic Need Impulses. There are two main streams of phylogenetic need impulses. One moves toward successful interpersonal relationships and the other demonstrates an aptitude for successful interaction with environment. These are:

A. *Libido.* One's libido is the variable but continuous flow of psychic energy which causes him or her to act out person-to-person attractions, usually in the form of lustful feelings that lead to sexual pleasure and climax if successful, or to sexual frustration and displeasure if unsuccessful; it is derived from primitive biological urges; its intensity is most often regulated through hormonal influences; it is one of man's Natural endowments for perpetuating the race [59]; and it is found to exist in all of the vertebrate classes.

B. *Intuition.* One's intuition is the variable but continuous flow of psychic energy [60] which carries a genetically loaded aptitude for reason into the state of consciousness. Deriving from primitive biological urges [61], it entertains incoming sense data by readying the state of consciousness for reason. As a precursor to the superego, it forges and maintains the neural pathway which carries intellectual attitude and substance to the state of consciousness. It too is a Natural endowment for perpetuating the race: it does for man much as instinct does for lower animals; and its action is what enables the emergence of the human self. To refresh our memory, the following is the explanation of superego which was given in Section 10.

Superego. The superego is often referred to as man's inner policeman and conscience; it is the psychic component which brings forward the attitudes gained from past experience and enters them in the conscious state as guides to deliberation in the present; such attitudes include principles, ideals, and other values which were gained through long-standing experience in family, church, school, and other relationships in society and Nature; it produces the feeling of "I should."

The Conscious State. The conscious state is the full state of awareness; it is the location of the ego; it is the state in which some perceptions and all conceptions are scrutinized by the ego and found to either reconcile or conflict with existing id [62] and superego impulses: into it flow unmet ontogenetic and phylogenetic need impulses, superego and intuitive need impulses, unmet sensory need impulses, and a generous amount of sense data that provide a graphic display of the environment. The conscious state is where in normal situations all cognitive emotional response impulses have been or are being transformed into the psychic energy values [63] (ideas) whose interplay becomes the essence of reason, judgement, self-realization, and the state of mind which we view as cognition. That part of the conscious state which performs through the activity of emotional reactions and associated nervous impulses exists in Actuality. In the next section, we will begin to consider the part of the conscious state which exists in Reality.

> *Conception does in Reality what perception does in Actuality...gather information.*

SECTION 17: THE PHENOMENAL SELF

Viewing Personality From the Inside. Join me in an imaginary visit to the newly delivered boy named Joe, and inasmuch as our trip can involve make-believe, let's give three of his organs the ability to verbalize their problems: these are the adrenal gland, the liver, and the thymus gland [64].

Referring to Sigmund Freud's infantile stages of development, this visit would extend from the beginning of the neonatal stage (first month) to the end of the oral stage (about the first year).

Here is what the adrenal gland might be saying: Hey you guys! We have a whole new ball game here. I need help. During the nine months between Joe's birth and delivery [65], his mother's body transferred a well-balanced diet into his blood. That diet was keeping glucose, salt, and water balance well within the normal range, and it was doing great in controlling the sodium and potassium which are so necessary for the normal development of his central nervous system. All I had to do was sit back and twiddle my thumbs. But now his mother has dumped him out and cut the vital cord. All she's doing to help him now is to stick a cow-milk nipple in his mouth and cover him with a blanket. If we don't get to work and keep Joe's blood sugar within 70 and 140 [66], he's going to drift into a diabetic coma; and even if we can keep the sugar in balance, his central nervous system will not develop properly if it lacks the proper amounts of sodium and potassium. I can do a lot to control these things, but I need help.

Here is what the liver might be saying: Right! I too was having a pretty easy time of it during that nine month trip, that joy ride down the uterine canal. And when Joe's mother dumped him, covered him with a blanket, and stuck that rubber nipple in his mouth, I thought that my capacity to store glucose would be enough to help you keep his blood sugar within the normal range, even though his pancreas was still learning how to release the insulin which acts as a catalyst in the movement of sugar into his body cells. What upsets me are those times when Joe's mother spurts that strange concoction into his mouth. One time it would have too much sugar: another time it would have too little. Why won't she use her own mammary papilla and let him have close to the same diet that he had during the trip? Yes, I agree. We need help.

And here is what the thymus gland might be saying: I understand your problems and I am trying to do the job that Nature put me here to do--which is to help you maintain Joe's cell, tissue, and body metabolism until the whole endocrine and central nervous systems become developed enough to be brought on line. The hypothalamus is developing nicely, and will be mostly on line before the end of Joe's oral stage. Knowing this is a signal to me that his thalamus and cerebral cortex are also getting ready for business. So tomorrow I plan to send distress stimuli to the intuitive emotional reaction formation and ask that it notify the thalamus to get the id started in diverting aptitude response impulses from their existing target --the mouth ganglia in the cerebral cortex--and have them forge a neural path up to the conscious level. This way they can make the conscious state ready for reason. And when the hypothalamus gets developed enough to assume the hunger function, its hunger impulses won't have to end in the cortex, but can be diverted by the id and sent up to the conscious level where the need impulses will be less apt to induce crying: rather they will be met by Joe's growing reasoning ability, and become expressed [67] by words and gestures whose meanings the folks can understand and interact with. You see, it will only be a short while before Joe will be able to manipulate the environment and get what he really needs. No longer will he have to lie with a nipple in his mouth, just hoping they get things right. Then will be the time when he will be able to point his want and smile his pleasure and utter words of love and affection and belonging and being and joy. That's when his assertive personality will have flowered, and when his dad will look down and say, "That's my boy."

So hang in there. It will only be a little while before Joe will be able to take responsibility for this whole body which he shall call "I" and "me" and "mine." Then you guys may return to your normal tasks, and after that, go back to twiddling your thumbs. As for myself, you can always find me. Just look for the scar on Joe's inner chest wall.

The Puppet Master Episode. Before leaving our make-believe visit with Joe, we should look in upon his thalamic area and envision where his conscious state lies. What was going on in it, as the first hunger need impulses began to enter? Actually, at that time, it was pretty empty. There were few if any sexual impulses coming in. There were no superego [68] or elimination need impulses coming in. Aside from developmental errors on the part of the hypothalamus and the thalamus, the conscious state had only intuitive aptitude impulses, hunger need impulses, and sense data impulses to deal with. This is what Joe's conscious state was like when the puppet master episode began.

What is the puppet master episode? That is the period when the ego state is just beginning to form. In Joe, it was the time when one or more of his cognitive emotional reactions would react to sense data impulses that describe objects in the environment and produce response impulses which, under the guidance of his intuitive emotional reaction impulses, would be passed up to the appropriate ganglia in the cerebral cortex to effect motor impulses that would move the objects described. For example, seeing his left toes, Joe would send response impulses up to the left toe ganglia in the cerebral cortex and effect motor impulses that moved the left toes.

The puppet master episode [69] begins near the end of the neonatal stage and lasts well into the oral stage. During that time, Joe was really having a ball. Every waking moment you could find him pulling strings, that is to say, sending response impulses to the cerebral cortex, and then waiting to see what moved. If he could talk at that time, his words would probably be something like these: Hey! This is great. I can now move that bottle so as to get the nipple in there straight. I can kick that blanket off when I get too warm. I can see that I must be something, because I can make things happen. But why can't I move mom's hand, or dad's? When Joe reached this point in his development, when he began to distinguish between himself and the environment--that was the point which marked the end of his puppet master episode and the becoming of his phenomenal self.

Emergence of Self. Again, let us put words into Joe's mouth and hear him say something like this: I'm getting confused. When I started this puppet master thing, I was under the impression that I could physically control everything my sense data described. Now, I feel like the captain of a boat who is just finding out that he doesn't control the whole environment, but just his boat. I want to know what's going on. Exactly what am I a part of? Am I like the captain, having to remain tied to the dock until supplies come aboard; or must I get on my hands and knees and go after them? And what about all those things that mom and dad say I am--a Smith, a boy, a Christian, a child of God, a Texan, an American, a good boy, a sweet thing, a chip off the ol' block, handsome, cute, hungry, wet, and in need of change? I don't have the foggiest notion of what they are talking about, but I do know that I can get them to say certain things when I smile and other things when I cry. So what I am going to do is to concentrate on my cry and smile behaviors and try to remember the words and gestures that they evoke; especially those that please mom [70]. Somehow, my love and trust in her seems more secure when she's happy that I smile. Maybe if I pay particular attention to words and gestures that bring me pleasure, I will be able to ask why, when, where, and how questions and find out what the heck they were talking about when they called me all those things.

During the early part of his oral stage, Joe's conscious state was bewilderingly void of word meanings. There was a bevy of words coming in via sense data, but no learned responses to greet them. Only the intuitive emotional aptitude (for reason) impulses were controlling the psychological action at the time. Then gradually [71], as the bevy of words kept coming, Joe began to associate words with the hunger needs that were being gratified at the time. These successes became temporarily saved by his cognitive emotional reactions [72] which responded to new arrivals of these words with impulses that constituted his strands, or fabric, of reason [73]. At the very beginning, these strands of reason interacted with the aptitude impulses and underwent energy transformation from nervous energy to psychic energy[74]. The result was an idea. And when enough of these ideas joined together, a conceptualization of self appeared. Joe's phenomenal self [75] had become a Reality whose use of ideas produced a self realization that would later be expressed by terms like "I," "me," and "I am."

We must bear in mind that what we refer to here as intuitive emotional aptitude impulses were genetic recordings of successful superego impulses in Joe's ancestral past. In returning to the present, they acted much like an ignition in getting his self operating; but after it had a chance to create and save a number of similar self-realization ideas, superego began to form in a polarized manner and send its own attitudinal values into the conscious state, thus making the intuitive impulses unnecessary for the perpetuation of self. This soon became Joe's permanent learning process, where ideas would be created in his conscious state and saved as new additions to his superego operation in the Reality medium.

Joe's phenomenal self is the protuberance of his superego into his conscious state when he is both awake and asleep; it is his Real self; it exists only in the Reality medium; it is the real counterpart to the actual self; and, as will be discussed in the next two sections, it contains all of the characteristics of life which occur in the actual self, save for those that involve the physics of matter.

This is not a study of psychology any more than it is of biophysics or Natural history or the history of Western

Civilization. Although it relies heavily upon all of these fields, it takes from them only as much information as is required to introduce the reader to the philosophy of Affective Realism. I believe that we have gathered enough information from bio-physics and psychology for the reader to envision the existence and vital importance of the phenomenal human self. We will therefore not be viewing Joe's development through the remaining infantile stages. If you are not a student of human personality, you may want to refer to child psychology books and study child development further.

SECTION 18: PSYCHOANALYTICAL VIEWS [76] OF THE EGO STATE

The difference Between Psychoanalysis and Affective Realism.   There would be no difference between Psycho-analysis and Affective Realism if it were not for the fact that psychoanalysts work with the understanding that Actuality and Reality are the same thing while affective realists work with the understanding that they are not the same thing. It should then be reasonable to think that all one has to do to envision the model of the ego state from the viewpoint of Affective Realism is to imagine the psychoanalytic model and modify it so as to accommodate for the difference between Actuality and Reality. That is what we will be doing here [77].

The Static Model of the Ego State. My introduction to the psychoanalytic model of the ego state was when the professor had us imagine the old nursery rhyme about three men in a tub --the butcher, the baker, and the candlestick maker. She then had us remove the butcher and put a policeman in his place, remove the baker and put a beggar in his place, and remove the candlestick maker and put a wise man in his place. Her last step was to inform us that in psychoanalytic terms the policeman represents the superego, the beggar represents the id , the wise man represents the ego, and the tub represents all or part of consciousness. The id, the superego, the ego, and all or part of consciousness are the components of the *ego state*. This "tub" view is the static model of the ego state.

Concrete science has not yet arrived at the exact configuration of the ego state. But this did not mean that the psychoanalytical study of human personality had to stop. On the contrary, psychoanalysis has been growing ever since Sigmund Freud started it late in the 1800's. Today, it is one of the major theoretical tools used in the medical profession to assess functional mental health problems [78]. It has also contributed greatly to fields that work with normal range human behavior [79], for instance, educational curriculum development, educational philosophy, teacher training, and school counseling.

What one must understand is that for over a hundred years the human ego state has been recognized and dealt with in most segments of the intellectual world, although we have yet to find exactly how it fits into the thalamic area of the human central nervous system.

Formation of the Ego State. If you will think back to the time when our subject, Joe, was in his neonatal stage of development, his ego state was practically empty. All it contained was an id whose expressions of need were almost entirely made up of hunger impulses (The libido was then being directed upon his body), and whatever existed in the manner of ego and superego development had not yet become actuating factors. Yet during the next twelve months [80], all three of these ego state components, the id, the superego, and the ego, would simultaneously grow and interact to become the players in Joe's operable ego state.

The Action Model of the Ego State. One thing that tends to be overlooked is that if one's personality develops normally, its id and superego are going to be tenaciously inclined to unite in producing the ego. Putting this in other words, Natural Selection has provided human personalities whose ids and superegos unite for the purpose of survival. Where they unite, the personality will survive, and where they divide, the personality will not survive. The production of the ego in the ego state is much like the production of light in a light bulb [81], when the wires are united, light appears; and in the ego state, when the id and superego are united, the ego appears. Similarly, the veracity of the components, the force of the energy used, and the purity of the medium will determine the strengths of light and ego that are produced. This "light bulb" view is the action model of the ego state.

You may have noted that insofar as Western civilization has tended to save all human personalities we are touching upon a very sensitive subject. Although this study's primary concern is with the highly veracious and tenacious ego state, which provides for a mental condition that is often referred to as self-actualization [82], and which we will be considering as the mode of higher reason, we must give passing notice to the troubled ego states that exist within the minds of almost half of the American adult population. The contention here is that while some of these ego state problems have genetic causes, the vast majority of them root in culture and are therefore avoidable.

A Graphic Example of an Ego State Conflict. Perhaps the best examples of how the human mind falls into discord are those that are found in id-superego conflicts, and the most graphic of these seem to be the ones that occur in celibate and married clergymen. One good illustration was the case where a beautiful woman sitting in the front row of the congregation placed her legs in such a provoking manner that the clergyman's libido broke loose from the harmonious relationship he had set up between his id and superego. The result was that as he began to cathect [83] libidinal energy toward the woman and develop feelings of sexual want for her, his superego would step in and register its taboo with feelings of anxiety and inhibition. Finally, his conflict became so severe that he came in for counseling. The way used to solve his problem was to have him verbalize his want feelings concerning the woman for a while, and then have him verbalize his should feelings regarding her.

Gradually, he was able to reconcile his want and should impulses; his anxiety and inhibition were gone; and he had regained the ability to self-actualize while preaching. Interestingly, it happened that at subsequent church meetings he preached from the pulpit at the other end of the altar.

Psychological Defenses. There are a number of mechanisms [84] that every human mind may use to help keep its ego state operating in the normal range of behavior. These are called defense mechanisms because they work to keep threatening sense and recall data from the attentive wit of the ego. We will be considering two of these mechanisms--projection and introjection [85].

We do not have to go far to find defense mechanisms in action. In fact, we don't have to go anywhere. We can just stop to consider our own mechanisms. So in view of this and the probability that you and I are operating in or near the mode of higher reason, why don't we reflect upon our own thinking and note how we handle threatening intellectual sense data? Since I am doing the "talking," let's have me be the provider of threatening sense data and you the reader be the one who sets defense mechanisms into action. The substance in the following paragraph (paragraph A) is designed to trigger your projective mechanism [86] and the substance in paragraph B is planned to trigger your introjective mechanism.

A. To summarize this short discussion on the merits of psychoanalysis, it might be said that Sigmund Freud committed grave errors, foremost of which was the way in which he failed to mention the established fact that the human soul is located in the heart, as literature so aboundingly reflects.

B. To summarize this short discussion on the merits of psychoanalysis, it might be said that Sigmund Freud led the intellectual world to a

new horizon, from which the explanation of
human existence appears inevitable and straight
ahead along the road of concrete science.

Human Cognition. In this study, human cognition is defined
as being the emotional level which exists while the ego state is
in the process of reasoning through to value judgements and
executing them in manners which promote unification and harmony between the id and superego. We should be mindful of
the fact that in this study our focus is on personalities whose
ego states are operating in or near the mode of higher reason
and have a minimal number of nonbeing values [87] pressing in
via sense and recall data. In other words, our focus will be on
the interactions between the three ego state components when
there is a minimal need for psychological defenses other than
introjection and projection [88]. With these things in mind, I
ask you to envision the action (light bulb) model of the ego state
and consider your own performance while reading paragraphs
A and B.

If you found yourself grimacing while reading paragraphs
A and/or B, it would indicate that your intellect was probably
not in alignment with the reasoning found in this book. If such
was the case, and if the grimacing was not accompanied by
unusual emotional feelings [89], then it may be safe for you to
continue reading. But if you did experience raised emotions,
particularly those expressed by anxious feelings, then I caution
you to stop: the **RED LIGHT** [90] is on, and you will be wise
to turn it off before reading further.

If you found yourself grinning while reading paragraph A,
it may be a signification that you allowed me to hook you into
becoming a needful figure in a Gestalt experience [91]. It may
indicate that you allowed me to set you up to expecting some
ridiculous sense data, that is, sense data whose load of information would be out of alignment with the reasoning in this
book. When your ego discovered this lack of alignment, it
responded by prompting laughter: or to be more specific, it
prompted laughter because your superego was advising that the

experience was only make-believe and that the line of reason in this book was still as introjective as ever. If you found yourself hooked into this positive Gestalt experience, you may want to copy paragraph A and have it read by someone who has not been set up; then observe the early response. If that person gears to concrete science, his or her response should indicate a psychological rejection mechanism that is being played out through some form of verbal and/or nonverbal behavior. By viewing this, you may get some idea of how you would have reacted had you not been set up.

If you felt pleased while reading paragraph B, it would indicate that your ego state was buying (introjecting) the load of information which sense data was laying upon it, that your superego was ready to consider its acceptability as data to incorporate with existing affect, and that you are probably feeling an interest in reading further.

A Two-Approach Overview of the Ego State. Imagine, if you will, the human thalamus and hypothalamus sitting near the center of the skull and at a level about even with the nose. This is what we previously referred to as the thalamic area and the location of the cognitive arena. Now, with the action ego state model in mind, let us continue in imagination and consider the contents of the cognitive arena. What we see is an ego state whose id is functionally geared to the thalamus and hypothalamus. What we don't see is how the superego and unconscious tie in to the central nervous system. We know that they must lie in or near the thalamus, because the id's gearing to the thalamus and hypothalamus anchors the entire ego state to the thalamic area. What we have been able to do so far, then, is to use the Biophysical and Psychoanalytical Approaches to develop an eclectic view of the ego state being functionally geared to the central nervous system on the id side, but dangling free on the superego side. The superego side is dangling free in the sense that it contains the superego, which is able to feed information to and recall information from the unconscious; yet we still have to determine if and how this side attaches to the biophysical portion of human personality, other than through the id.

As for how the ego emerged, we must begin to prepare for the realization that human personality straddles two mediums-- Actuality and Reality. We have to touch upon this matter here because part of the ego state lies on the Actuality, or id, side of the A-R Interface, and is best scrutinized from this two-approach view. If you will bear in mind that the biological propensities have been unfolding throughout child development, as with projection and introjection, and if you will recall the period of omnipotence and what we referred to earlier as the puppet master episode, you may see how the Actuality side of the ego state has derived from those early stages of development. In other words, the Actuality side of the ego state is a biological phenomenon that emerged during the period of omnipotence, and has matured to become the puppet master all grown up. This is what we will be referring to as the *actual self.*

Projection of Self. Insofar as we are reasoning so close to the emergence of the actual self and the manner in which it is expressing propensities that originated during the period of omnipotence, it should be pointed out that the projection of self is not only one of these propensities, but that it is the mechanism which humans may use most in interactions with the environment. Watching television or reading a book or hearing one tell a story are typical examples of where the individual projects himself or herself into the situation being studied. But is this possible? How can it happen? The answer is that, in Actuality, it is impossible and can not happen; however, you can't tell that to the actual self, whose cloak of omnipotence still holds self to include all that is perceived. The trick of it all is that while the infantile puppet master was playing with cerebral cortex strings (thalamic radiation fiber tracts), some of the earliest ideas [92] relating to self-conception were created. Foremost among those early ideas was the idea of omnipotence--which the superego would keep bringing back to the ego state and prevail as a cloak of omnipotence upon the actual self. This cloak was the seed which developed into the main subject in our next, the three-approach, overview. But before leaving our present discussion, let me structure the idea of projection a bit further.

As things now stand, concrete scientists have little reason to believe that energy leaves any of the senses and *cathects* upon objects in the environment. This means that such things as the projection of self and projection of blame--a form of rejection --can only be cast back into the unconscious and returned by the superego for ego state assessment. For example, a television program, whose information you have been extracting from sense data, loses your interest. Your ego responds by effecting motor behavior that will change the channel. The point is that the projection never leaves your head, and its only contact with the outside world is the motor activity that your biological format strategically effects. The play in all psychological projections is only carried on between the biological format, the ego state, and the unconscious state.

Using this two-approach view of the ego state is giving us a clearer understanding of how the id gears to the central nervous system. It is giving us some idea as to the possible origin of the actual self. However, it does not explain the dangling effect, or lack of rooting, on the superego side of the ego state. So let us advance to the next level of eclectic overview and see if we can't find at least part of that explanation.

A Three-Approach Overview of the Ego State. This is the view [93] one gets when the Biophysical, Psychoanalytical, and Phenomenological Approaches are joined to give an eclectic overview of the ego state. By bringing the Phenomenological Approach into the picture at this time, we can begin to get some plausible explanation for the dangling side of the ego state, and at the same time, come closer to understanding the structure of the ego state as it exists in real life. To do this, we will be focusing on the conceptualizations of the phenomenal self and the transcendence of self.

In order to conceptualize the phenomenal self, one must envision the living human body as standing alone in the Universe, then consider the structure of the thing inside the head that makes it able to initiate human activity the way it does. Viewing only from the Phenomenological Approach, it can be seen that this thing must be able to control reason, judgement, and all voluntary (motor) activity; and in order to do this, it must be in gear with the biophysical parts of the human body. Furthermore, it must be able to project itself into places that have been, are being, or will be experienced during the course of mortal life. This thing is what some followers of the Phenomenological Approach [94] refer to as the *phenomenal self.*

Similarly, in order to conceptualize the transcendence of self, one must envision the living human body as standing alone in the Universe, then consider how the self expands itself to include all of the biological structures of the individual's body. In other words, it transcends from being a mere speck in the middle of the brain and becomes the whole body. It does this because there is nothing to suggest that it can't. On the contrary, in their emphasis upon such things as cleanliness, grooming, looks, and attire, our human societies consistently reinforce this transcendency. Thus the infantile stage of omnipotence unknowingly lingers on.

As for where the phenomenal self is centered, one need only ask where inside the human head the structure is that can do all of the jobs that the phenomenal self can do. The answer is that it is the superego at the dangling end of the ego state: for this is the place where human reasonings and judgments are either received or generated and rejected or introjected (accepted) into affect; where attitudes from the past become manifested in the present; and where, in the midst of all of this, ideas are created. But as for knowing where the superego and the unconscious exist, we will have to advance to the four-approach overview, which is one of the subjects presented in the next Section.

In closing this Section, we should express thanks to Sigmund Freud and the host of other scientists and philosophers whose pioneering along the Trail of Reason gave us a path to follow. And as we move toward the end of this book, I trust that you the reader will join me in recognizing how, in its search for truth, this longstanding team of scholars has been moving mankind ever forward along the road to human destiny.

SECTION 19: VIEWING THE EGO STATE THROUGH AFFECTIVE REALISM

As was pointed out earlier, Psychoanalysis and Affective Realism differ only in that psychoanalysts work with the understanding that Actuality and Reality are the same thing, while affective realists work with the understanding that they are not the same thing. The position taken in this study is that the reasoning in Psychoanalysis and Affective Realism is exactly the same until we come to this next, the four-approach, level of eclectic [95] overview.

Before going on, however, there is an important distinction to be made clear. It lies in the fact that Psychoanalysis is one of the seven approaches to human personality and may be brought into construct, that is, into eclectic view, with any or all of the other six approaches at any time. The same can be said for any of the other six approaches. But Affective Realism is not an approach to human personality: rather, it is a philosophy which is founded upon all seven of the above approaches when they are joined to give an eclectic display of human personality. This means that as affective realists you and I can entertain any of the seven approaches and arrive at interesting ideas and concepts; but we will not know their validity until we are able to bring them into construct with at least one of the other six approaches. If you think back, you will note how that has been the procedure we tried to follow in this book.

The Four-Approach Overview of the Ego State. This is the view one gets when the Biophysical, Psychoanalytical, Phenomenological and Existential Approaches are joined to give an eclectic overview of human personality. This is the view which allows us to conceptualize a human personality standing alone in the Universe and consider its existence in a Greater Scheme of Things than what our animal senses make out, that is to say, what our animal senses make out to be actual truth, and what we commonly refer to as Actuality.

In the first part of this chapter, there was considerable discussion given to the way in which man's animal senses witness the truths of Nature, most notably, how the Natural Laws of Cause and Effect and Natural Selection sometimes collaborated to produce new and improved rackets for survival. It was found that after more than two billion years of production, Nature has yielded millions of species of plants and animals; it was found that existing species had survival rackets to keep them from extinction; and we found ourselves, humanity, to have perhaps the best racket of all--intelligence. Now is the time for us to look beyond our animal sensibilities and inquire into the existence of such intelligence.

Also in the first part of this Chapter, there was considerable discussion given to the Interface which exists between two distinctly different mediums--Actuality and Reality. We noted that one of these mediums, Actuality, is filled with matter and energy, and that the other, Reality, is filled with energy and some yet to be explained form of anti-matter--a low or no mass substance. And then we noted the Interface, the A-R Interface, which lies between the two mediums. In this study, we are viewing how these two mediums interface at places where active exchanges of values are ongoing throughout mortal human life. These places exist as what we have come to regard as ego states; or to be precise, they are points of interface between the human ids and superegos.

Recalling the action (light bulb) model of the ego state, we can say that the filament represents the A-R Interface, that one electrode represents the id, and that the other electrode represents the superego. However, in saying this, we must adjust the two-approach and three-approach overviews of the ego state so that they will cease to have the superego end of the ego state left dangling, and instead, let it root in the Reality medium. This is what we are doing here in the four-approach overview. We are determining what this dangling end roots into. So let us consider the Existential Approach and see what it can bring into our growing view of the ego state.

You will recall our discussion in Chapter Three where we differentiated between being and nonbeing values by pointing out how being values are in correspondence with Actuality and how nonbeing values are not. That was where the point was made that the most valid degree of being is reached by the human mind whose conception of Reality is an exact duplication of its perception of Actuality. When a human mind behaves this way, it is said to be self-actualizing. Now let us bring these understandings into construct with what has just been said.

Viewing from the Existential Approach, it appears that there are two mediums involved in the emergence of a human personality: one is Actuality, the other is Reality, and they interplay at a point in the Interface which we have come to regard as the human ego state. This brings us to what may be the shortest and most encompassing definition of a human personality. *A human personality is a place in the A-R Interface where the interplay of human values becomes a fellowship between Actuality and Reality.*

Recall also where it was said that the phenomenal self is a protuberance of the superego into the conscious state. Now let us carry this discussion a bit further and point out how the superego--the phenomenal self--deals only in real values: for example, in such tictoc time values as seconds, minutes, and hours; in such other dimensional values as length, width, and depth; and in such existential values as past experience, present experience, and future experience. What we must level with is the fact that these are values of Reality, of Reality alone, and in mortal experience, they have never been, they never are, and they never will be found on the other side [96] of the A-R Interface, not even when they are being conveyed via symbols from one human personality to another.

As we bring this four-approach overview into focus, there

are eight considerations that tend to recap the story of human existence. These are:

1. **The Nature of Human Existence.** How the arrival of several billion humans on this earth fits in to the Grand Scheme of things is a matter which we may never completely understand as mortals. However, as mortals we have managed to make a start in that direction.

   After about 350 years of working within the framework [97] of inductive science, mankind has been able to gather many if not most of the truths about human existence as it actually occurs on earth. We have been able to amass a body of concrete information which provides an understandable account of the physical and biological forerunners of what lies before and within us today. We now know much of Nature's history and how mankind emerged as a fruit of her labor; we now know much about the human body and its survival needs; we now know much about the Measurable Universe and the laws of physics which prevail throughout; and we are now beginning to understand human metamorphosis and how it is happening before our very eyes.

   Man now has a body of concrete information which has been growing and revealing and ever-pointing to the eternal components of humanity. For the past million years or so, this great amassment of knowledge has been recorded in ideas which have been organized into concepts and usually passed along to each new generation. Especially during the past 350 years, this amassment has mounted; and as might be expected, the intensity and breadth of the insight produced was bound to provide an awakening to the eternal aspects of human existence, if indeed they exist. That is what is happening today.

   One way of assessing the human situation on earth today is to compare it to a giant popcorn popper--where five and one half billion kernels are getting ready to pop. As will be discussed later, this "popping" should have started two thousand years ago, but somehow Aristotle and others neglected to put the right kind of reason, inductive reason, into the science which Aristotle himself had fathered.

2. **Two Mediums Available to Human Reason.** For the better part of a million years man gave eye to his existence. Then in the Stone Age, he pondered his existence; in the Bronze Age, he pondered his existence; in the Iron Age, he pondered his existence; in the Ancient Age, he pondered his existence; in the Dark Age, he pondered his existence; in the Middle Age, he pondered his existence; and when he advanced into the Age of Reason, he was still pondering his existence, as we are doing today. Albeit long, the road to human destiny has had man marching to the ontogenetic and phylogenetic drummings of Nature, keying upon the beckonings of God, and deliberating over human existence most of the way.

Today, in gleaning the past, we find that many of man's existential ponderings involved religious values, most notably, those involving abiding faith, ritual, and worship. But with the arrival of the Age of Reason, man began three secular endeavors that centered on human existence. One of those endeavors was to review the works of the ancients, particularly those of Plato and Aristotle, and try to build upon the valid reasonings of the past. A second endeavor was to commence a study of human values, for example, of secular principles [98] and ideals, and attempt to spread more light on the matter of human existence. And the third endeavor was to begin a scientific study whose method of thinking would be inductive reason. Largely as a result of these three secular endeavors and the religious thrust within the Christian churches, that is, the spirited drive toward God and Christ, our God and intellect-oriented Western Civilization surged into world domination, and notwithstanding its many infusions of delusions from within and without, it still stands strong today.

Over the past 350 years, there has been an intellectual explosion of valid ideas and concepts concerning human existence, as is shown by the advances in biology, medicine, and psychology. Nevertheless, despite his new insights and intellectual horizons man has advanced through the Ages and even to this day believing that he is operating in only one medium. What we are finding today is that what seems to be one medium is actually two mediums, that what we thought of as a sameness of meaning between the words Actuality and Reality is a myth, and that if we are to stay with truth, we must prepare for the understanding that Actuality is one thing and Reality is something entirely different.

After all of those ponderings, after all of those deliberations over human origin and destiny, man has finally advanced to the point where he can differentiate between that part of his existence which is actual and that part which is real.

3. **The Essence of Human Personality.** Earlier it was said that perhaps the shortest and most encompassing definition of a human personality is that it is a place in the A-R Interface where the interplay of human values becomes a fellowship between Actuality and Reality. To many, this will be seen as a ludicrous idea, but to you who are concrete scientists and/or true Christians, the realization should be upon you that in a Greater Scheme of Things, human personality is exactly the way it has just been defined.

What you and I must come to grip with is the fact that our personalities straddle two mediums, Actuality and Reality, and that as mortal human beings our animal senses and feelings of need keep us in tow with the Actuality medium. Moreover, we must understand how it has only been after we had gathered enough intellectual vision, or insight, on the Reality side of our personalities that we have become able to conceptualize what human existence is all about.

4. **The Living Ego State Specimen.** You who are con-
    crete scientists may have future use for the static and
    action ego state models. For example, if you are a
    psychology teacher who is ready to introduce the ego
    state, you may want your students to envision the
    static ego state model, the three men in a tub situa-
    tion, which finds the three ego state components--the
    id, ego, and superego--functionally geared together
    upon a sea of consciousness. You might then explain
    that your description of the component functions is
    completely accurate, although the tub configuration
    is only vaguely correct. You may then want to
    advance to the action ego state model, the light bulb
    situation, and explain how the electrodes represent
    the id and the superego, how the filament represents
    the ego, and how wakeful experience occurs when
    energy begins to flow. But these are just models of
    the ego state. Now we must find that part of human
    anatomy which by all measures is the living ego state
    specimen.

    The living ego state specimen must have the fol-
    lowing qualifications: it must be located in the brain
    area, preferably near the center; it must lie along ner-
    vous (afferent) pathways leading from the spinal
    cord to the cerebral cortex; it must be functionally
    geared to the hypothalamus; it must be the cross-
    roads for most if not all of the senses; and it must
    have two complexes of nerve fibers, radiations, con-
    necting it with the cerebral cortex. There is only one
    structure in human anatomy which can satisfy all of
    these qualifications, and that is the thalamus. The
    thalamus and its immediate vicinity is the location
    where ego state functions occur. Hence in general
    terms it may be said that the thalamus is the living
    ego state specimen.

    What we have just been discussing is that part of
    the ego state specimen which lies on the Actuality
    side of the A-R Interface: it is what we call the thal-

amus. What concrete science must now look into is the fact that the thalamus is only the Actuality side of the ego state specimen. Now it must investigate the A-R Interface and the Reality which lies beyond. The position taken in this study is that, after advancing human intelligence to such a point, man will have broken through the shell of mortality which his animal sensibilities have him presume to exist, and thus take another crucial step toward human destiny.

It has been previously indicated that such things as the Super Collider and advanced cloud chamber technology must be brought on line before concrete scientists can truly comprehend the A-R Interface and move beyond it to investigate the properties of human Reality. It was also indicated that the formidable mental health and nonbeing problems in the United States may be producing a national mentality which would impede American scientific progress. If that happens, then the folks in other countries will have to step in and assume the lead. All things considered, however, it appears that a step in human progress as great as this should involve all of the members of all of the nations.

5. **The Actual Self, the Phenomenal Self, and the Real Self.** During the rest of this study, we will be referring to the ego state in terms of the actual self, the phenomenal self, and the Real self. But this should not imply that we are going to be leaving such things as the id, the superego, and sense data behind and move on to new components of human personality. It is not that at all. All we will be doing is to bring together all of the organismic need and sense data impulses which enter and leave the Actuality side of the ego state and say that it is the point of brokerage which we will be calling the actual self. We will be following the same procedure on the Reality side of the ego state and refer to its value broker as the Real self. And as for the phenomenal self, it will be helpful if you bear in mind the filament of the

action (light bulb) model of the ego state, because its function is very similar to that of the phenomenal self and the process of cognition [99].

Perhaps the most striking lack of similarity between the action (light bulb) model of the ego state and the living ego state specimen (the thalamus) is that while the energy flows rather constantly through the action model of the ego state and produces a steady glow, it flows in an irregular fashion through the living ego state specimen. This irregularity is sometimes the result of a feeling of organismic want rising to the point where it is winning the battle (with the superego) for control of the ego state and proceeds to effect motor behavior that will satisfy the need without waiting for illuminating advice from the superego. Another irregularity occurs when the superego rejects energy carrying unacceptable sense data. And still another example would be when the superego foresees failure for an ongoing behavior and puts an end to it. Such changes in energy flow between the id and superego provide an irregular "glowing" of the ego.

In the future, we will be using different terms to say essentially the same thing as was said above. The difference is that we will be giving recognition to the relationship between Actuality and Reality. Thus for the remainder of this study we will be saying that such changes in energy flow between the actual self and the Real self provide an irregular "glowing" of the phenomenal self. And you will recall that whereas psychoanalysts find the superego rooted in the unconscious, in this four-approach overview of human personality, we find it as a protrusion of Reality into the conscious state; and as such, it becomes the phenomenal self which can not only project itself against Actuality (rejection) and back into Reality (projection of self), but it is the creator (conceiver) of the building blocks of Reality--ideas, concepts, and constructs.

6. Ego State Tenacity. Something else that was discussed earlier is the tendency for the id and superego to adhere to each other. Now, here in the four-approach overview of human personality, this tenacity is seen as a condition where the actual side of a personality is clinging to the A-R Interface from its position in Actuality and the real side is doing the same thing from its position in Reality. Our main concern in this study is how this tenacity between Actuality and Reality affects the operation of the human ego state, or to say it more precisely, how it affects the relationship between the actual self and the Real self. Yet it should not go unnoticed that this tenacious relationship may extend beyond the ego state and occur between the actual and real parts of the entire human body. I know nothing about that, except to say that if it is a possibility, concrete science will eventually make it known.

A further concern which this study has for ego state tenacity is how it is affecting the mind of you the reader. I am confident that if you are reading this book as a true Christian you are handling ego state tenacity quite well; for you are one who has accepted Christ for what He is, and you are prepared to go wherever valid reasoning will take you to find Him. You have followed His advice; you have cast aside the pagan dogmas and nonbeing values which lead toward hideous devils and supernatural gods; and, with your readiness to let Actuality be what it is and Reality be what it is, you have become mentally prepared to witness the Reality of humanity as being Nature's most illustrious production.

My main concern is for you who are concrete scientists; because what has brought you to reading this book is more than likely your reliance upon ego state tenacity. In other words, your personal demand for demonstrable causes has made your ego state become one which requires that your conception of Reality be an exact duplication of your perception of Actuality. In this regard, you and all of the other concrete scientists have had the "tiger by the tail" for the last 350 years. You have considered "...the lilies of the field...." [100]. You have revealed the demonstrable causes of humanity right up to the doorstep of its destiny; and, in doing all of this, you have developed a lustful anticipation for the next demonstrable cause. For you to move concrete science forward and recognize the A-R Interface as the immediate "river to cross" will very likely be the next major step in human progress. The irony, however, may lie in your failure to acknowledge the A-R Interface as being the dividing line between Actuality and Reality in your own personal ego state.

How reminding this is of the Scriptural saying that the day will come when he who is most will be least and he who is least will be most. And how regretful it would be if it turns out that some concrete scientists develop such compulsion for ego state tenacity, and such unquivering acceptance of the idea that Actuality and Reality are one and the same, that they move intellectually into human destiny, never having relaxed their compulsions long enough to consider their own roles in making human destiny an achievement, and in helping the paradox of human salvation to become understandably true.

7. **Personality Formatting.** In this study, the term "format" is used to indicate the general makeup, or plan, of the biological structures that Nature has developed to transfer information between the Actuality and Reality mediums within a human personality and from one human personality to another. We have found the thalamic area to include the structures (namely the thalamus) which transfer information between Actuality and Reality within one human personality. Now we will consider those biological structures that provide for the transfer of information from the Reality of one human personality to the Reality of another human personality.

The personality formatting which Nature has

provided to facilitate the transfer of information from the Reality of one human personality to the Reality of another human personality is located in the thalamic area and the cerebral hemispheres of the central nervous system. It appears as an immensely complex gathering of nerve fiber radiations, tracts, and relays; of nonaffective, affective, and cognitive emotional reactions; and of fleshy lobes, caverns, and valleys whose role in strategically linking and distancing all of the above helps make this gathering one of Nature's most incredible accomplishments. But despite the complexity of this gathering, its job description is easy to understand: it is to facilitate the transfer of information from Actuality to Reality, from Reality to Actuality, and from one human Reality to another. We will be referring to it as the *biological format*.

One should know that an affective realist never leaves the roost. By that, I mean that he or she will always, and without the slightest exception, be working from his or her own personal ego state. Subsequently, the more we know about our ego states and how they function within this tremendously complex biological format, the more astute we will become in handling our personal affairs and in helping others to do the same. Perhaps the first step one can make in this matter of astuteness would be to visit a University or medical school book store and pick up late editions of college or professional level books on human anatomy, physiology, biophysics, and human neurophysiology. There, one will find that much if not most of personality formatting has already been investigated and documented.

8. **First Things First.** The matter covered in this next consideration is something that everyone would like to know about. It is something that everyone can know about. It is something that everyone should know about. However, it is one of those things that can only be understood by those who have done the

first things first. If you are one of those who have just picked this book up and not read the earlier chapters, and if you are finding that what you read is being introjected easily and kindles your interest, then you have probably done the first things first. You have done what is necessary to ready your mind for the full truth of your existence. You have prepared yourself to accept the Reality of Almighty God and Christ, and you should have no problem in reading the rest of this book.

On the other hand, if you have just picked this book up to read, and have a mystic god in mind and a lack of concrete science to guide your thinking, then you had better be careful. My advice to you would be to either go back to page one and start reading or close this book and consult others as to what the phrase "first things first" really means. If you disregard this advice and become nervous or anxious as you read, then you should have the good sense to know that you may be putting your mental health in jeopardy, and should discuss your feelings with a licensed professional student of human personality before pursuing this book's subject matter further.

SECTION 20: ETERNAL LIFE

A Mythical Belief. When you view into sense data, you are taking note of sensible objects in the environment and your actual body. This is O.K. Your thinking is accurate up to this point, because you are viewing Actuality. Your error begins when you view into sense data and start thinking that Reality is being viewed as well--which of course is an understandable but wrong assumption.

What makes it seem that Actuality and Reality are the same thing is that your ego state produces affective realms--frames of conception--so fast that your phenomenal self emerges as your personal stereoscopic viewer, and the conceptions that you realize reflect upon both the matter and energy of Actuality and the physical dimensions of Reality (length, width, depth, and time). The result is a human personality in action. The result is also a myth in the making, where humans live their lives thinking that Actuality and Reality are the same thing. And the end result of all of this is that we have five and one-half billion humans possessing this stereoscopic ability [101] and the value systems it both promotes and delivers.

Omnipotence. The phenomenal self does not just happen. It has a very definite cause, and that is to be found late in the neonatal or early in the oral stages of infantile development. The phenomenal self is what begins to emerge when the child generates his or her earliest ideas--one of them being the idea of omnipotence. Omnipotence--the idea that everything my senses perceive is a part of me--is what lays down as the founding value in each of our personal Realities and casts influence upon our thinking throughout all of mortal life. This influence is discussed further in the caboose [102], but what we should consider here is how the phenomenal self builds upon the founding value, asserting the value of omnipotence during the rest of the oral stage and throughout all of child and adult life; and in doing this, it becomes an entity in itself.

What Is the Phenomenal Self? Earlier it was suggested that the phenomenal self is what the Real self becomes when it protrudes into the conscious state. This is true. But it would also be correct to say that the phenomenal self is what the actual self becomes when the ego state is "turned on" and allowed to operate. Furthermore, it would be correct to say that the phenomenal self is the condition which exists during an act of cognition, that is to say, during those moments when the actual and real selves are deliberating over the substance of the next and upcoming ideas. The following message about the snowplow seems to apply here.

THE SNOWPLOW

There had been a heavy snow[1] during the night, and
early the next morning the snowplow[2] driver began
to clear the road. It was fortunate that tall stakes[3] had
been previously placed on both sides of the road, so
he could see where to plow. What happened was that
as he plowed a bank of actual snow[4] was made to
gather on the left side of the road and a bank of real
snow was made to gather on the right side, thus making the road[5] clear[6].

After an hour of plowing, the driver came upon a
police car with flashing lights and the patrolman[7]
standing in front, motioning for the snowplow to
stop. The patrolman said they were checking all
snowplow driver identifications, to see if the driver
was representing the community on the Reality side
of the road or the community on the Actuality side of
the road. To this, the driver responded in astonish-
ment, "Reality! Actuality! I don't know what you
are talking about. I'm from the town of Actual
Reality--which includes both sides of the road."

The patrolman reacted with a smile, "Yes, I know
what you mean. I used to live in Texarkana, and
when people asked me which state I was from, I
would tell them that I am a resident of Arkansas
because I don't have to pay as much property tax
there, but I buy my groceries in Texas because it does
not tax food. But as I recall, when I was living in
Texarkana, I rarely ever thought of which state I was
from. I considered myself to be from Texarkana. So
I guess you have a point. Still, I must check your ID
to see which side of the road you reside on. That
should be enough."

The snowplow driver pondered, and then said,
"Well, my ID is going to tell you that I was born on
the actual side of the road, that I eat and sleep on the

actual side of the road, and that my house and all the marvels of Nature are on the actual side of the road. But to be frank with you, most of my learning was done on the real side of the road. The schools are over there. The church is over there. Even my day job as an electrical engineer is over there. So I would hate to have to say that I was from either the actual or the real community. I'm from both. And that is why I would want your report to say that I am from the community of Actual Reality."

To this the patrolman responded in amazement, "You must be one of those phenomenal people that I have been reading about. You come from both sides of the road."

"Right," the snowplow driver added, "I'm a phenomenal self."

"A phenomenal self!" echoed the patrolman, "then this means that I have a very important message to give you. It is that insofar as your plow is piling white snow[8] on both sides of the road, you are in good shape. You are heading for the Big City[9]; and if you keep moving the way you are, you are destined to get there. However, there are two problems that you may encounter if you claim to be from the actual side of the road. One problem is that if you identify your self with your carcass, which is part of Actuality, you are going to die when it dies. The other problem is much the same: it is that if you identify with Actuality, and if it should suddenly disappear, for example, into the black hole, then you would go right along with it. On the..."

The snowplow driver interrupted, "If you're trying to scare me, you are doing a good job of it."

"No, it's not that at all," continued the patrolman, "what I was going to say is that, on the other hand, you have been following the high stakes; you have been keeping the real snow on the right side of the road as white as the actual snow on the left side; and in doing these things, the essence of you--as a phenomenal self--has been introjecting into your Reality. You may not realize it, but ever since you were a child, your personality has been duplicating you and depositing the creation in your Reality. So if you want to avoid the experience of death, all you have to do is identify with your real you. Otherwise, you will experience death along with your carcass[10]. But never fear. You are of great value to the folks in the Big City. In the event you do not take heed, then someone will come out to rescue the real you; although it may take some doing to revive you (the phenomenal self). My main concern is for all those snowplow drivers who are moving away from the Big City. Maybe you can help educate them on how to get to the Fold of Reality[11] and use it as the sure way to receive eternal life.

The End

Death and/or destruction come to all actual things. Eternal life and/or existence come to all real things.

THE SNOWPLOW LEGEND

1.	snow	objects of value
2.	snowplow	ego state
3.	tall stakes	
	a- on actual side	principles of concrete science
	b- on real side	principles of Christianity
4.	actual snow	perceivable values
	real snow	conceivable values
5.	road	A-R Interface
6.	clear	identifiable
7.	patrolman	affective realist
8.	white snow	Reality is an exact duplication of Actuality
9.	Big City	Greater Reality
10.	carcass	the actual part of a human personality
11.	Fold of Reality	where Reality is an exact duplication of Actuality

The "Eye" of Reality. What is the "eye" of Reality? There are several different ways of answering this question. One way is to say that there are five and one-half billion "eyes" of Reality on earth today--one for each living human being, and in addition, there is one for every human who ever lived to be more than a few weeks old. In this context, we would say that the "eye" of Reality is the nucleus [103] of every individual's Reality, and that each individual Reality is a cosmic cell in the Grand Scheme of things. But perhaps an answer to the question which is less lofty and deals specifically with you and me is this next one.

What is the "eye" of Reality? The "eye" of Reality is the "I" and "me" whose presence we feel throughout life; it is the superego whose protrusion into the conscious state has it become the Real self in the ego state; and after the transcendence of values, it becomes the phenomenal self which balloons throughout one's carcass, and, when viewed in the mirror, appears as "I" and "me," and if you are standing there, "you."

The word "carcass" was just used to impress upon you that what you have thought of as your body has been reconstructed in your Reality. You have a real human body, and it will be with you forever, just as you reconstructed it over the years. The problem which some people have is that they try to make their thirty year old real bodies "jive" with their seventy year old carcasses, which is one way to develop unnecessary mental and physical problems.

You may have noted that what we have been discussing in this consideration are matters for subsequent studies. Their understanding is something that falls beyond the objectives of this study. However, I do want to mention the "eye" of Reality, because some readers have already become mentally awakened to their personal Realities. I am sure they will want to keep these matters in mind while reading the remainder of this book.

For those readers who have not yet had their Realities come in to view, it might be helpful to know that viewing one's Affective Reality has nothing to do with imagination, recall, and construct development. Imagination, recall, and construct development are cognitive acts: they occur because the individual decides to have them occur. But when one begins to view his or her Reality, there is no conscious act of decision. Assuming that the commitment to Almighty God and Christ and a commitment to demonstrable cause are in effect, the only thing required to bring one's Affective Reality in to view is more true intellectual information, which will eventually tip the "scale" and make Reality as viewable as Actuality.

How to Get Out of This World Alive. This chapter is an introduction to just how one gets out of this world alive. What it amounts to is that any human who has generated a conception of self will survive mortal death and only his or her carcass will die. However, this does not mean that everyone will go on to an eternal life of "milk and honey." What one introjects into his or her Reality will determine that.

If while looking through a slit in the curtain, it took you one second to complete a visual image of a passing car, you would have drawn about three percent of the image's information from Actuality and about 97 percent of it from Reality.

Study of matters like this may lead to an understanding of the relationship between the cognitive emotional reactions and the ego state.

Chapter Five

The Table of Reason

SECTION 1: WHAT IS THE TABLE OF REASON?

In the first three chapters of this book, we were considering some of the religious and historical aspects of humanity. In the fourth chapter, we were considering some of the biological and physical aspects of human personality. In this chapter, we will be considering human Reality and the part it plays in the human phenomenon. This is one way of saying what we have been and will be doing in this study. But there is another way of describing our work, and that is to consider the levels of reason that we have been and will be working at.

In the last chapter, our level of reason was getting very close to concrete science and its mountain of discovered facts. In other words, we were trying to develop immediate, or first generation, generalizations from the factual matter of concrete science. This is a challenging level of reason for most people to operate at. But because one of my jobs in writing this book is to provide a God-oriented philosophy that would bolster the existing front line trench philosophy of concrete science, this level of reason is an essential part of our study. It is essential in that it provides us with an inducted philosophical basis to which we may connect the deductions from our philosophical and religious universals. In doing this, we will be stepping up to the level of reason which joins generalizations that derive through induction with those that derive through deduction [104], thus providing ourselves with new horizons of understanding. For instance, we would bring the deduction that Jesus Christ is our personal Savior into construct with the induction which shows Him being the Vector of Reason that leads us to the Fold of Reality and the presence of God. This middle level of reason is what we will be calling the Table of Reason.

If you find this explanation of the Table of Reason hard to understand, don't worry about it. What the Table of Reason is and how it can be used are two different things, and our concern will be with the latter. Simply stated, we will be using the Table of Reason as the meeting place for our scientific and religious understandings. This chapter is developed to help the reader bring his or her Christian ideals and principles into construct with the Laws of Nature and the principles of concrete science.

Almighty God and Christ are the main ideals in Christianity: They are also the two main Realities in the Grand Scheme of Things. What we will be attempting to do is to bring Their idealistic and realistic measures together in one common understanding. Our axiom will be that the truth is the truth, no matter how you look at it.

SECTION 2: HOW OUR TABLE OF REASON WILL BE SET

Use of The Reality Construct. At the beginning of the last chapter, we referred to the Reality construct quite often. Then as we moved along we referred to it less and less, and finally, not at all. The idea was that if a reader was ready to psychologically acknowledge his or her Reality, a Reality construct should not stand in the way. However, with average intelligence and with the Vector of Reason to lead the way, it took me thirty-seven years to fill my Reality construct with enough valid intellectual values to tip the scale [105] and allow me to view my personal Reality. For me, this has been the toughest intellectual "nut to crack." Thus you may understand when I register the suspicion that probably not over ten percent of the readers will have succeeded in this venture up to this point in the book. Nor can we overlook the likelihood that many people have been reared to face their Realities, or have previously developed such ability through other means, notably, through genuine decisions for the Reality of Almighty God and Christ. In such cases, they may have already achieved the goal of this book and regard much of its substance as being "old hat." With these things in mind, it nevertheless seems important that we regroup and have this study return to using the Reality construct; for sooner or later, it will become full enough (with valid intellectual values) to tip the scale and bring the phenomenal selves of most other readers in to clear view of their personal affective Realities.

General Layout. In the last chapter, we considered some of the philosophical matters that may help concrete science to continue its investigation of human personality. We found these matters along four approaches--Biophysical, Psychoanalytical, Phenomenological, and Existential--and we attempted to join them so as to provide an eclectic display [106] that would allow us to visualize the configuration of human personality. These are the four structural approaches to human personality: they take note of its structure during mortal life.

In this chapter, we will be considering three more approaches to human personality--the Humanistic Approach, the Gestalt Approach, and the Behavioral Approach. These are referred to as the functional approaches because they have to do with how a human personality operates during mortal life [107]. It should be pointed out, however, that in order to avoid a baffling mountain of complexity, this study will only be considering human personality while it is performing in the normal range of behavior [108]. Abnormal behavior will be of no direct concern to us here, although it is clear that after mastering the substance of this chapter a professional student of human personality may be better able to visualize the departure of clients and patients from the normal range of mental behavior.

We will not be discussing the functional approaches as units of study. This is because they will all be used in the development of this chapter. We will be using the functional approaches as we consider the ego state in action, for example, and in some instances we will number them so as to indicate further discussion in the caboose.

What the Functional Approaches Take View of. As we move along in this chapter, you will find the three functional approaches to be viewing three inseparable factors of human personality when it is performing in the normal range of mental behavior. One of these factors is the expression of ontogenetic and phylogenetic needs, as viewed from the Gestalt Approach; the second is the interaction between the individual personality and its environment, as seen from the Behavioral Approach; and the third is the issuing of human values, as noted from the Humanistic Approach. These three factors are inseparable [109] in that if one of them becomes missing or disabled, the others will become negatively affected as well, and the personality will regress toward the vegetative state [110].

If you are a professional student of human personality, you will no doubt want to keep the four structural approaches and the three functional approaches in mind as we move along in this chapter. When all seven of these approaches are joined, so as to provide an eclectic display of human personality, you will have a conceptualization which is as good [111] a basis for validating ideas as the demonstrable cause basis which we have in concrete science.

Viewing the Eclectic Display Is Not Necessary for Nonprofessional Students of Human Personality. You may be a housewife or a farmer or a lawyer or a barber or a man or woman of the cloth. You may have a strong desire to look more deeply into the structures and workings of human personality; yet after reading the last chapter, you may have found yourself unable to imagine the eclectic display of human personality. Or you may have found yourself having difficulty in understanding the concepts and principles of concrete science, most particularly, its conception of demonstrable cause. What you should know is that while the eclectic display of human personality becomes a basis for validating psychological and philosophical reasoning, and demonstrable cause becomes a suitable basis for validating reasoning in concrete science, there is still another basis for validating ideas, and that is what many refer to as pragmatic reasoning.

SECTION 3: PRAGMATIC REASON

A True Christian Is a God-Oriented Pragmatist. One definition of pragmatism is that it is a philosophy which finds the practical bearing of an individual to be one of the main sources of influence that provide meaning to ideas and the conceptions which they give rise to. Such influence is an essential factor in determining how the individual thinks and acts; moreover, it becomes a practical test for assessing the full measure of one's belief. These principles of pragmatism very nearly coincide with those of Christian Doctrine and the personal philosophies of true Christians.

Before Charles S. Peirce (1839-1914) and William James (1842-1910) presented this philosophical meaning, the term "pragmatism" had a number of meanings, for example: those alluding to an order issued by the king; expertise in business; and a genuine concern for the lives of others. What Peirce and James did, just before the turn of this century, was to revive the intellectual's interest in human experience; only this time, the emphasis was upon the practical bearing of conceptions and the human experiences that help them to occur. So it appears that Peirce and James settled upon the word "pragmatism" because it indicated one whose interaction with environment involved an active faculty of reason.

Back then in the late 1800's, pragmatism presented a dramatic new direction for philosophical thought; for in placing a greater importance upon environment, it was deflating the Copernican notion held by Immanuel Kant (1724-1804) [112] --that perceivable objects merely orbit the faculty of knowledge.

You will recall that around the time of the American Civil War the intellectual world was just beginning to react to Darwin's theory of evolution, and that a part of its response was to review the thinking of Jean Jacques Rousseau (1712-1778) and his romance with Nature. It was during the remainder of the 19th century that the works of Peirce and James emerged; and as that happened, the idealism of Kant and others waned in influence, the Industrial Revolution had gotten under way, the infant flock of biological sciences was becoming established in the universities, and soon would come such things as electronic communications, automobiles, aviation, television, and the Atomic Age. Meanwhile, under the tutelage of John Dewey (1859-1952) and his followers, pragmatism became central in most of the American educational philosophies and in many of those in other free-world societies.

Thus to summarize the intellectual progress during the 19th and 20th centuries one might say that the members of advanced societies were bringing the true relationship between Actuality and Reality into perspective. Or to put it another way, and with regard to human personality, the intellectual world was awakening to the fact that valid reasoning requires an interplay of values between both Actuality and Reality [113], and not just in one or the other. This is the bit of understanding that the philosophy of pragmatism was bringing people to enjoy. As the saying goes, "It takes two to tango," so does valid reasoning emerge from the interplay of values between the faculty of reason and the environmental field upon which it works. Only now we are bringing things into greater focus and finding the interplay to be between the actual self of Actuality and the Real self of Reality. When the interplay is harmonious and in balance, self-actualization exists.

You who live in advanced nations are more than likely participating in a human society which is predominantly pragmatic. These nations became advanced, not only through education, but through intellectual awakening to the truth which lies in the practical bearings of everyday life, and which validates the realizations we call ideas. Nor can we say that the resulting human progress came through mortal human toil alone. I can attest to that. But by-and-large we mortals have been allowed to grow in our virtue and wither in our folly. And here we are today, ready to "sit" at the Table of Reason and take view of that which each of us will be carrying on to eternal life--our unique individual Realities.

So here is another way of arriving at the Table of Reason. It is for a Christian to just be his or her pragmatic self. For as multitudes have already noted, Jesus of Nazareth [114] was himself the most perfect pragmatist to have walked the face of this earth; and when humans accept his teaching without reservation, they automatically assume his pragmatic manner of valid reasoning and become placed in the mental position for witnessing how its unveiled Vector of Reason [115] is a line extending to and from Almighty God.

What I am suggesting is that a true Christian's personality is already prepared to arrive at the Table of Reason. He or she can do it without having to perform all of those conceptual labors of concrete science, philosophy, and psychology. Such intelligence is vital in that it becomes foundational in the programs of formal education, for example, in curriculum building. But for Christians, it may merely stand as verification of what they have already gained through pragmatic reason. Can it be that the least of us in formal education may have, in pragmatic reason, the surest way to the Fold?

The success of Christianity has come through its members'

acceptance of the existing truth which they find in the name of Christ. Indeed, their religion has guided them to the Table of Reason. Now all they have to do is behave as the God-oriented pragmatists that they are, sit at the Table, and enjoy the eternal view which at this point only their personal Realities can provide.

Ego State Harmony. The personalities of true Christians and concrete scientists are where ideal truths become those that can be demonstrated. This is the human value which puts them upon common intellectual ground and brings them into harmony [116] with each other--both sociologically and psychologically.

SECTION 4: THREE MODES OF REASON

Secular, Central, and Religious Modes of Reason. Unlike the traditional belief that humans think in either the secular or the religious mode of reason, this study holds to the position that the more correct mode would be the one which takes valid ideas from the secular and religious modes and becomes referred to as the central mode. Consider the following definitions:

> Secular Mode . Refers to the worldly as opposed to the spiritual and to the temporal as opposed to the eternal: it includes all nonreligious activities, as in governmental and economic functions.

> Central Mode. A mode of reason where God-oriented values are derived from demonstrable cause and/or the eclectic display and/or pragmatic experience: an actualization of self: a mode of reason where the realization of human values reflects complete agreement between Actuality and Reality: a socialization whose central doctrine reflects complete agreement between Actuality

and Reality in the minds of its members: a mode of reason which takes values from the religious and secular modes, but only when they are consistent with the standards expressed above.

Religious Mode. Concerning religious affairs, as in systems of faith in and worship of God.

The philosophy of Affective Realism holds to the central position without reservation. This means that human minds that use this philosophy will have turned faith in God into acceptance of Him, and worship of Him into service. It will also mean that human minds that use this philosophy will have turned the Godless, often dollar-sign, philosophy of secular technology into the God-oriented philosophy which stands as the front line trench of concrete science. But there is more to it than that.

We humans sometimes say one thing and then do another. For example, in our relationships with God and Christ, some of us Christians say, and are even convinced, that we have turned faith in God into acceptance of Him; yet our intellectual awakening to the Reality of human existence has moved us up to the side of the "pool", but we still need the bit of faith that there is something to jump into. One of the objectives of this book is to help ease the reader into the chair which stands at the Table of Reason. When that is done, the Vector of Reason will become felt and known to exist, and the Grand Scheme of Things will have another functionary to serve while still living as a mortal.

On earth today, there are thousands of people who have been thinking in the central mode of reason, just as there have been others in the past. In the olden days, they were viewed as prophets, forecasting things to come. Today, they are seen as evangelists, doing much the same, but also bringing people to a decision for Christ. The authentic prophets of old were functionaries in the Grand Scheme of Things, as are the authentic evangelists of today. But now we are about to witness a new era in human progress. It will be where the central mode of reason thrives and builds upon the three bases from which valid reason is drawn--demonstrable cause, the eclectic display, and pragmatic experience--and the long-foreseen awakening to the Greater Reality will be at hand.

We must be mindful of how Jesus Christ Himself anticipated the time when the meaning behind His name would become more clearly understood, and when people would recognize the universal nature of such meaning, that is, how it exists in all human minds regardless of the fact that the word "Christ" is absent in so many religions. We must also be mindful of how the word "Messiah" [117] was given to Jesus by the first Christians, how in later translations the word "Messiah" [118] was changed to "Christ," how the word "Yeshua" was changed to "Jesus," [119] and how to this day the English and Romance languages have not only stayed with this Greek-to-Latin translation, but it has been carried to most other languages around the world.

Now is the time for all humans to focus on the meaning of the words "Christ" and "Messiah," and find it also expressed in the central mode of reason as being the Vector or Reason [120]. Now is the time for all members of all other religious systems of faith and worship to search their doctrines for this same meaning and help bring all mankind together as one group operating within the central mode of reason and professing as one--that insofar as the Vector of Reason is a Reality, so must Almighty God be the same.

A final word on this matter is that I find great comfort in being able to realize the Vector of Reason while operating in the central mode of reason, and then turn my thoughts to religious affairs and find that the reasoning behind the terms "Vector of Reason" and "Christ" is the same. This leads me to appreciate the insight which Jesus of Nazareth was trying to get people to possess. It provides me with the luxury of having in my Reality the two greatest pillars of wisdom--the principles of concrete science and those of Christianity. With these things in mind, and as a member of a quaint little church in New Hampshire, I say let's keep our churches just as they are and permit them to change only in the minds of their members, as faith in Almighty

God flowers into acceptance of Him being Real, and as worship of Him transforms into service and membership in His Greater Reality.

SECTION 5: GOD IS REAL

In June of 1954, I received the Bible which I now have. That was the time when I first turned to the idea that God Almighty is Real. What had happened was that after twenty-nine years of living with the idea that God was some mystical entity in the sky, my frustrating search for the True God left me with one possible place to search, and that was Reality. Could it be that God Almighty is Real? As it turned out, this became the correct hypothesis; for by using it, I could bring my insight as a science teacher in to complete agreement with that which I received from Scripture.

For the next thirty-seven years I stayed with the hypothesis that God is Real, and then my ego state tenacity finally relaxed enough for me to take view of my personal Reality. The caboose [123] carries this discussion further, but here we will be considering only those things that are relevant to one's personal view of Reality, and foremost among them is the fact that Almighty God is as Real as you and I.

Reality Recapitulation. To envision the Greater Reality is what most humans aspire to. I know this when I say that such a view is not listed as one of the objectives in this book. This is because the entire book, including its objectives, are heading straight for this view, as a tide of information heads straight for the shores of understanding.

One thing that may help us at this stage of enlightenment is the matter of recapitulation. Recapitulation is defined as being a situation in which the principle details in an ongoing development are repetitions of those in a previous development. Rousseau referred to cultural recapitulation in explaining the development of human societies, as did Friedrich Froebel

(1782-1852). And of course all students of Natural history are introduced to recapitulation when they study how, in developing from simple to complex, ontogeny recapitulates phylogeny.

If we would be correct in assuming that recapitulation also occurs in the Grand Scheme of Things--as with ontogeny recapitulating phylogeny--then we may have some indication of what to expect as our intellectual tide moves ever closer to shore. As we become enlightened on how human selves generate their own Realities and become their respective nuclei, why then would not God Almighty have done the same in generating the Greater Reality?

How comforting it is to know that if we can value our carcasses enough to recreate their "spitting images" in our Realities, then God Almighty must be able to do the same thing in the Greater Reality; only He has the wherewithal to add "spitting image" carcasses to our real bodies and accept us as members in the Greater Reality which interfaces with perhaps the very same Actuality. Thus one may see the reasoning behind the Scripture which says that we are the children of God.

In addition, it is reassuring to think that because we can physically manipulate our carcasses and other objects in Actuality, so must God be able to do the same--as it has been with His involvement in some of the awesome physical changes that have occurred here on earth.

SECTION 6: REALITY ANALYSIS

Earlier I mentioned how alone I felt when I learned that I was completely alone in the Universe. You may recall that I also explained how the feeling of being alone only lasted a short while; and that I quickly realized how as an Actuality I am alone, but as a Reality I am surrounded by my wife and children and the great number of people and things that I encountered over the years. They are all in my Reality, just as I experienced them in my days of mortal living, and they will remain there throughout eternity.

Certainly this subject of Reality content will be investigated by other affective realists, and among their findings will be valid explanations of such things as love, hate and reaction formations [121]. In this study, we will be considering only the dimensions and broad measures of content in a human Reality [122]. The subject will be me.

Safeguards in Reality Analysis. The most important safeguard in Reality analysis is to be sure that the subject gathers all information through the projection of self. A subject should never attempt to move the "I" of personality from its mooring in his or her carcass and into its Reality. This is because the "I" of personality is the "eye," or nucleus, of its Reality, and to break it free from the carcass would bring about an immediate collapse of the ego state and the arrival of the vegetative state of living. Projection of self is the only way that a mortal human being can make analysis of his or her Reality and be able to talk about it later.

A second safeguard is for the subject to behave Naturally-- as he or she would do while watching a television program or reading a book. In these cases, the subject is projecting his or her phenomenal self into the program being watched, or read about. In Reality analysis, the subject is projecting his or her phenomenal self into Reality. And this is where the simplicity of the psychological mechanics can be seen. In all three cases --in watching television, in reading a book, and in Reality analysis--the phenomenal self is projecting into Reality. The only difference is that in watching television and reading a book the programs are being placed into construct, but in Reality analysis the phenomenal self is being projected throughout the "whole ball of wax" of Reality. This is discussed further in the caboose [123].

A Description of My Personal Affective Reality. What you are about to read is a description of my Reality. It will include discussions of the dimensions and broad measures of content that I can take note of. It will not be discussing the ego state mechanics that I find to be operating in my personality. A detailed discussion of these mechanics is given in the caboose [123].

It is extremely important for you (the reader) to know that all of the information that I gathered about my personal Reality came through the projection of my phenomenal self. I shudder to think of what would have happened to my ego state had I attempted to do it any other way.

Dimensions of My Reality. I find my Reality to have at least seven dimensions. They are:

1. Length
2. Width
3. Height
4. Time
5. Being
6. Nonbeing
7. Incidence of Effect

I have written a description of what appear to be the seven dimensions of my Reality, but that has been removed from this book. There are two reasons for this. One is that my description is based upon my personal experience, and lacks verification by other studies; for example, that which comes through the survey of many descriptions. The other reason is that if this study is moving upon a virgin intellectual ground for concrete science to explore, the worst thing that I could do would be to cast error into the works of scientific investigation. The way things stand right now, the human population is pretty much caught up in coping with and solving problems of its own making. The position taken in this study is that concrete scientists should set base lines for investigation before the field of observation is disturbed, that is, before their actions "stir the pot." The dimensions of human Reality constitute one of these base lines.

It is hoped that you the reader will send us a description of your Reality's dimensions [122]...or better, if you were to start your own study. But be sure to take steps that will assure valid base lines of operation.

Content of My Reality. The broadest description that I can give of the content of my Reality is that it is made up of values [124] that derive from Actuality and/or misconceptions by my self or the selves of others. It has no spontaneous values.

The next broad description finds each of the values in my Reality to be part of one of two groupings. One grouping lies on the left side of my field of view and the other grouping lies on the right side [125]. The grouping on the left side contains reflections (ideas and concepts) of the *being* experiences that I had since my ego state began to function, back early in the first year of postnatal life. The grouping on the right side contains all of the *nonbeing* experiences that I had since that first day of self-conception. Let us review what is meant by the terms "being" and "nonbeing."

Being. A being experience occurs when one's conceptualization of an actual object is an exact duplication. For example, if you were to conceptualize a female body with the aim of showing exactly where her body stops and the external world begins, you would be having a being experience; and every time you refer back to that conception as a foundation for reaching a value judgement, you would be having a being experience. In my Reality, all of my being values are in the grouping which lies on the left side of my field of view. This grouping is what was earlier referred to as the Being League.

Nonbeing. A nonbeing experience occurs when one's conceptualization of an actual object is an apparent or invalid duplication. In this case, if you were to conceptualize a female body with the aim of showing where her body appears to stop and the external world begins, you would be running the risk of having a nonbeing experience. And every time you refer back to that conception as a foundation for reaching a value judgement, you would be having a possible [126] nonbeing experience. In my Reality, all of the possible and obvious nonbeing values are in the grouping of values--the Nonbeing League--which lies on the right side of my field of view.

Kinds of Human Values. The building blocks of my Reality are the ideas that have been flowing into it for the past seventy years, the walls are the concepts that I managed to shape (reason) these ideas into over the years, and the rooms are the constructs that my reasoning shaped from these concepts. This is one way of explaining what my Reality is like. Another way of explaining it would be to say that my ideas are the basic units of my Reality, much as atoms are the basic units of my carcass --my personal piece of Actuality, with its atoms, molecules, cells, tissues, and organs. These actual and real basic units, and anything that they can be built into, are what this study views as the two kinds of human values [127] that lie within the scope of human reason. In my personality, the real basic units, and whatever they can be built into, are the *real human values* that comprise my Reality; the actual basic units, and whatever they can be built into, are the *actual human values* that comprise my carcass; and beyond that, in my environment, lie five and one-half billion other humans with the same or similar conditions.

Setting Value. Many of us have been having trouble making distinction between human values that are actual and human values that are real. We have been thinking that actual and real human values belong to the same order of things, and that was what sent some of our reasoning into a tailspin. Much like putting all of the eggs into one basket and then calling the basket the chicken, we have been putting our newly created ideas into Reality and assuming it to be Actuality. Actuality and Reality are two different things, two different mediums; and until we can come to realize this, our reasoning will be contaminated by varying degrees of misconception. As things now stand, we mortals all have varying degrees of misconception represented by the nonbeing values in our Realities. Thus it must be said that all mortal Realities contain both being (valid) and nonbeing (invalid) values that exist as ideas, concepts, and constructs. These "being" and "nonbeing" values are what this study refers to as *foundational real values* [128].

Human abortion is a good example of the misconception of value. Some Americans have taken time to consider the actual female body, or are taking the word of those who have; while other Americans are considering the female body as it appears to be. The result is that two camps have formed in American society. One camp is filled with citizens whose conceptualization of the female body is an exact duplication of the actual thing; the other is filled with citizens whose conceptualization of the female body is built upon what appears to be the actual thing. Thus a debatable issue has risen between the two camps --the debatable issue of abortion.

What Is a Valid Issue? In this study, a *valid issue* is defined as being a cognitive condition where the flow of reason travels from a known valid source to one valid end (conception). In researching the prenatal development of the human child, for example, concrete scientists made such development a matter to reason through, and in so-doing, they began an issue, a flow of reason, which conceptualized the entire development--from the production of egg and sperm to the moment of delivery. What is important for us to realize is that those concrete scientists were applying inductive reason to the hilt in every step of investigation. In other words, they insisted upon demonstrable cause all the way. The result was that their ego states were generating ideas and concepts that were exact real counterparts of the actual objects of study. This illustrates how concrete scientists generate being values--ideas, concepts, and constructs--in following a valid flow of reason (a valid issue). In this case, it was the valid issue of prenatal development.

It is also important for us to note how valid issues only exist in the Being League, or realm of being values. In my Reality, the Being League is the group of human values which lies at the left end of my field of view. All of its values were placed there by me--either as a concrete scientist or as a pragmatic person with a strong gearing to the Christian mode of reason.

I enjoy working within and from my Being League because I know that most of its values are valid; hence any matter that becomes an issue (a flow of reason) will probably extend from a valid beginning--as from concrete or pragmatic experience-- to a valid end (a valid idea, a valid concept, or a valid construct). Such are valid issues, and only through invalid reasoning can they be debated.

What Is a Debatable Issue? In this study, a *debatable issue* is defined as being a cognitive condition where the flow of reason either begins at an invalid source of information and ends as an invalid concept or it begins at a valid source of information but becomes contaminated by misconception during its flow of reason. We will be using the case of human abortion to illustrate how a debatable issue can emerge.

Perhaps the main event which brought the American people to the debatable issue of abortion was when our concrete scientists reasoned through the matter of prenatal development and made the American public aware of how it works. This meant that the idea of the father depositing the new child in the mother's womb--the capsular theory--had to be discarded as a myth. However, it opened the door for another misconception, another myth, which passed down through the Ages. That was the mythical belief that human birth occurs when the child is delivered from the mother's womb. And with this misconception came the debatable issue which divided the flows of reason in American thought and made them travel toward two different ends. One of these ends was the conception that the mother had a right to destroy her baby, and the other was the conception that the baby had a right to survive. A debatable issue had emerged.

Some will say that we are nit-picking here, that birth of a child comes when he or she becomes a free agent in the nurturing outside world, and that to reason otherwise would lead to nothing more than an insignificant detail. On some matters, I might agree with the notion of insignificant detail. However, on this matter, the matter of birth, I chose the branch of reason which supports the life of a human [129]. And I am sure that you will agree that the life of a human does not start at the moment of delivery, but at the moment of fertilization [130] in one of the Fallopian tubes and no later than in the uterus. Nor can we overlook the fact that the inside of the birth canal is a part of the external world, and anything that develops freely within it is outside the mother's body.

SECTION 7: RESOLUTION OF DEBATABLE ISSUES

There are two main categories of human issues--those that are social in nature and those that are personal in nature. This study does not go into the resolution of social issues at the interpersonal and group levels of interaction, for instance, as they would be found in lover quarrels and in sessions of Congress. Our concern will be for how social issues become resolved in each lover's mind, in the mind of each congressman and congresswoman, and in the mind of every other mortal human.

The contention here is that social and personal issues only exist in human Realities. They do not exist in such things as books and documents and computer discs. Books and documents and computer discs are mere pieces of Actuality that contain meaningful information which human perception can pick up and forward to the biological format and the actual self of the carcass. In this respect, they belong to a human culture of Actuality, but they are never part of a human society. A human society is a culture of Reality, and exists only in the Realities of its members.

This idea that a human society only exists in the Realities of its members may seem unbelievable; but when you stop to consider the founding value--that of omnipotence--and the way in which it leads our phenomenal selves to accept all things perceived as being part of our Realities, the true worth of our power of reason, our intelligence, begins to show through [131]. In everyday living our founding values stay the course and lead us to believe that our society is out there, a part of Actuality; but in truth we are projecting upon a society that we created in our personal Realities. The paradox lies in the way that we have affixed our conception of Reality so completely to such things as books and documents and computer discs and our very own carcasses, that we tend to think that Actuality and Reality are the same thing. This made society seem to be a part of Actuality as well as Reality. The truth is that many of us have been caught by the colossal myth which holds Actuality and Reality to be the same thing. But gradually, down through the Ages, man has been able to add increasing validity to his intellectual foundation, his foundational values. He has managed to expose most of the myths in such foundation; but he still has the big one, the colossal myth, to see through. That is where we are today.

To me, the greatest irony lies in the possibility that some of humanity's greatest concrete scientists, social scientists, and philosophers have become so taken by the colossal myth that they might very well work themselves into the middle of human destiny and never realize the help they have given in service to God and the good of mankind. In fact, this axiom seems to apply: The more valid one's intellect becomes, the more valid intellectual values it will take to see through the colossal myth.

A Closer Look at Human Issues. We have explained the difference between valid and debatable issues as being where valid issues begin at sources of valid information, as in the works of concrete scientists and pragmatic Christians, and become flows of reason which end as valid concepts; whereas debatable issues either begin at sources of invalid information and end as invalid concepts or begin at valid sources of information but become contaminated by misconception during their flows of reason. All mortal humans have Realities that contain varying numbers of both valid and debatable issues.

But what about the makeup of an issue, a flow of reason? Is it something that we already understand and can explain in detail? Or is it an unknown that concrete science is getting ready to investigate? The position taken here is that the make-up of human issues lies right at the front line trench between concrete science and the unknown. No one knows the exact makeup of human reason, yet. However, if the fast rate of progress which is being made in the fields of mathematical physics, electronics, and computer science is any indication, we shouldn't have to wait much longer.

The view taken here is that the basic units of reason go on to become the building blocks of Reality. These are what we refer to as *ideas*. And although we don't know exactly what ideas are, we do have reason to believe that they constitute the elemental basis for Reality, just as atoms constitute the elemental basis for Actuality. One such reason is that it does not seem logical for the Grand Scheme of Things to have the Laws of Nature stop at the A-R Interface and start as an entirely new and different set of laws on the Reality side. If this reasoning is correct, then we may expect the Law of Cause and Effect to be operating on both sides of the Interface; we may expect that the real substance of ideas consists of such things as the anti-particles that some physicists claim to have noted; and we may be sure that the spontaneous emergence of ideas is itself an obtuse misconception.

Issues Lie in Fixed Positions. What gives a human Reality the ability to take on dimensions is the fact that all of its parts take permanent position in the overall structure. All of these parts consist of ideas and concepts that group together according to their validity. In my Reality, all of the valid concepts lie in fixed positions at the left end--as shown in my field of view-- and all of the possible and obvious invalid concepts lie in fixed positions at the right end. Those at the left end have become my Being League of values and those at the right end have become my Nonbeing League of values.

In the above paragraph, we were placing a human Reality in a static position. We were stopping our tictoc time clocks and considering one frame of reference, or instant view, without time passing [132]. Now, after turning tictoc time back on, we are going to see how ideas and concepts not only remain in fixed positions, but how they are part of issues whose positioning is also fixed. When I view into my Reality, even tictoc time appears to be fixed, because nothing is moving. All of my creations--my ideas, my concepts, my constructs, and my issues-- are frozen into fixed positions, and when viewed as a group, they constitute my Reality, my fixed Reality.

Tictoc Time is Real Time. It exists only in a human Reality. It does not exist in human Actuality, that is, in the human carcass. When we view the external world with our real time clock running, we see things in motion and tend to think that real time is being expressed, as in seconds and minutes. What must be understood, however, is that the time which occurs in such motion is actual time; it is a property of motion; and because matter only moves in the present, it too exists only in the present. So when we conceptualize the relationship between actual time and real time, it likens to a boat speeding across the lake--where the motion of the boat displays the rate of happening and the wake which forms behind is a history of the happenings. The motion of the boat represents actual time and the wake represents the resulting real time. Or to put it another way, the boat represents the present, when actual time is a property of motion; and the wake represents the past, when the property of motion is real time expressed as a history of events. Tictoc time [133] is that part of real time which exists at the very beginning of the past, when ideas are created.

Those concrete scientists who intend to assemble valid information as a foundation of an issue leading to a valid conceptualization of human Reality may find that this threshold between actual and real time is a good place to start, because it is located at or near the A-R Interface and is where ideas are created and the flows of reason begin.

Some will say that this idea of two different kinds of time is nonsense, but let us see if the proof is not in the "pudding."

Physical and Affective Realms. Fortunately, human personalities have come into being, and their specialty lies in the ability to take "snapshots" of actual happenings--around thirty per second. In this study, these "snapshots" are referred to as *realms*. Those realms that gather all of their qualitative values from actual happenings, that is, experiences with Actuality, are called *physical realms*. They help give rise to those ideas that derive value from Actuality. Their counterparts in the attainment of values are called *affective realms*, which help give rise to ideas that derive value from past experience (Reality). Physical realms draws value from Actuality on the actual self side of the ego state and affective realms draw value from Reality on the Real self side of the ego state.

Actual Time, Realms, Tictoc Time, Ideas, and Issues. One way of explaining how all these things relate to each other is to consider their overall relationship in one play of a football game. If we might consider time only as it deals with the play itself, actual time begins to occur at the snap of the ball and information regarding the subsequent happenings is brought as sense data to the actual self of the viewer's ego state; physical realms [134] begin to form at the viewer's A-R Interface; tictoc time commences on the Reality side of the A-R Interface; the whistle blows; the physical realms merge to become an idea of what happened; and the idea becomes the latest entry to the flow of reasoned ideas which is what we call an issue. In this case, the issue is the overall flow of reason, whose substance is the matter of winning the game, and whose resolution is determined when its ending is established as either a win or a loss.

Most cognitive experiences group into issues where actual motion, comfort, security, and/or survival become both the means of progress and the desired end. In each human individual, these issues tend to unite, or combine, to form the real aspect of his or her style of living [135].

Issue Length Ranges from Split-seconds to a Life-span.
When a person dodges a speeding car with a behavior that is
initiated by his or her ego state, an issue will have emerged. It
could include as little as two ideas--one to size up the problem,
and the other to provide information on how to solve the problem. When the phenomenal self acts upon this information by
committing the carcass to service, the issue is in process, and in
as little time as a fraction of a second, it has become resolved.
If the person feels relief, then the issue would have succeeded,
indicating that a positive Gestalt had just occurred. But if the
person feels pain, then the issue would have failed, indicating
that a negative Gestalt had just occurred.

Many human issues extend over long periods of time. Your
public school education [136], for example, was and may be
one of your *main issues.* Your college education is or may
become another main issue in your life. But your *master issue*
is the one you become involved with in the pursuit of God and
eternal life [137]. What must be understood is that every idea
that one adds to his or her issues becomes fixed forever. The
message which this study is trying to present is that one cannot
alter any issue in his or her Reality. All that can be done is to
discover misconceptions and invalid foundations in ongoing
issues and either validate their substance for present and future
use, or declare them untenable and join a main issue that has a
valid foundation. This study finds that two main issues stand as
valid secondary issues in the pursuit of God. One is founded
upon the teachings of Jesus of Nazareth and the other is founded upon the findings of concrete science.

Cognitive Experiences Occur in Relation to Ongoing Issues.
Most human experiences are stimulus and response reactions
that occur below the level of cognition, as with spinal cord
reflex actions, nonaffective emotional reactions, and those
involving the biological format at the subconscious level. Still
other experiences will be anticipated as a result of prior experi-

ence with a given real or actual setting, as when one loads his or her cognitive emotional reactions with affective realms that will provide for immediate response while crossing the street. But whenever the ego state becomes involved in the initiation of stimulus-response behaviors, acts of cognition occur; which means that ideas are created, reason is set in motion, and the resulting flow is what we refer to as an issue. All newly created ideas either start a new issue or enter into an ongoing one; they can never be added to resolved or abandoned issues; although resolved and abandoned issues can reveal affective realms and/or ideas to the individual's projecting self. Whether this is a matter of reflection or actual transfer is yet to be determined.

A Normal Human Reality Contains a Multitude of Ongoing Issues. If my Reality bears any resemblance to yours, and to all the other human Realities on earth, then we may assume that one way of accurately describing a human Reality is to say that it is loaded with issues. In fact, when I became able to look into my Reality, what I first saw were the hills and mountains of New Hampshire, as viewed from the family hill. Then, while projecting further into my Reality, I came upon specific episodes in my past. After studying some of these episodes, I soon learned that my projection was arriving at ideas and conceptions that had "captured" the actual and/or real happenings which occurred during each episode.

Eventually, I came upon the idea of projecting along my real time line, or history of events, and it was then that I learned what an issue really is. An issue is a sequence of ideas and concepts that starts at a founding cluster of ideas and ends at a goal or solution to a problem. Or as has been previously noted, an issue is a flow of reason.

After numerous projections into my Reality, I always found myself arriving at ideas and concepts while they were integral parts of issues. In fact, that is all I ever did arrive at--ideas and concepts while they were integral parts of issues. This has led me to think that issues are the main constituents of Reality, and furthermore, that they may be the major source of the energy and qualitative values that give rise to the assertive element of human Reality--what has been previously referred to as the nucleus, or eye, of Reality.

As for the exact number of issues in my Reality, I have not the slightest idea; although I feel sure that it must range in the millions if not billions. Many have been either resolved or abandoned and lie as derelict nonbeing issues [138] in my past; others have merged to become foundations for my master and secondary issues; while still others arise as ongoing issues for meeting current and foreseeable problems, for example, when and how to file my tax return and how to get the camera copy of this book ready for the printer. And as for my nonbeing issues, I know that I have some; but when I spot one [139], I try to ignore it, and let it lie dormant in my Nonbeing League. Subsequently, for the last four decades, my Nonbeing League has been dwindling [140] into the past.

Today, I find my known ongoing issues to be united under one "roof," which is to say, I find them to be operating as secondary issues within one master issue whose target is Almighty God.

SECTION 8: A CORNERSTONE ISSUE

The following is a description of a being issue that stands out as one of the cornerstones in the foundation of my concrete science issue.

A THREE YEAR ISSUE

During the winter of 1943, I was a high school senior with a big problem. Hitler was taking just about everything he wanted and it became clear that I would be drafted into the army if I didn't volunteer in some other branch of service. After pondering my situation, I decided that if Hitler was going to take my life, I should get into a military program that would help me first take many of his followers. That led me to the idea of becoming a bomber pilot.

What happened in my Reality was that I realized a problem which was not going to go away. I had to come up with a plan. What I came up with was a plan whose ending, or goal, was to become a bomber pilot. The moment I committed to that plan, my problem's solution became the end, or objective, of an issue [141]. It was the issue of becoming a bomber pilot.

In my military issue, the foundation was to gather enough information to qualify me for the aviation cadet program in what was then the Army Air Corps. Back in the winter of 1943, I frequented one of the local roller-skating rinks. It was there that I met some of the aviation students who were taking college training at the university. As it turned out, they were the ones who helped me devise a plan of action--the beginning of which was to lay foundation. Upon their advice, I boned up on such things as mathematics, the principles of flight, and dead reckoning navigation. In May of 1943, I took the cadet entrance exam at the nearby army air base. After passing that, the foundation component of my military issue was established.

On the day after my eighteenth birthday, I found myself on a train headed for Miami Beach and six weeks of basic training. The flow of reason component of my military issue was under way. During the next fifteen months, I went through all of the stages of pilot training, and in November of 1944, I received my wings.

In August of 1945, President Truman ordered the dropping of the first atomic bomb. I was separated from military service in December of 1945, at which time, my military issue became joyfully resolved. In January of 1946, I entered Syracuse University as a freshman, and my military service issue became a cornerstone in the foundation of my college education issue.

God Almighty and Christ are Real

SECTION 9: THE LEAGUES OF BEING

For a good portion of this chapter, we have been flying in the clouds of philosophy. By that I mean we have been trying to bring inducted generalizations into agreement or disagreement with philosophical deductions (from universals) and/or religious principles. Now we are going to drop down to "earth" and consider the live, or ongoing projections of our own phenomenal selves, and in so-doing, view our own Realities as they exist in real life.

If you are a concrete scientist, you may be getting an idea of where this is taking us. It reminds me of what Cicero (106-43 B.C.) may have meant when he said that we are babes in the morning of time. We are finally reaching that point where we will not only be able to search for a concrete understanding of the ego state from the outside, as we are doing in our biophysical exploration of the thalamus, but we will now be able to "climb" inside our personal Realities and examine the ego state from the Reality side of the A-R Interface. In doing this, we will be awakening to a Greater Reality that may be just as reasonable as the Actuality which we know so well; and we too may have to agree with Cicero--that we are still babes in the morning of time.

The Valid Point of View. This brings us to the reason for this book's jacket saying, "For True Christians and Concrete Scientists [142]." True Christians have been following the teaching of Jesus Christ in a pragmatic manner, while concrete scientists have been following the course which demonstrable cause has provided. Both of these systems of investigation have been making a beeline for our Real God.

What we must become clear on is that the path followed by true Christians (that of pragmatism and faith) and the path followed by concrete scientists (the central mode of reason) are the only two valid tracks to follow. Expressing this in terms of human issues, the true Christian and concrete science tracks are the two main secondary issues within the master issue whose goal is our Real Almighty God. This is the only valid master issue one can belong to. Expressing this in terms of being, the Real God master issue is the essence of the Being League-- meaning that all of the member issues are valid secondary issues, and become collectively known as the Being League of values, in spite of the possibility that some [143] of their con- stituent ideas and concepts are of nonbeing value. Those who operate within the Being League will usually acquire the valid point of view [144].

One way of telling when people are operating with the valid point of view is to see if they are debating the issues which exist in their Realities. Issues that require verbal defense are most often supported by people who lack the valid point of view, and issues that do not require defense will always be promoted by people who possess the valid point of view. In other words, issues that require defense are working from invalid founda- tions and/or with invalid modes of reason; whereas issues that do not require defense are working from valid foundations and with valid modes of reason.

Take for example the matter of Aristotle and the housefly. Concluding that garbage pails produce houseflies, Aristotle rea- soned in an invalid manner. He used deductive reason, and in so-doing, failed to recognize the causal relationships that exist in protoplasmic development. Subsequently, his failure to use the correct method of reason--inductive reason--led him to many invalid conclusions [145].

There are two points to be made here. One is that while Aristotle was operating within a God-oriented master issue, as was shown by his associating the Law of Cause and Effect with God, the science which he fathered--deductive science--became bogged down in its investigation of Actuality. His advancing foundation [146] of knowledge was becoming contaminated with misconceptions, thus leading him to an invalid point of view concerning Actuality [147]. When he let deduction become his method of scientific reason, he was allowing him- self (his "I" of Reality) to derive apparent truth from his foun- dation of universal truths and commit it to value judgement without further inquiry. Instead, he resorted to demonstration of the apparent fact that houseflies are produced by garbage pails, and that is what he called "science" [148]; for after all, he reasoned, if you can demonstrate an apparent fact, then correct conclusions and applications will follow. The point being made here is that actual truth originates in the object beheld, and real truth originates in the mind of the beholder.

The second point to be made is that concrete science does just the opposite of what Aristotle was doing. A concrete scientist does not allow himself or herself to make value judgement as to the origin of a thing--in this case the housefly--until the earliest cause has been reached. The problem is that concrete scientists have always been able to arrive at earlier causes in the study of protoplasm, but not the earliest cause...not yet. However, they are now approaching the limits of Actuality, and must consider what it takes to continue the matter of cause on the Reality side of the A-R Interface. In their determined attempt to avoid value judgement on the matter of earliest cause, they have been leaving a trail of accomplishment that is headed for the earliest, or first, cause--what we refer to as the Real God. In this, they have been taking the valid point of view.

Using pragmatism and faith, true Christians have been following the same kind of non-judgmental trail which heads for the Real God. This is what is meant when we say that true Christians and concrete scientists have been making a beeline for God, and in so-doing, they have been taking the valid point of view.

Issue Deception. Aristotle's scientific inquiry into Actuality was misleading to many of the intellectuals in ancient Greece and Rome, and to medieval Catholics. But the practice of exerting an invalid point of view didn't stop there.

Consider how deceiving it is today when proponents of nonbeing issues become so taken that they feel absolved from responsible thinking and begin to attack valid issues from invalid foundations. Take for instance the case of human abortion. The unborn child is in the beginning [149] of an issue whose mortal ending will come with the death of his or her carcass, and up until the time society begins to press invalid notions into his or her Reality, it is one of the most valid issues that a human can possibly have; for it is occurring before the flow of reason stage begins. Yet so many of our legal and political minds reason to save the self-serving issue [150] of the mother and destroy the valid issue of the child [151].

The lacking of a valid point of view is due to one or both of two things. Either the person has allowed an invalid foundation to form for the issue in question, or an invalid goal has been agreed upon. Whichever the case may be, an invalid point of view will have been acquired.

Concrete Science and the Valid Point of View.   Like Aristotle, today's concrete scientists are all operating within the Real God master issue. Some are there because their Christian religion and concrete science are placing them there, while others are there because their concrete science is holding them there in spite of their non-Christian ideals and goals. Nevertheless, as with Aristotle, most of today's concrete scientists are operating with an invalid foundational idea. Aristotle's main misconception was the idea that scientists could arrive at the truths in Actuality through deductive reason. Concrete scientists corrected for that by changing to inductive reason; and as history shows, they went on to reveal many if not most of the truths in Actuality. Yet they remained with the invalid assumption that Actuality and Reality are the same thing--the colossal myth.

Perhaps the biggest difference between Plato and Aristotle was that Plato recognized ideas as being real things and went on to discuss Reality; while Aristotle thought ideas to be nothing more that fleeting things, and he stayed with the colossal myth. The colossal myth was no great problem for Aristotle, however. He never got far enough into the valid understandings of Actuality to note that there was a colossal misconception in his science issue's foundation; hence it may not have been a factor in his move toward an invalid point of view. Furthermore, he explained all mental activities as being functions of the human carcass. And yet he was using his Reality all the while in formulating such things as logic, ethics, and his several modes of deductive reason...never stopping to consider what was really going on.

Today's concrete scientists are placed in a much different position. Having revealed the Actuality of the human carcass right up to the A-R Interface itself, they will have to do one of two things. Either they discard the colossal myth and accept Reality for what it is--in which case they may use their own personalities for experimentation; or they will have to approach Reality through a make-believe, or theoretical, construct and use volunteers as subjects. They must do one or both of these two things. Otherwise, they will have allowed the colossal myth to deprive them of the valid point of view.

The Assertive Component of Reality. The assertive component of Reality has been described as the "eye," or nucleus of one's personal Reality. It can also be added that the assertive component is the "I" of one's personal Reality: it is that part of human Reality which brings reflections from the past to the Reality side of the ego state; and in this action, it holds an ongoing or recalled issue in gear with the ego state, thus becoming the Real self of the ego state.

Taking from my own experience, I find that my "I" of Reality can function in at least two different ways. First, it can project across my A-R Interface and help to give rise to my phenomenal self. And second, it is mobile in the sense that it can travel anywhere within my Reality. Everything else--the issues and their constituent ideas and concepts--are in fixed positions.

The Nonbeing League. One of the broadest scans of my personal Reality is when I bring my Being League and Nonbeing League into view at the same time. My Being League is always on the left side and my Nonbeing League is always on the right side. This is what I see when I am facing my Reality and examining the field of view, much as watching a television screen.

Now let me explain what I see when my phenomenal self sends this viewed information to my biological format. In my carcass, my Being League is always showing in my left frontal lobe and my Nonbeing League is always showing in my right frontal lobe. This makes me wonder if this positioning of my leagues of value has anything to do with the fact that I am right-handed. If there is a relationship, then it might mean that left-handed readers will have their Being Leagues showing in their right frontal lobes. If you are into statistics, you may want to do a survey and use the normative approach [152] in a study of this kind of subject, a study in comparative realism.

Abnormal Human Behavior. It was noted earlier that this study does not get into matters of abnormal human behavior. It only considers normal-range human behavior [153]. Now, we have come to the question of nonbeing values. Do we include them in this study? The answer is no. This study does not get into the matters of nonbeing, except to say that any human who is not operating within a Real God master issue is a possessor and victim of nonbeing values--which include a lack of the valid point of view and a large assortment of invalid ideas and concepts. However, this is not to suggest that people who operate within a Real God master issue will not have nonbeing values to contend with. All humans who operate in the Being League of values will have at least some nonbeing values to deliberate over. The question is, do they debate the issue involved, or do they go into the issue, find the nonbeing value, and purge it from the psychological or social exchange? The point is that conflict does not exist between valid issues.

Allow me to use my own Reality to illustrate what has just been said. The left side of my field of view is filled with my Being League; but the right side is empty except for a dot-sized Nonbeing League; and what makes it appear so small is that it occurred over sixty years ago. I was a little crook back in elementary school--a time when free candy and toys and money to get them were all that mattered. They became the goal of my master issue and the top priority in my Nonbeing League of values.

What I find interesting is that I am able to project my phenomenal self back to that Nonbeing League and seemingly [154] draw it up to the present, thus permitting me to see it big as life on the right side of my field of view or in my right frontal lobe.

Upon reaching junior high school, I began to give serious consideration to my existence. It was then that I started to lay foundation for the God-oriented issue which grew to become my Real God master issue. This established me in the Being League, where I have been operating ever since.

But although I was operating in my Being League during those junior and senior high school years, I had managed to carry a bunch of "trash" from my Nonbeing League. It wasn't until the mid 1950's that my issue foundations had shed enough nonbeing values for me to live a fully honorable life. So concerning the kids in the "street," perhaps you will understand when I say that I will have to be among the last to "throw stones."

A final word on nonbeing values is that every one you muster will be a part of your real baggage forever. There is simply no way that a human can get rid of an introjected idea, except with the help of God. All a human can do is to shed nonbeing (invalid) values [155] from his or her advancing issue foundations, replace them with being (valid) values, and let them, the nonbeing values, lie dormant in his or her history of events.

SECTION 10: TOOLS FOR REALITY EXPLORATION

We have discussed what appear to be the seven dimensions of Reality--length, width, depth, time, being, nonbeing, and incidence of effect [156]. There may be more. However, from my present point of view, I can only discern seven. Nevertheless, with these seven dimensions and what we now know about them, we can tell that there is no standard configuration for human Reality; rather, each of the five and one-half billion human Realities on earth has a unique configuration. This is at least partly due to the fact that most humans have not been able to evaluate the issue foundations which they were basing value judgement upon. Those who have come closest to having a sameness of Reality configuration are members of groups with high degrees of solidarity, as may be found in the sciences, in the religions, and in family life.

The state of humanity today is largely a matter of growing dependence and declining self-reliance. If history is any indication, human progress can only continue if these trends are reversed. It is essential that we help the reversal of these trends by giving the human individual enough valid intellectual values to bring the balance between Actuality and Reality back into play in the human ego state, and this will not be done until the colossal myth is slain. When this happens, then every man and woman and boy and girl will have the opportunity to purge invalid values from their issue foundations and thereby ready their Realities for the eternal trip ahead. The following tools will be needed in that effort.

Tools for Reality Exploration. The tools which I have been using to explore my Reality are discussed in greater detail in the caboose [123]; but in this section, I am only going to say what these tools are and how I have been using them. Both of them involve the use of my phenomenal self in the process of projection.

One of the wonderful things about human personality is that an individual does not need to know about the details of how these tools work. All he or she has to do is just think, and the tools will do exactly what the thought requires. For those readers who are not in need of specific detail about these tools, I would say that they don't even have to read this section. But I can't say that because there are at least two danger zones that I ran in to, and they should be pointed out to all readers. What it amounts to is that those who are able to face their Realities should know at least the substance of this section before they start exploring. These tools are:

1. *Projection of Self.* This is like standing on the shore and viewing the ships out on the water. The human phenomenal self can act like a telescope and bring a distant ship up to close view, and at the same time project itself upon the ship, just as though it were there. The explanation for how we humans can do this goes back to the founding value--the feeling of omnipotence which we picked up during early childhood. What is happening during the projection of self is that the phenomenal self is positioned at the actual self on the Actuality side of the A-R Interface and projects itself across the Interface and upon objects in Reality. This is the same process as that which occurs during the projection of self into [157] sense data, which bring information about objects in Actuality; except, in this case, real values have already been given in the development of physical realms and ideas, thus allowing projection to be a "straight shot" to the targeted real values [158].

2. *Retroprojection of Self.* This is like jumping from the shore into a motorboat and driving out to where the ships are on the water. In this case, the phenomenal self straddles the A-R Interface so that part of it is in Actuality and part of it is in Reality. The part which is in Reality identifies with the Real self and becomes free to travel anywhere in the Reality...again, a matter of projection. I refer to this motorboat effect as my putt-putt; because although I don't know exactly what it is, or how it works, I use it to scoot about in my Reality--from the present back to the age of two years and from my Fold of Reality to my pit of nonbeing. In order to use this tool, one must have discarded the colossal myth.

A WORD OF CAUTION. Upon first discovering my putt-putt, I went all over my Reality, and was soon to realize one important use for it. I found that whereas I could only get a stationary view while using my projection of self, I could gear my putt-putt to the timing of physical realms and ideas that were created during a selected episode of my past and recover the exact motions that I experienced. For example, while taking basic flight training in 1944, I became particularly fond of a plane numbered 337. I found that I could putt-putt up to myself during preflight procedures--meaning that my putt-putt was staying with me as I walked all the way around the plane. One important thing that I have learned about retroprojection is that it provides me with much more recovered detail than I can ever get with the projection of self.

This brings us to the word of caution. When I first began to use my putt-putt, I did all of my exploring within my Being League. But then the time arrived when I became obtusely reckless. I decided to putt-putt over to my Nonbeing League and see what was going on there. For as long as I was reviewing such things as my stealing of candy and money, that little trip wasn't so bad. However, when I putted all the way to the right side of my Nonbeing League, I arrived at my pit of nonbeing. One second at the pit was all that I needed to convince myself to never return; for what I saw were such things as men with giant eyes instead of heads and several arms protruding from their shoulders and knees...evidence of my childhood lust for weird tales and comic books.

The position taken in this study is that retroprojection should be used only for research purposes until more is known about it. What you the reader should know is that you can putt-putt around your Reality just as I have been doing, but let me explain that before I could do such retroprojection I had to establish my phenomenal self on the Reality side of the A-R Interface. It was like building a bridge across a stream. Once it's set up, then you can cross over at any time. My advice is that you not build that "bridge" and do all of your Reality exploration through the projection of self; because that way your phenomenal self will be operating from the Actuality side of the A-R Interface, just as you do while projecting into a theoretical construct. What must be made clear is that until retro-projection is confirmed to be a safe thing to do, one should have a psychiatrist on hand to advise and give medical aid if the need arises [159].

The second danger zone I putted into was my Fold of Reality. Everything went fine for as long as I stayed with my concrete science issue. I could see where my concrete science issue was in contact with my Fold of Reality. I could see the self-actualization and Vector of Reason experiences I had while writing this book. But then, again, I made an obtusely reckless mistake. I thought that I could see something off in the distance, so I putted away from my concrete science issue to have a better look. And it was then that I learned a lesson which should be passed on to you. It was the understanding that my "I" of Reality had to be a function of an ongoing issue in order to operate; or to be more precise, it had to be geared to a flow of reason; for once it lost that contact, it saw only bits and twists of what may be best likened to a bowl of scrambled bacon and eggs--scrambled Reality. We will have more to say on this subject in a later section. What must be made clear here is that the "I" of Reality is a function of an ongoing flow of reason, and in this function, it becomes the nucleus of one's Reality and the "I" of his or her personality [160].

SECTION 11: GENERAL MIND SETS

Mind set has been described as being an established state of mind. In everyday life, there are numerous minds sets to be found. You can find them emerging as a result of such backgrounds as the individual's culture or sex or education or size or health. In this study, we will be considering what might be called the *general mind sets*. There are two general mind sets that a human can develop. One is the *ego mind set* and the other is the *phenomenal self mind set*.

Here is another wonderful aspect of a living human personality. It is that one does not need to know all of the fine details about the two general mind sets in order to use them. But it is necessary to know enough to tell them apart. The caboose goes into greater detail on each of the general mind sets. The following discussion should be enough to help tell what they are and when one is using them.

The Ego Mind Set [161]. This is the outlook which people have toward life in general when they are abiding in the colossal myth--the notion that Actuality and Reality are the same thing. We refer to it as the ego mind set because it was the outlook which Sigmund Freud found people to have when he established Psychoanalysis and used the term "ego" to symbolize the center of cognition. This is the mind set which has predominated over human life--probably since the beginning of our species.

When one's ego mind set is in operation, he or she will be thinking in terms of recall from memory, imagination, and a realization of self and perceived things as being both actual and real.

The Phenomenal Self Mind Set [162] is the outlook which people have toward life in general when they have discarded the colossal myth--that Actuality and Reality are the same thing. With this mind set, one sees Actuality for what it is and Reality for what it is. For instance, he or she will be able to view any man-made or Natural physical object through the process of perception, just as it is done with the ego mind set. But in addition, that person's mind will view prior experiences with actual things, events, and conditions. Those who use the projection of self will get a fairly good view of most if not all prior experience. However, the resolution becomes much clearer when they use retroprojection; although, for me, it was only rarely with studio quality [163].

Some will say that this same thing can be done when using the ego mind set. This is true. All humans with normal mentality will get imaginable recall of past experiences--some more than others. And why shouldn't they? The psychological mechanics are the same with both mind sets. The only thing different is that people who use the ego mind set have no other place to look for Reality than out there in the perceivable world, in Actuality...because they are hung up on the colossal myth. The result is that the colossal myth compels them to think that they are recalling imaginable information from an unconscious reservoir of ideas on the Actuality side of the A-R Interface. This causes a needless loss of resolution and energy, as the phenomenal self tries to gather the information through a wall of denial--a window frosted with myth [164].

Further study on the matter of general mind set should show if there are relationships between genetic and cultural influences and variations in general mind set that would account for such things as group differences in aptitude, recall ability, and readiness to face Reality. Until that information comes, we must not rule out the possible need of changing the term from "general mind set" to "general but variable mind set."

Dual Mind Sets. After twenty-seven years of counseling, I have not yet met a client who was using the phenomenal self mind set. All of them were using the ego mind set. However, that was no problem in my counseling until about three years ago, for I too was using the ego mind set. But when I became able to use the phenomenal self mind set, I found myself having to gear my thinking back to the ego mind set, which was always the outlook of the client. From the first, I had no problem gearing down [165] to the ego mind set. However, I had a hard time getting back to the phenomenal self mind set. The way I solved this problem was to ask myself if there is a difference between an actual value and a real value, and if it is true that Reality is created through the process of cognition? Upon realizing that the answer to both questions was yes, I found [166] myself slipping right back into the phenomenal self mind set.

SECTION 12: THE FOLD OF REALITY

What is the Fold of Reality? Earlier, the Fold of Reality was explained as being the place in human mentality where corresponding values of Actuality and Reality are in exact agreement at the A-R Interface, and that it is where the Vector of Reason becomes noticeable. In this section, we are going to discuss how human Being League issues tend to coalesce with the Fold of Reality. The way this happens is that nonbeing values become purged from Being League issues, thus providing completely valid issues to the growth of the Fold of Reality.

There are probably several if not many different ways of explaining how human issues relate to the Fold of Reality. For example, there may be ways of explaining how musical and artistic issues relate to the Fold of Reality: this study is centered on how intellectual (reasoned) issues relate to it.

The view taken here is that answers to questions concerning the relationship between intellectual issues and the Fold of Reality are now available at the philosophical level, and that a new frontier for concrete science lies "just around the corner." We may be just months away from being able to construct a working model of the Actuality side of the human ego state [167]. What is needed now is some idea of the mechanism which a working model will be hooking up to. In other words, what is there on the Reality side of the A-R Interface that we can expect the artificial actual self to be gearing to? Locating the A-R Interface in the area of the thalamus will be among the first things to do. It is submitted that this task can be accomplished much easier if there is someone on the Reality side to deliver real impulses that can be identified from the Actuality side. The Fold of Reality appears to be the Reality component with the highest concentration of energy, hence something to key on to. Perhaps some of the preliminary information can be provided here.

The Real Value Range. As mentioned earlier, I have no idea of what your real value range is like. So what will be described here is my own. It will be interesting to know the likenesses and differences between yours and mine. It might be a useful beginning in the field of Reality analysis.

Viewing into my field of view and using my broadest scan, I see my Fold of Reality as being flush with, if not part of, the left wall of my Reality. Immediately adjacent on the right side of the Fold is my Being League. Then there is an open space ranging all the way to the right side of my Reality. When I bring my time line [168] into the picture, I can see my Nonbeing League as a dot near the right wall.

When I view the entire value range on a scale of 1 to 10 beginning at the left wall, my Fold extends to "1," my Being League extends to "3," the open space extends to "9.5" where lies my Nonbeing League, and the right wall stands at "10".

Cursory Effect. My "I" of Reality leaves a cursory effect whenever it retroprojects throughout my Reality, that is to say, it appears to be produced by an organized electronic system, much like the cursor we see on a computer screen. In an instant, I can make it travel from my Fold to the right side of my Reality; I can make it travel slowly or in an instant from something I did yesterday to the day my younger brother was born--sixty-seven years ago; and I can make it travel anywhere in my Fold, my Being League, my open space, and my Nonbeing League at will--much as a bee can fly about in a garden.

There may be some significance to be found in the fact that I can move about in my open space just as I can move the computer cursor about on a clear file whose inset symbols "⏎" have been moved to the right margin. The indication here is that I can retroproject to any points in my Reality that have been previously visited by informational characters--those that occur in recording ideas, concepts, and open spaces. I marvel at how similar the functions of Reality are to those of computer and electronic apparatuses.

Coalescence of Issues. When I first started to view the issues in my Reality, I was under the impression that they were fixed in place. I kept that impression until it came time to study the relationship between the Fold of Reality and the issues which lie in my Being League. After pondering this relationship and not being able to generate enough insight to start this subsection, I asked myself, "Where have I gone wrong? Where is my misconception?"

You see, I was working with an issue at that very time. It was the issue [169] whose objective was to determine the relationship between the Fold of Reality and Being League issues. What I had to do was to check that issue over and see where the misconception was. It didn't take long to find. Where I went wrong was in getting the idea that human issues are fixed in position--like trees and telephone poles. When I realized that they were not completely stationary, but had one part [170] that could move with time, my Vector of Reason let itself be known, while that entire issue coalesced with my Fold of Reality. Today, when I want to visit that issue, I have to go into my Fold of Reality to find it.

That experience with issue coalescence led me to some important understandings concerning human Reality. One was that while the Vector of Reason may become a factor in many other changes in human personality, it is most definitely present when a being issue coalesces with the Fold of Reality. Another understanding was that being issues respond to a polar situation--as a bunch of compass needles will respond to the polarity of earth and always point to the north pole. And still another understanding was that although being issues are highly compatible, they are not completely valid; otherwise they would have already coalesced with the Fold of Reality, and there would be no ongoing Being League--only Fold of Reality.

This is perhaps the fastest way for me to explain the relationship between the Fold of Reality and Being League issues. It is to "stand" right there [171], have the relationship demonstrated before my "very eyes," and then relay what I saw to others. This relationship is a case where a being issue would be completely valid, were it not for the presence of one or more invalid constituent ideas. Once those invalid ideas are discovered and rendered invalid, the issue itself becomes completely valid and coalesces with the Fold. Thus the Fold gets a bit larger and the Being League gets one issue smaller.

Some of you who are still operating with the ego mind set are no doubt thinking that what has just been said is crazy talk, or at least a pipe dream. But don't be like the people in Washington who lobbied against the launching of orbiting satellites on the very day that Sputnik went up; or the throng who watched Columbus sail away--obviously to fall off the end of the earth; or the ego mind setters at Calvary. And to those of you who have slain the colossal myth, let me say, welcome to the philosophy of Affective Realism and the field of Reality analysis.

A Final Note. There are other aspects of my Reality that could be discussed here. One is what I think of as scrolling--where I can look upon my Reality as a giant roll of conceptual content and unroll it to get view of my entire conscious life history. Another aspect is that the Fold of Reality wall lies in a straight line, while the Nonbeing League wall (the right one) varies on the range scale from 10 to about 1. However, it seems pointless to discuss such things until other people have made assessments of their own Realities. Then we will be able to know which assessments are consistent with all others and which ones reflect individual difference.

Also, you should know that I am an average mortal human. I make mistakes. If I am living true to form, there will be a number of mistakes found in this book. I will accept them as my badges of mortality and as things to get rid of in preparation for the eternal life.

SECTION 13: CALL TO THE FOLD

My first job in writing this book was to reaffirm the real existence of Almighty God and Christ [172]. My second job was to provide a God-oriented philosophy that would help bolster the existing front line trench philosophy of concrete science. And my third job is to call all mankind to the Fold of Reality.

In the last two chapters, we covered some rather profound ground. What made it profound, however, was not the subject matter; rather, it was the lack of readiness to accept Reality for what it is. The ego mind set, which views Actuality and Reality to be the same thing, has blanketed humanity, probably from the start, and has cloaked our intellectual vision just enough to obscure the truth about human existence. But now, more than at any time in the history of man, people are questioning the philosophies of old and arriving at conceptions that were missed--as is shown by the convergence of Eastern and Western philosophers on the expanding horizons of concrete science. This is where mankind is today--just ready to leave the wallows of excessive pleasure and need, and enter the Age of true happiness and morality and honor and self-reliance and responsibility and fellowship with our real God and the Greater Reality. The only thing that can prevent this from happening is for the majority of people to remain with the ego mind set and the colossal myth.

The most effective way of destroying the colossal myth is for the individual to evaluate his or her Being League issues and invalidate all of the misconceptions. This way, the valid issues will coalesce with the Fold. The result will be that the Fold will develop more intellectual clout and the myth will fall. When we say that we are going to call people to the Fold, this is what we are asking them to do--to evaluate their Being Leagues, invalidate the misconceptions, and let the valid issues coalesce with their Folds. In doing this, they will be able to slay the colossal myth and let Reality be what it is. If the majority of people on earth can do this, then the good life will come and be with us for hundreds if not thousands of years. If they don't, then they had better listen for the click [173].

This third job is one where every man, woman, and child on earth must be called to the Fold of Reality before the end of this century. Why this century? Why Not? In spite of the ego mind set's persistence over the past two thousand years, man has developed a tremendous amount of intellect. If that wasn't enough to slay the colossal myth in the minds of most humans, then why not? Why not make the call to the Fold, so that invalid notions may be purged from human issues and enable all of us to experience the Vector of Reason which has been cloaked in darkness by the colossal myth. Then surely most humans will see enough truth to slay the myth.

With these thoughts in mind, I ask you to come aboard and join in making the call; for this is not a one-man job, or a job for the leader of a group, or the members of a single group. It is a job for the members of any and all groups who have the slightest idea of what the subject of this book is all about.

SECTION 14: A NOTE TO EGO MIND-SETTERS

Ego mind-setters are people who believe that Actuality and Reality are the same thing. Phenomenal self mind-setters are people who have noted the difference between Actuality and Reality. The great majority of mortal humans are ego mind-setters and a scant minority of mortal humans are those who have managed to acquire the phenomenal self mind-set. This is where humanity stands today. Yet if mankind is to survive much longer on earth, it must enter into a massive departure from the ego mind-set and begin using the phenomenal self mind-set. The determining factor will be how well you and the billions of other ego mind-setters execute this change in human outlook.

As an introduction to Affective Realism, this book is almost completed. Of the three jobs it had to do, the first two are done. It reaffirmed the Reality of God Almighty and it provided some philosophical information which should help bolster the front line trench philosophy of concrete science. All that is left to do is to provide ego mind-setters with a clear explanation of what is meant when we say, "call to the Fold of Reality." Hopefully the following discussion will do that.

Mind-set Grading. In making the trip back and forth between the ego mind-set and the phenomenal self mind-set--that which recognizes the difference between Actuality and Reality--I came upon something which leads me to think that in some cases there may be grades of acquisition. There may be cases where an individual has moved partially away from the ego mind-set, but not quite up to the phenomenal self mind-set. What led me to this suspicion was that at one spot on that trip I could look at a landscape, for example, and then cast a sketchy image of it upon the wall or a piece of paper. All I had to do was pencil in that sketch and then start shading or painting. Could it be that some ego mind-setters have managed to acquire this unique grade of acquisition--this ability to bring Reality in as a factor, but not to the degree that the ego mind-set had become lost? Could it be that this mind-set grading occurs in other fine arts, for instance, in music, in sculpture, in architecture, in ceramics...and in literary pursuits of knowledge as well?

What crosses my mind is that this concept of mind-set grading may be pointing to a whole assortment of mind-sets from whence one can start an approach to Reality. In writing this book, I started from what might be called the basic ego mind-set and reasoned my way up to the phenomenal self mind-set. But that was just one approach to Reality. While toying with my frame of reference, which I liken to a television, I found that there were many "buttons" I could push and each time get a new view of Reality. This suggests that there may be many approaches to Reality--each one different from the one used in this book, but equally as important.

You may be operating from one of these higher grades of acquisition--which is to say, you may be advancing toward the phenomenal self mind-set through an aesthetic or literary approach. This may be why you have difficulty following this philosophical approach. I know that I would be as lost trying an aesthetic approach as I am in trying to understand classical music. For all I know, those who are following the artistic approaches may have already reached the phenomenal self mind-set in fine art or literary art terms. If such is the case, then perhaps we should try to share our values at that level, and in so-doing, find it an easier mode of communication.

Moreover, it should be emphasized that Christianity became the backbone of Western Civilization by forwarding the message of Jesus Christ. It did this, not only through Scriptural review, but through such fine and literary arts as music and art and sculpture and architecture and prose and poetry. Many if not most of our artistic approaches to Reality have followed the Christian track to God.

What must be understood is that now is the time for all humans to apply their unique talents for reaching the Fold of Reality. Now is the time for us to pack our Folds as full of valid insight and beauty as possible. And this is what is meant when we call all mankind to the Fold.

Being Least May Be Most. One of the biggest differences between the ego mind-set and the phenomenal self mind-set is that they cast different perspectives concerning the matters of wealth and possession. Many of today's ego mind-setters place great value upon such things as money and diamonds and houses and cars. But to those who operate in the phenomenal self mind-set, the greater value is placed upon the things that are going to last for eternity, and these include such things as love and hate, service to God and service against Him, responsible behavior and irresponsible behavior, and justice and crime. Good or bad [174], these things are real values; they are with us in mortal life; yet when mortal death arrives, only they and the realizations of their respective Actualities will still be in existence, while the actual values will have passed away...money and diamonds and houses and cars. What it comes down to is that the people who cast their lots with worldly wealth and possessions are going to have little if anything in their Folds after the click of death comes upon them.

The true Christian and concrete science tracks to God bring one to understand that the Fold of a human Reality contains only valid eternal values. Only those values will go on to coalesce with the Fold of the Greater Reality, and only the individuals who possess them will be able to follow.

In everyday life, we see people placing greater value on worldly wealth and possessions and lesser value on service to God and the betterment of mankind. Those people are gathering things that are actual in nature but real in deed. The actual things do not themselves get into Reality, but the deeds of self-realization which place value on them are real; and all real values are eternal. It then follows that many who place greater value on actual things may be committing acts of self-service [175] that result in the production of nonbeing values, and those who place greater value on real things--as in love and responsibility to God and mankind--are committing acts of service to others that result in the production of being values. Being values are the ones that coalesce with the Fold of Reality. Thus you will see how the person with fewer actual values may have spent more of his or her mortal days gathering being values through service to God and mankind, and therefore have more to contribute to the Fold. Hence being least [176] may be most.

Here again is what we mean when we call all mankind to the Fold. You may not yet have acquired the phenomenal self mind-set, but you have built enough Reality construct to know what is meant when we think of the Fold, the Being League and the Nonbeing League--the three reservoirs of real human values. You may not know for a fact that the human Fold is the only component of human personality that will go on to coalesce with the Fold of the Greater Reality and thereby enter the individual into a vastness of insight and beauty which lies beyond our imagination; but you have come close enough to Affective Realism to suspect that such is the case, and that the coalescence between the human Fold of Reality and the Fold of the Greater Reality stands just ahead. I submit that with what you now know about the Grand Scheme of Things, and with your commitment to serve Almighty God, you, as a responsible person, must join in making the call.

What we must do is to go our ways, make the call, and

advise others of this responsibility to the Real God and to themselves. Beyond that, their choice of destiny will be theirs to make. And other than to answer questions, our attempts to inform might be getting in the way; for it is the truth which people see for themselves that moves them toward the Fold.

I once heard a student say, "Yes, professor, you can lead a horse to water, but you can't make him drink!" The professor replied, "Sure you can! You stimulate his thirst." The mere idea of the subject which you and I have to promote is enough to stimulate the thirst for answers which we are prepared to give. If readiness for an answer is what valid education is all about, then the world has never been more ready for our [177] answers than now.

Moving to the Fold. One way in which a person can move to the Fold of Reality [178] is to follow the teachings of Jesus Christ. This is the main way in which Western Civilization came to be what it is today--people following the teachings of Jesus Christ through faith and acceptance. Here, we are discussing another way of moving to the Fold. It was the way that Jesus Christ wanted to follow at the time, but found the people too low in intellect to follow [179]. It involved the use of reason in following a trail which has since been cleared by concrete science. It is regarded here as being one valid intellectual pathway to the Fold of Reality.

During those earlier days, something happened that led people astray from the mark, from the Fold of Reality. Along both the Christian and concrete science tracts, it was the problem of misconception. Along the Christian track, great numbers of people fell to the belief that God Almighty is supernatural in a mystical sense, and this led them to gather invalid religious values. God Almighty is as Real as they are; and in a real sense, just as Supernatural. Along the concrete science track, everything was going fine until the front line trench reached the A-R Interface. This is where concrete science is today. Many concrete scientists are still hung up on the colossal myth. They believe that Actuality and Reality are the same thing; hence, in their judgement, there is no A-R Interface. Mystic values and the colossal myth--are these the two great barriers that stand between the pursuit and realization of our Real Almighty God? If they stand, humanity will fall; but if they fall, humanity will go on to have many more years of progress and fellowship with our Real God. History, or lack of it, will tell.

Validating Issues. A final thing to consider about one's moving to the Fold is the matter of human issues. If we were operating within the phenomenal self mind-set, it would be easy to find an invalid issue. Like searching through a deck of cards, all we would have to do is check each idea and concept until we come to the ones that are invalid. Upon invalidating them, the issue becomes valid and worthy of coalescence with the Fold. But from where we stand, in the ego mind-set, we can't see issues; we can only sense their presence as they press superego impulses upon our ego states.

We must remind ourselves that the differing of issues is what confuses human minds and causes marriages to break up and churches to divide and social conflicts to erupt and countries to war against each other. What it amounts to is that if we can bring all human issues upon valid ground, then there will be no confusion or division or conflict or war; for valid issues compliment each other.

This brings us to the key which ego mind-setters may use to resolve human issues. It is to "listen" to our superego impulses, and when we find one that calls for defense, don't defend it, as you would be tempted to do, but sit back and share with others this inclination to defend and protect. The explanation for why you should do this lies in the way you counsel yourself, or ponder an issue. Let's pursue this matter a bit further.

When Sigmund Freud got into the study of human personality, he made frequent use of hypnosis as a means of getting into the patient's unconscious to find out what was going wrong. But eventually he discovered that hypnosis was not always necessary. He found that in cases involving mental snags (as opposed to hangups) he could just sit back and listen for signals in the patient's free association of words. He found that the patient would follow such signals right back into the unconscious and to the problem ideas. All he had to do was listen and follow along. Upon arriving at a problem idea, he engaged the patient in a discussion which would restructure that earlier event and thereby make the problem idea invalid [180].

We all have problem ideas in our unconscious (in our Realities), and there are several ways of getting rid of them. We can get rid of them by going in for professional counseling --where the Freudian free association of words would probably be used. We can discuss our feelings with relatives and good friends, and the problem signal will automatically lead the conversation back to the problem idea. Or we can do what is so popular in Eastern nations. We can simply meditate, and our own minds will follow the signal to the problem idea.

You who are true Christians may be just one misconception away from being able to work (reason) at the Fold of Reality, and in all probability, it is a misconception which has to do with human creation [184]. There are two things that you should know concerning this misconception. One is that not even the greatest one among us knows what he is; we are all looking for that answer. And the other thing is that there need not be a conflict between the six day creation which Moses proposed, the "consider the lily of the field" prescription which Jesus of Nazareth presented, and the findings of modern historical geologists and Natural scientists. There is no conflict because Moses was referring to that part of man which contains the Real self--his Reality; Jesus was referring to both one's Real self and his or her carcass; and the concrete scientists were pursuing the development of one's carcass. When you come down to it, all three were pursuing legitimate aspects of human personality. Moses (1571-1451 B.C.) [181] was viewing man as a Reality; Jesus was viewing man as a Reality with ties to Actuality; and our modern concrete scientists are viewing the biophysical aspects of human personality as a body whose carcass has somehow developed human characteristics. There is no misconception when you combine all three of these aspects into one clear view of human personality.

Jesus of Nazareth tried to explain all this to the people of his day, only they had not yet acquired enough intelligence to comprehend it. The result was that he had to fall back to a religious message--wherein he described a human Reality as being the Comforter, or Holy Ghost.

Mohammed (570?-632) thought highly of the teachings of Jesus, except that he did not accept the idea of the Trinity--the Father, the Son, and the Holy Ghost. If only Moses and Plato and Jesus and Mohammed could have been contemporary with modern concrete science; then they would have the view which we hold today--a Real Almighty God, a Vector of Reason which Christians refer to as Christ, and a ghostlike personal Reality.

You who are concrete scientists may very well lead humanity into the middle of human destiny and never realize that you have closed upon the Mother Load of Reason [182]. This you can do if you keep insisting upon demonstrable cause while working within your Reality construct, and at the same time, stay with the colossal myth.

What irony! To find a humanity whose scientific and religious tracks to God became stalled at the door step of its destiny--one because of the colossal myth and the other because of mystical misconceptions of God. God Almighty is Real. Jesus Christ is Real. Now you must abandon your myths and become as real as They.

Come to the Fold [183].

END

Affective Realism is the study of man as a Reality.

Reasoning is a function of Reality.

Ego mind-setters are people who see themselves as being part of Actuality. Phenomenal self mind-setters are people who see themselves as being part of either Actuality or Reality

Caboose

The Key. Our use of the key should not lead you to believe that we are going to lock the being ideas away from those that are nonbeing; rather, our use of the key will be to temporarily step away from the greater American social condition and see how far a diet consisting only of being values can carry us in the pursuit of human existence and destiny. We must bear in mind that there is not a human on this planet who knows what he or she is; we must recognize the fact that every member of American society who is in good mental health is as interested in human existence and destiny as we are; and that we should quietly follow the trail of being values to the top of personality mountain, find out what we are, and then return to a friendly human society and give the word and call.

1

Construct. A systematic uniting of ideas whose contents are sense and affect related: a consolidation of smaller ideas into larger formations of ideas and concepts.

2

Paradoxical understandings are understandings that seem unbelievable but are true.

3

Deductive and Inductive Reason. Let us become clear on two of the methods of reasoning. One is deductive reason and the other is inductive reason. Deductive reason is when one comes to understand a general idea and then derives specific ideas from it. Inductive reason is just the opposite: it is when one gathers many specific ideas and then derives from them a general idea which reflects the same truth in each one.

4

Aristotelian Deductions. You don't have to go far to find some of the Aristotelian deductions that have made it through 2300 years of testing and still manifest here in the present. If one has as much as an eighth grade education, he or she will have some of these deductions already in mind. Take evolution, for example: Aristotle is generally credited for discovering it at the philosophical level, that is, the level at which possible facts are discovered; and Charles Darwin (1809-1882) is credited for discovering it at the scientific level--the level at which actual facts are discovered.

Or consider the Law of Cause and Effect. Today, it is viewed as being one of the Laws of Nature. It was explained at the philosophical level by Aristotle, although it hasn't been until modern times that it became fully understood at the scientific level.

5

Concerning the Law of Cause and Effect. Aristotle maintained that any object in Nature that consists of matter and form is an effect which is caused. For as much as this concerns living matter, he did not know about protoplasm and the genetic determination of form. So, being convinced that Natural objects consisting of matter and form must each be caused, he attributed these causes to the Supreme Being or to something else in the Universe. This way, he made no room for spontaneous generation, while at the same time, he was able to take overview of the cause and effect relationships in Nature and come up with a conceptualization of evolution. Actually, there was not a whole lot of difference between Aristotle's evolution and Darwin's evolution. The biggest difference was that Aristotle ascribed a final cause to every object consisting of matter and form, whereas upon recognizing protoplasmic development, Darwin assigned all living effects to earlier causes. The question we are now left with is, what about the earliest cause, the first cause, the cause which created that first cell of life over two billion years ago? Scientists are faced with two possible answers. Might that first cell have been created when some nitrogen and some methane and some other things came together and spontaneously created it, in which case, we would have to grant the possible existence of spontaneous generation? Or should we attribute its cause to the Supreme Being?

6

One should not get the idea that Aristotle's science was all there was during the first three centuries B.C. On the contrary, there were numerous ancient researchers whose findings came under the heading of science. Unfortunately, however, their works investigated the "how," "where," and "when" of objects studied, but they hardly ever considered the "why's." Aristotle's science was popular, not because it was any good, but because he was a popular "guy." Archimedes (287?-212 B.C.), on the other hand, made use of demonstrated proofs and went on to disprove many of Aristotle's scientific findings, while having most of his own works survive until this day--as any physics student can tell you. Archimedes is credited as being the originator of mechanics in science.

And of course we should not overlook Hippocrates (460-357? B.C.), a contemporary of Socrates and the Father of

Medicine; or Claudius Galen (131-201 A.D.), medical writer and philosopher who acted to bring medical science together for that time.

Yet the fact remains that even though the Renaissance (14th century A.D.) revived Aristotelian science, it eventually gave way to the nationalistic and Humanistic movements, and only bits and pieces have made it through to today.

To summarize the demonstrative science successes between the years 400 B.C. and 1600 A.D., little can be attributed to Aristotelian science, more can be attributed to those working outside of Aristotle's deductive science, and up to the time of Francis Bacon, the practice of seeking "why" through the demonstration of cause was the exception and not the rule.

7

I can understand why **Martin Luther and Peter Ramus** said that everything Aristotle said was wrong. It is true that he "goofed" when he put deductive reason into the physical and biological sciences. That was wrong. And as we are about to find out, he was wrong in assuming that Actuality and Reality are the same thing. No doubt there will be a lot of people saying that he should have spent more time listening to Plato. But the view taken here is that Aristotle's part in revealing the intellectual potential of man tends to balance his wrongs.

Perhaps we can all agree that this would be a much different world today if Plato had chosen not to have students; because although Aristotle no doubt meant well by contending that ideas were fleeting things, he was perpetuating, if not creating, the false notion that Actuality and Reality are the same thing. Such nonsense was a believable myth 2350 years ago, as Aristotle's success has shown; it has been a believable myth for the past 2350 years, vexing man's intellectual search for truth; and today, it is a myth which even our elementary and high school students are made to accept.

8

A professional student of human personality is a person who

has been trained to assess the normal and abnormal conditions in a human personality. Some of these people have gone through extensive training for giving help to people with mental health problems, and are licensed to do so. These include psychiatrists, psychologists, and LPC's (Licensed Professional Counselors).

9

Cognition is a function of the ego: of or relating to conscious intellectual activity.

10

Self-actualization is a term that we will be using throughout this book, and each time we use it, it will be given a little more profound meaning. At this point, it is being used to indicate a person who is showing a readiness to abandon false ideas and face Reality for what it is.

11

Bacon, Montaigne, Comenius, and Rousseau were among the main 17th and 18th century philosophers whose works supported the rise of modern education and concrete science.

12

During the 5th century B.C. in Rome, the land owners, the rich and powerful, the politicians, and the religious leaders all belonged to a blood line class, or aristocracy. These people became known as *patricians*. All the people who didn't belong to this class were automatically cast into a lower class. Members of this lower class were called *plebs*. For centuries, the struggle between the patricians and plebs left the plebs on the bottom end of things--in money, in land, in political power, and in religious say. But gradually, things changed for the plebs, and eventually they took control of things, much as what happened during the Middle Ages. The lesson in all of this is that, given time, a group of humans whose callings are to God and political freedom will in the end prevail. The case of the plebs was not too unlike that of the humanists in religion and politics...religious freedom and city-states for the plebs and religious freedom and nationalism for the humanists.

13

Toward the end of the 15th century and the beginning of the 16th, scholars were beginning to take note of what an unmolested human personality would be like. The accepted leader of these scholars was Desiderius Erasmus (1466-1536). His spirited assault on Scholasticism led the monks to say that he laid the egg which Luther hatched.

14

Aristotle's conception of the Law of Cause and Effect was valid except that he failed to recognize the principle of earlier causes and substituted God as an immediate cause rather than to succumb to spontaneous generation.

15

If you agree with me that the Christian religion is the backbone of Western Civilization, then you may find this allegory interesting. It is a symbolic overview of the Christian religious development and that of concrete science.

16

Embryology: The study of the development of an individual from the fertilized egg stage to the time of delivery, or hatching.

Histology: A concrete science which studies groups of cells called tissues; usually a microscopic study.

Cytogenetics: The study of heredity and variation with methods from cytology (the study of cells) and genetics (the study of genes and chromosomes).

17

Family values: These include such things as beliefs, principles,

ideals, and attitudes that the family generates and displays--
both as a group and in the behavior of its members.

18
Individual values: These include the psychological values
which appear in a family member's behavior. They also appear
as behaviors of a peer group member, and are often the major
cause of family hiatus and disorder.

19
Jacob M. Schleiden (1804-1881) published on the Cell Theory
in 1838.   Theodore Ambrose Hubert Schwann (1810-1882)
published in 1839...a year later mainly because of the greater
difficulty in assessing animal cells.

20
The slayers of the capsular theory were those whose works laid
the foundation for the field which we now think of as cytogenetics. Their work was most frequently found in the fields of
Natural history, cytology, and histology.

21
Diploid: Having the somatic number of chromosomes, which
is twice that of the gametic, or haploid, number. The egg and
sperm are called gametes because they contain only one-half
($\frac{1}{2}$) the number of chromosomes that are found in body (somatic) cells.

22
One of the best examples of social rise and decline is the
Catholic Church during the Dark Ages, when upon its degrada-
tion to secularity the entire society declined, and when upon the
arrival of Scholasticism and the Holy Roman Empire the entire
society began to rise.

23
The word "central" will be discussed in Chapter Five; but for

now, let us just say that it is neither secular nor religious.

24

Like the old song says, "You got to accentuate the positive, in order to eliminate the negative." That is the manner in which this book is written.

25

Main Objective. What you are reading now is a section that I am writing after completing the book. After reading over the entire book, most of the chapters seemed to get the message across pretty well. With my latest overview, I could not see how to make further improvement to most of the sections. But this section--Tools for the Climb--stuck out like a sore thumb. It was getting into matters that we didn't have to cover. This book is not submitted as a psychology text, or a biophysics text, or even a textbook on philosophy. It is written as a philosophical message which is as complicated as necessary and as uncomplicated as possible.

26

Consider a horse, a cow, a chicken, a barn, and a house. When you think of them one at a time, you are thinking of ideas; and when you remove the tail from the horse, the udders from the cow, the left leg from the chicken, the roof from the barn, and the windows from the house, you will have changed the ideas completely. Similarly, if you were to take all five of these objects and consider them as a whole, you would have developed a conception of a farm. And if you were to put several farms together, you would have a conceptualization, or construct, of a farm community.

If you were flying over that farm community when you made your first assessment and noticed only that each farm had a horse, a cow, a chicken, a barn, and a house, you would have generated ideas of such things and gone on to develop conceptions of the farms and the farm community. What we must realize is that those first ideas and conceptions were bought (introjected) by your personality and invested in your Affective Reality. They are fixed for eternity, and only God Almighty can change them. So if after landing you were to drive out to the farm community and notice that at each farm there was a tailless horse, an udderless cow, a legless chicken, a roofless barn, and a windowless house, you would not be able to go back into your Reality and update, or correct, your original ideas and concepts. All you can do is to generate new ideas and concepts, and introject them into your Reality.

In a way, we humans liken to the old miser who never took money out of the bank. The difference is that, in our case, we can't take ideas out of our Realities: we can only go into our Realities and reflect upon them while generating new ideas in the process which we call *reason*.

The lesson here is that once an idea is created and introjected into Reality, it becomes fixed for eternity. This is what provides the essence of the Reality dimension which we will be calling the *incidence of effect*.

27

If you are a high school student or one who didn't go on to college, don't let these tools throw you. I know that if these terms were thrown at me fifty years ago, I would have been confused. What you should know is that, like jumping in at the deep end of the pool, this chapter is moving you in only one direction, and that is toward the shallow end of the subject. So keep this in mind. We will not be going any deeper.

28

The definition of *Affective Realism* is given in a later section...a philosophy which is founded upon the eclectic display of human personality. A definition is also provided in Section 2 of Chapter Four.

29

Founding value. The next section provides a fuller explanation of the founding value. Its shortest definition would be to say that it is apparent Reality.

30

Teleology. Concrete science treats design, purpose, and utility as properties of an effect after it comes into existence. Teleology centers on final causes of such properties; concrete science centers on the earlier causes of such properties and their ultimate First Cause--God.

31

Plane. The founding value is the idea of omnipotence which is created during early childhood of every human and remains in effect throughout life. In cases where, under the tutelage of the nurturing environment, the individual develops values that improperly or unnaturally root in the founding value, odd feelings of being may result and go on to support unusual adult behaviors. Homosexuality that is psychological in nature, and not the result of germ plasm propensity, may be the most striking example of this unnatural phenomenon.

One way to overcome this affliction is to acquire enough intellectual data and generate sufficient insight to challenge the founding value on this matter and destroy the misconception that made this illicit rooting take place. The life issue of the subject is what must be explored. The old saying that "The truth will set you free" seems to apply here.

32

Denial. Unconscious repudiation of a truth.

33

I got my copy of Russell's little book by putting a request on the Internet.

34

In his explanation of time as it exists in Nature, Russell gave some support to ideas that you may have picked up during science fiction shows. One, for example, described how a man could climb into a spaceship and travel at the speed of light for seven years, reach the next nearest star, slow down and circle it, then regain the speed of light and return to earth. After getting out of the spaceship, he would be astonished to find that his welcoming wife had become fourteen years older, while he had aged only a few hours. He wouldn't have aged more than a few minutes, however, were it not for the fact that he had to slow down while circling that distant star. The reasoning here is that light travels near the absolute velocity and any object traveling at that velocity would have little if any vectorial motion, hence less time to display.

35

We have said that Actuality includes every thing, event and condition that exists in the Universe other than the human selves and their respective Reality constructs. You will note that we did not say measurable Universe, which would suggest that it has limits and, as some astronomers would explain, includes everything within an imaginary circle cast by a beam of light. Recalling that in Nature the circle is the measure of distance, this conception of the Universe seems to work fine for astronomers; for in having a measurable Universe, they have reasonable things to work with; and the subject of other Universes is left for study at the philosophical level of reason. In our study, we are not considering celestial objects; we have no need for setting an outer limit to the Universe; so what we are doing is to take away the limit and let the actual Universe include our measurable Universe and all of the other measurable Universes that may be out there extending for Lord knows how far. For us, the Universe will be that giant, boundless space whose material contents we call Actuality.

We have also said that except for its nonbeing values, Reality is the human creation which is the developing counterpart of Actuality.

You may be picturing in your mind that Nature makes up most of Actuality, and Reality occurs as five and one-half billion mortal dots and let's say two billion deceased mortal dots in the space which is left in the Universe. I held on to this picture for a long time. But then, I finally came to the realization that our Nature may not take up that much of Actuality, and be nothing more that one of countless Natures where geologic and life forms evolve as Actuality.

36
Phylogenetic. Having to do with a broad evolutionary group, or phylum.

37
Ontogenetic. Having to do with the development of the individual.

38
Biological Format. The biological format includes all of the components of the human carcass that facilitate the expression of will and inclination of the Real self ("I" of Reality), namely the thalamus and cerebral cortex.

39
One way of telling if your *Affective Reality* is in full view is to see if it has become positioned in your frontal lobes. The error that I made at first was to think that I was viewing my Affective Reality with my eyes; but that was not the case; it was appearing behind my forehead.

Also, it should be noted that imaginative thinking and thinking in construct are instances where one "dives" into his or her Reality construct on specific matters. Such "dives" are permitted by the psychological defenses that one has in place-- meaning that they are all that he or she may safely perform. If you feel nervous or anxious while reading this chapter, you should stop and get professional advice. There is no hurry. Your Affective Reality is going to be with you for eternity.

40
Magnetic moment is a magnetic field whose lines of force move

in a circular direction and produce torque.

41

Over One Million Years. If this concept is unclear, you may want to read more about it in a college level Natural history book. Most public libraries have them.

42

Feral Children. Deprived of human contact: raised by wild animals.

43

Preparing for an Eclectic Overview of the Phenomenal Self. In the remainder of this chapter, we are going to be using five of the seven approaches to human personality to bring about an eclectic overview of the phenomenal human self: these are the Psychoanalytical, Biophysical, Existential, Behavioral, and Phenomenological Approaches. The remaining Approaches, Humanistic and Gestalt, will fit into the overview after we use the other five to bring it into focus. This is not too unlike a situation where you use five approaches to build a car, and then apply the gas and oil approaches to see how it performs.

44

There are also hormonal and other chemical signals that work in this manner.

45

In this study, we use the terms "state" and "level" to imply that one is operating *in* a state and *at* a level. For example, George was in the conscious state while driving at the subconscious level.

46

As mentioned in Section 10, the term "emotion" denotes a physiological departure from homeostasis before, during, or after acts of will, accident, and/or disease.

47

Proprioception. The function of certain sensory receptors in activating muscle movement, as in the winking of an eye and muscular action within the heart.

48

Sleep occurs when these nervous processes become fatigued.

49

The conscious state is the place where the senses report the state of the body in relation to the external world when an unlearned response, or the revision of an unsuccessful learned response, is called for. Successful learned responses are usually initiated by affective emotional reactions at the subconscious level. When such responses are unsuccessful, they will be diverted to the id side of the ego state at the conscious level. There the need will be deliberated and met with an act of cognition. The conscious level is also where emotional needs and responses become felt.

50

The distinction between an emotional condition and an emotional reaction is that an emotional condition includes all of the nervous and/or chemical activity that is going on in a specific place: an emotional reaction is what that specific place becomes when incoming stimulus impulses and outgoing response impulses gear to the emotional condition within it.

51

During the last few sections, we have been viewing human personality from the Biophysical Approach. We came to view the thalamic area as being the place in the biophysical state where the psychological state is rooted, and we have used Sigmund Freud's term, the id, in naming this root connection. Now, we are going to move to the Psychoanalytic Approach and view the biophysical and psychological states as part of one Natural phenomenon. Upon doing this, we will find that our study has arrived at the Phenomenological Approach to human personality. Then, having these three approaches as our base of reason, we will bring the Behavioral, Gestalt, Existential, and Humanistic Approaches into the picture and see what human personality looks like as a Reality. We will have then come to the end of the Trail of Reason.

52

Ancestral Past. There are two important things we should note about man's ancestral past. One thing is that impulses reporting survival needs of the individual usually flowed upward to the highest point of command. Today, we find that most of man's survival need impulses flow into the thalamic area: many originate in the spinal cord; a relatively few originate in the medulla; and a great many originate in the hypothalamus, where need information is received from body organs and sent to the thalamus and on to the cerebral cortex for response. The other thing to be noted about man's ancestral past is that while all of that development was going on, simple reflex action was becoming replaced by emotional reactions in meeting the survival needs of the individual, as is now shown by the functioning of the thalamic area.

53

What we are referring to here are the need impulses that move from the medulla to the thalamus. Back in man's ancestral past, and before the development of the new brain, this kind of impulse was geared to other nervous systems, the sympathetic and parasympathetic, and were used extensively in deciding matters of fright and flight. Such lower mammals as the rabbit still use these nervous systems today; but when man began to rely on thalamic area decisions, this primitive system of response became almost obsolete. I say almost because human anatomy still has nerve fibers connecting the reticular formation and the thalamus. On occasion, impulses will get passed along to the thalamus, and whenever the id intervenes and passes them up to the conscious level, they will sometimes cause inhibitions and nightmares.

54

Cognitive Arena. What is being presented here is a logical layout of the cognitive arena. The actual layout has yet to be determined by concrete scientists.

55

As was mentioned earlier, when a nonaffective emotional reaction fails to achieve balance on its own, it will pass the stimulus impulse along to the cerebral cortex where a symptom of the cause of the stimulus response--for example, a pain--will become felt at the source and realized at the conscious level. This would be an indirect response.

56

These response impulses are issued below the conscious level of awareness if the proper responses had previously been learned, in which case, the learned response impulse will go out and effect the appropriate motor activity (behavior). An example would be an itch on your hand. The first time you feel the itch, you would realize it and move to scratch it; but the second time you feel it, your other hand would have already been moving over to scratch it. These can be temporary learning episodes, or, if as in hunger the stimulus impulses arrive regularly, the response may become permanently learned.

57

In this study, we break awareness down to two levels--the conscious level of awareness and the subconscious level of awareness. Both have open and ongoing relationships with the individual's internal and external environments.

58

The main difference between a need stimulus and a need impulse is that the term "need stimulus" indicates that the need must be met and the term "need impulse" indicates how it will be met.

59
Race. A group of individuals possessing the same traits: descending from a common line, or ancestry, as with the Caucasian and Oriental races.

60
Psychic Energy. In this study, psychic energy is considered to be any form of controlled energy flow which is directly involved in the transfer of data to and/or from the ego state on either side of the A-R Interface: it is the controlled counterpart of the loose, or renegade, energy flow that gathers during moments of distress, as in attacks of anxiety and depression.

61
Man began living on this planet over a million years ago. Before that, his ancestral development extended back to the beginning of the Vertebrate Subphylum, about 500 million years ago. And before that, it went back to the beginning of the Chordate Phylum, probably not over a billion years ago. We could trace still further back, but because man's biophysical ancestry lies within almost a billion years of chordate development, this should be sufficient for us to recognize how Natural Selection was given a chance to prove its point. That was that if a plant or animal racket for survival worked, it would be around to be tried another day; but if the racket didn't work on a regular basis, then it would no longer be around as a survival factor.

Today, you look around and see only plants and animals that have successful rackets for survival. It has to be that way, because if a forebearer's racket for survival failed to work regularly, the existing plant or animal would not be here as testimony to a line of successfully adapting rackets which extends back hundreds of millions of years.

There are as many rackets for survival as there are species of plants and animals; for example, members of the dog species can smell, members of the cat species can claw, members of the pine tree species grow tall, and members of the fern species thrive in the shadows below.

This study is concerned with just one of these rackets for survival. In lower animals it is seen as an inherent aptitude for successful interaction with the environment, and each species has its own unique version of it: it is called *instinct*. Today, many biophysicists view instinct as a symptom of successful emotional balance in the making, where inherent aptitude triggers response impulses that effect successful motor behaviors and reduce the body tension which caused the stimulus impulse to occur...all being done below the conscious level. The contention here is that somewhere in or near the mammalian thalamus there is a nervous formation consisting of instinctive emotional reactions that are genetically "loaded" with the above-mentioned aptitude.

Instinct in human personality is less apparent. This may be because man's ability to reason turned out to be a better way of interacting with environment. But then, it may also be that early man only lost the overt expression of instinct, and that it still exists behind the scenes of cognition, operating in a covert manner.

Could it be that the instinctive emotional reactions that are now found in most other mammals are also present in the human? Could it be that the inherent aptitude response impulses in man do not first flow from the thalamus to the cerebral cortex, but forge a neural path through the entire length of the id, through the unconscious and subconscious levels, and arrive at the conscious level ready to set the psychological stage for reason and promote the emergence of what has come to be known as the ego, or self? In addition, this would explain how successful reasoned responses lead to the gathering of affect which is geared to the intuitive neural path at the unconscious level. This affect consists of affective emotional reactions that are programmed to issue learned responses to new stimulus impulses. In substance, this gathering is what we refer to as intelligence: in form, it is referred to as the superego.

As for the exact location of what would now be called intuitive emotional reactions, it would be either in the reticular formation near the beginning of the reticular-thalamus neural pathway, somewhere along the way, or in the thalamus near the pathway's end. If research finds that none of this exists, and that the entire intuition concept is wrong, then what is found to be the correct facility would have to fill the bill in terms of cause and effect: it would have to be the developmental cause of the superego, intelligence, the foundation of reason, and the emergence of self. If that correct facility should turn out to be the actual cause of all of these effects, and at the same time remain in alignment with man's ancestral past, then I would drop the intuitive concept like a hot potato and stay with the demonstrable facts.

The importance of intuition, or whatever the correct component may turn out to be, compares to an automobile ignition starter. A Human personality may not be able to start without it.

62
Id impulses include the phylogenetic and ontogentic impulses.

63
We have increasing understanding of the electrochemical activity in emotional reactions; we understand much of the biophysics of their stimulus and response impulses; but we have little if any understanding of the physical nature of the psychic energy values which we call ideas, although our recognition and use of them is proof that they exist. Surely they will be the main objects of study in the fields of mathematical physics and biophysics as human progress moves ahead.

64
These are only three of the many body organs engaged in the maintenance of human metabolism. The objective here is to show how human personality exists as an ever-changing living phenomenon, inside as well as outside; and to further show how the living human body is a colony of cells, tissues, and organs whose joint purpose is to help the colony survive.

65

Birth and Delivery. Birth is when a new individual human is created: that is when the sperm joins the nucleus of the egg, thus producing the basic number of chromosomes. Delivery is when the child leaves the womb.

66

70-140. This is a range which is programmed into instruments that measure blood sugar. A reading of less than 70 would indicate a hypoglycemic condition--too little blood sugar. A reading of above 140 would indicate a hyperglycemic condition-- too much blood sugar. In laboratory measurement, this range of blood sugar falls between 100 and 150 mg. per 100 ml. Under normal conditions, the liver works to maintain this range; but when it is exceeded, upper centers in the spinal cord and the hypothalamus involve the sympathetic nervous system in the production of symptoms, for example, sweating and paleness.

67

This is where culture begins to play its role in helping the child meet felt needs by manipulating his or her sense data in ways that will convert the expression of felt need from animal cry to human word, and in a manner that will introduce words as symbols of reason. This is also where the unique gestalt-centered family style of living begins to develop in the infant child...one new member of a close-knit group.

68

Superego and elimination impulses are learned. At that time, there had been no prior learning in the cognitive arena, and therefore no learned impulses were entering the conscious state. This should not be confused with the nonaffective learning that may have begun in the cerebral cortex well back in prenatal development.

69

Psychoanalysts refer to this as the period of omnipotence.

70

Psychoanalysts look upon this as the point in infantile development when, realizing the separation between himself or herself and mother, the child experiences the feeling of dependence and compensates by casting his or her self-love (narcissism) upon the mother. Before this time, the child directed libidinal energy upon himself or herself; but now, it is being directed upon the mother and will remain that way throughout life. Some refer to this attachment between mother and child as the psychological umbilical cord. It is perhaps the best illustration of the axiom which states that love is an outward manifestation of an inward dependence.

71

In psychoanalytic theory, this is the point in infant development when the ego begins to emerge. It is the time when the child begins to anticipate the delivery of food and the pleasure that follows. It is also the time when frustration is first experienced. Thus the normal ego emerges as a variety of feelings are experienced by the child, most notably, isolation, dependence, love, gratification (pleasure), anticipation, and frustration. The reasoning here is that if frustration persisted, there would eventually be no living child, hence no ego; and if the food always arrived before anticipation could become felt, there would be no importance placed on gratification, hence no ego, and all of the other feelings would not have had a chance to develop.

You will also note how other approaches to human personality tend to meet here. For example, the feeling of gratification would be seen from the Gestalt Approach as being a case where the needful figure meets the benevolent ground and a gestalt climax is realized as pleasure; or if viewed from the Behavioral Approach, it would be a case where a desired ego behavior would be rewarded; and if viewed from the Humanistic Approach, it would be a case where parents would consistently place greater value and emphasis on some words and gestures, and less on others.

72

The biophysical elements of these successes are later established in affective emotional reactions in the thalamus and/or cerebral cortex and brought back into action upon recall. What is being referred to here as a success is any stimulation by sense data and/or superego impulses upon cognitive emotional reactions that are strong enough to cause response impulses to be emitted. In this instance, a success will involve the conveyance of values irrespective of validity.

73

This is where human intellectual values leave the biophysical state of Actuality and enter the superego state, or Reality. Or to say this more precisely, it is where the essential meanings of intellectual values are conveyed from sense data in the biophysical state of Actuality to the development of ideas in the superego state of Reality. If we were to view this from the Biophysical Approach, it would appear that we had reached the end of the "road" and that some other phenomenon must be coming into play.

74

When we view this point in infant development from the Existential Approach, we find that the child's perceived self-image--that which the senses say he or she is--is joined by a conceived self-image which is presented into the conscious state by the superego. The perceived self-image lies on the Actuality side of the A-R Interface, the conceived self-image lies on the Reality side, and the ego emerges to become the balancing act between the two. Altogether these constitute the ego state.

75

When we view this point in infant development from the Phenomenological Approach, we find that all of the things said above are true and that the phenomenogist of today would have only one thing to add, and that might be, "We told you it would turn out to be something like this." Phenomenology did its part way back in the fifties and sixties, when it planted within us questions like these: That thing which dwells inside your head, that self--what is it? How did it get there? Is it a Natural phenomenon, or something else? Shouldn't we try to find out? Phenomenologists are the point men and women along the course of human progress. The questions they might ask today would no doubt be like these: Now that we know how a human operates, what other great scheme is he or she a phenomenal part of? What comes next for the inquiring mind of man?

76

The psychoanalytic model of the ego state which we will be using has four main parts. These are:

1. **Part or all of the conscious state**.
2. **The id**--includes all phylogenetic and ontogenetic need impulses; they provide an "I want" feeling.
3. **The superego**--includes all attitudinal impulses gained from past experience, e.g., principles and ideals; they provide an "I should" feeling.
4. **The ego**--the seat of reason and the component where value judgements are made; it is at the highest mode of reason when the id and superego are in harmonious balance and psychic energy is at the optimal level.

77

There are a number of other theoretical models of human personality coming from the fields of psychology, psychiatry, anthropology, and sociology, but the one which we gear to here is that of classical psychoanalysis. We do this, not only because psychoanalysis appears to be most valid, but because it first seeks to find out how human personality works, and then goes out to see how it performs in the process of socialization.

78

A functional mental health problem is one that results from a disturbed ego state, where its components--the id, superego, and ego--fall out of harmony and/or have breakdown. A problem of this nature involves discord within the psychological process, and should not be confused with an organic mental health problem which involves biological debilitation, as with special need personalities.

79

Workers in these fields have to contend with the fact that in some segments of the American child and adult populations the number of mental health problems is high, sometimes approaching fifty percent. Lack of learning readiness and retention ability may be due to emotional conditions that are either the cause or result of the ego state falling out of the mode of higher reason. Professionals who work with such segments should be on the lookout for individuals who are having difficulty keeping their ego states in balance.

80

This is the period when the child's identification with significant others first occurs, usually with the mother. This is also the time when the child abandons his or her narcissism and begins to incorporate environmental values into the first manifestation of self conception. If genetic propensity toward homosexuality can be ruled out, this point in an infant's development is when abnormal sexual identification is most likely to occur. Anna Freud's (1895-1982) finding that the individual tends to identify with the aggressor may apply here.

81

This section makes use of two ego state models. One is the static model and the other is the action model. The static model is the one which has the three ego state components--the superego, the id, and the ego--sitting like three men in a tub. The value of this model lies in our being able to stop all action and consider the function of each component and the impact it may have upon the others. The action model is the one which places all three of the components into action, the result being very much like what happens in a light bulb when it is on. The value of this model is to show how the emergence and strength of the ego component depends upon the veracity and tenacity of the other two components--the superego and the id--and the purity of the medium.

82
Explained in psychoanalytic terms, self-actualization would be the mental condition one is in when his or her id and superego are united and working together in or near complete harmony.

83
Cathect was a term used by Sigmund Freud to indicate the investment of libidinal energy in a object.

84
There are about two dozen psychological defense mechanisms. Every human personality has at least a few of them as part of its repertoire of character-building factors.

85
Introjection and projection are the two main psychological defenses which all humans pick up late in the neonatal stage or early in the oral stage of infantile development. Introjection first occurs as the behavior of swallowing; then, during the start of concept development, it generalizes into the psychological process and becomes the mechanism by which information is taken in and incorporated with existing conceptual affect. It is a defense in that it not only promotes acceptance and reduces hostility by significant others, but it promotes survival through intellectual achievement, as in the pursuit of occupational and religious goals.

Projection first occurs as the behavior of rejecting, that is to say, spitting out, things that would otherwise be swallowed; yet it soon generalizes into the psychological process and becomes one of the main defense mechanisms for protecting the ego from threatening sense data. In children, and in some adults, projection becomes a matter of casting the threatening sense data upon someone or something else, as in the laying of blame. However, in more composed personalities, it will appear in the form of unobtrusive behaviors, for example when the listener recalls a nonexistent task to be done or an appointment to be met. In less composed personalities, it will be found in utterances like, "Do you really believe that?" and "How can you say that?" And in uncomposed personalities, it may appear as a blunt order, for instance, when one says, "Shut up!" or "Mind your own business."

Today, millions of American homes have been thrust into family hiatus because one or both of the parents unthinkingly vented emotional conflict in the presence of the child. The child, also unthinkingly, introjected such conflict and tried to meaningfully incorporate it with affect. When, again unthinkingly, the child found himself or herself stuck with some introjected information that would not meaningfully incorporate, disorder sat in.

At first, such disorder may be displayed by guilt feelings. Then, if the parent continues to vent, not responding to the guilt signals of distress, the child may experience a masking out of the positive feelings which emanate from the parent ideal, most notably, those of love, respect, admiration, belonging, reliance, and trust. A frequent result is that the child acquires projection mechanisms that will protect his or her ego from more threatening sense data--the alternative being to engage in workable relationships with other adults or within the peer group itself. In either case, the result is family hiatus.

As psychoanalytic theory points out, it must be clear that human development never stops at the end of one developmental stage and begins all over with a new set of propensities; instead, it modifies those that are already in effect. This means that while swallowing in the oral stage of infancy is the advanced level of introjection for that age of childhood, the development continues on, year after year, so that when that individual is forty, his or her inclination to swallow has differentiated and become established in other parts of the developing personality, for example, in love-making, and in the ego state's readiness to incorporate useful and reasonable information into the intellect. This same general pattern applies to projection, where at first it is nothing more than the spitting out of the bad; but at the older ages, it becomes the rejection of useless and unreasonable sense data, and thus acts to reduce intellectual contamination.

What many parents fail to realize is that human personality is one continuous development from fertilization (birth) to the grave. Moreover, they fail to understand how Natural development always moves toward balance, how they themselves are the causes of hiatus, and how, if they would start meeting the child's intellectual wants with positive and useful and reasonable sense data, Nature would guide both the child and the family back into solidarity.

86

The Projection Defense Mechanism. This mechanism manifests in two different ways:

A. Rejection. This is when the self projects up to the incoming sense data, but no further into Actuality. In some cases, the self will simply reject unwanted sense data. In other cases, it will reject the unwanted sense data by seemingly projecting it back onto objects in the environment.

B. Projection. This is when the self projects itself into the Reality construct, usually as a means of gaining pleasing experiences from introjected encounters with environment, as in reading a book or watching television.

87

Nonbeing Values. Values that are not validated by actual things, events, and/or conditions: these may include apparent values.

88

Psychological Defenses. These also include intellectualization, repression, suppression, rationalization, regression, and others.

89

Emotional Feelings. Notably, nervousness, anxiety, and depression.

90

RED LIGHT. If you feel anxious or nervous while reading this book, it may mean that your psychological defenses are warning you that the subject matter in this book is inconsistent with your Reality construct. If this is the case, then you would be wise to stop reading and discuss things with a licensed professional student of human personality.

91

Gestalt Experience. A Gestalt experience has two major components--a needful figure and a benevolent ground. In this case, I tried to maneuver you into becoming a needful figure, that is, one who needs to read a paragraph whose substance is consistent with your Reality construct. When that need was met with sense data carrying such substance, you responded with a gratifying feeling--probably a smile.

92

This matter of idea creation and the transformations which occur at the A-R Interface during such creation is perhaps one of the first places that nuclear physicists will be looking--the reason being that changes in state involve either energy release or energy absorption, as in evaporation and condensation of water.

93

Around the turn of this century, a number of scientists decided to stand back and observe the human body as a Natural phenomenon. There stood the human body, doing all the things that humans do--singing, talking, reasoning, playing, working, mourning, studying, worshiping, and so on; yet where in the Grand Scheme of things could they find an explanation for how humans were able to do these things? To make a long story short, these scientists were engaged in a study which came to be known as phenomenology, and which would soon divide and give rise to two of the seven Approaches to human personality. Those who thought the explanation was to be found inside the human personality became members of what was to become known as the Phenomenological Approach to human personality, and those who thought it was to be found outside the human personality became members of what was to become known as the Behavioral Approach to human Personality.

94

It might be remembered that the study of phenomenology gave rise to two of the approaches to human personality. One approached the structure of human personality (phenomenological) and the other approached its behavior (behavioral). Here we are approaching personality structure; hence we will be using the Phenomenological Approach.

95

Eclectic View. Bringing two or more views together into one common view.

96

Humans Perceive Actual Values. The only exceptions to this would be real values that might arrive as perceivable, hence actual, objects furnished by real beings other than man; and as far as I know, this is yet to happen to me.

97

This study holds the framework of inductive science and the framework of concrete science to be the same thing--a time span of about 350 years, starting with the discovery of the cell. This was a time span whose beginning came right after the work of Rene Descartes (1596-1650), who is generally considered to be the father of the Modern Era.

98

Secular Principles and Ideals. Include such values as the principles of physics and governmental law, and ideals that reflect the highest degree of beauty and morality.

99

An example of this would be the comparison of the lighting of a room and the holistic body control which humans experience.

100

"...lilies of the field..." (Matt. 6:28)

101

Stereoscopic Ability. Some of the early students of the Gestalt Approach to human personality concentrated on how this stereoscopic ability operates during perception, for example, how the optical display of figure and foreground occurs during different experiences.

In this study, we are considering how this stereoscopic ability operates during conception. Here we are considering how the actual self develops an image from id and/or sense data (perception) and the Real self draws from affect (the individual's Reality) in developing a self-image which the phenomenal self must rule to be either a needful figure or a benevolent ground. This is the mental activity which accounts for much of the individual's manner of interaction with the external world--which includes his or her carcass.

102

It should also be kept in mind that the founding value was generated at a time when there was little if any A-R Interface in operation. This enabled a firm bonding to occur between the founding value (a part of Reality) and what was soon to become the actual self (a part of Actuality) before the Interface could become a preclusive factor. When you combine this realization with the understanding that during personality function, all factors impact in the present, this bonding between the founding value and the actual self provides for the omnipotent phenomenal self's emergence on the Actuality side of the ego state in a manner which is consistent and identifiable with the Real self which protrudes into consciousness on the Reality side of the ego state. Along with intuition, this helps ready the conscious state for ego state development and the production of stereoscopic ideas--the building blocks of Reality--which the phenomenal self unthinkingly attributes to Actuality and the actual side of the ego state. Thus endures the mythical belief that Actuality and Reality are the same thing.

103

Nucleus. Control center of a cell: in this study, it is viewed as being the control center of a human Reality. This is its basic definition. However, we assign other names to it, depending upon its function at any given time. These names are:

1. **"I" and "Me"**: These symbolize one's "I feeling" and "I" of personality when the holistic, or phenomenal, self is in process. In this function, one's nucleus of Reality is not only projecting into his or her carcass and taking command of the whole body (thanks to the founding value), but it either accepts or rejects command of any sense data that reach the ego state, for example, that which gives word of the football team or political candidate.

2. **"I" of Reality**:   Here the nucleus of Reality functions as the Real self when the ego state is in the process of cognition (reasoning).

3. **"Eye" of Reality**:   When the nucleus of one's Reality takes on the function of gathering information from his or her history of events, the term "Eye of Reality" is used...indicating that graphic information is being recovered. We don't go into this subject any further, except to note that the "Eye" of Reality performs an information gathering function in pursuing Reality which is very much like the function of our animal eyes during perception. Could it be that the human personality has the potential for perceiving both Reality and Actuality as they stand separated at the A-R Interface? Is this the mental condition which some of our more able minds have already reached?

104

Generalization. We use the term "generalization" here because Christ is a functional part of every human personality. The problem has been that many people don't realize it.

105

To tip the scale means to allow one's phenomenal self to operate on both sides of the A-R Interface. This is discussed in detail in item 123 of the caboose.

106

The eclectic display is the image which forms in one's mind when the four structural approaches are joined so as to give an overview of a human personality. It will be seen that the basic structure of a human personality is made up of four major components: these are Actuality, Reality, the A-R Interface, and a human ego state. All other components of human personality, for example, the senses and the biological formatting in the thalamus and cerebral cortex, will fall in to place as the display is constructed further.

107

Reality Analysis. Here is something that may be important to those who have become able to face their personal Realities. They may be having difficulty finding the eclectic display when they return for a later viewing. At first, this was my problem. I couldn't find it in my Reality. What happened to it? This was the second thing that I found missing in my Reality. The other thing was my real body. I couldn't find that either. Then I realized what had happened. I had matriculated both my eclectic display and my real body into my carcass. So now, when I want to view either of them, I know to find them coexisting with my carcass.

This brings us to the doorstep of a study which may someday be called Reality analysis. It should be particularly useful to folks in such fields as criminal justice, mental health, education, and the entertainment industry. The first lesson to be learned in such a study is what we are finding out here. For example, you can use a diagram as a means of describing the eclectic display and real body, but don't expect it to be recorded in your Fold of Reality. The reason for this is that an individual's Fold of Reality contains only exact duplications of actual counterparts. Human beings save everything they conceive of; but such a diagram is probably not exact enough and will be found somewhat afield from the Fold, yet certainly not as far away as the threshold of nonbeing. The Natural counterpart of one's eclectic display and real body is his or her carcass, and that is where we must look for them if we are to keep operating at the Fold of Reality.

A person might think that the practice of Reality analysis is something that human progress will come to in a hundred years or so, and that it is not a viable consideration at this time. Such a notion is wrong. Reality analysis is already with us in the works of technology. A prime example is the process developed by experts in electronics and computer graphics, a process known as virtual Reality.

108

Normal Range Behavior is that which occurs when the performer's personality possesses a lack or minimum of debilitating factors, for example, psychological defenses and genetic propensities that have negative effects on cognition.

109

Perhaps one of the best examples of this inseparability is the case where a thirsty man in the desert sees a mirage. If the mirage exists because of his condition, and not as a result of atmospheric conditions, then the indication may be that because his sense data is not bringing word of a benevolent ground, his phenomenal self creates an idea of a mirage that will serve the purpose. However, the result is that his mirage fails to provide for gratification (Gestalt climax); his environment fails to provide positive reinforcement, that is, reward for valid thought and action; his ego state is left holding an invalid idea; his personality ceases to operate at or near the level of self-actualization; and his mind begins to regress toward the vegetative state. In a way, you might liken human personality to a balloon in the sky, where, if its gas becomes lost, it will collapse and fall to earth. If even one of these three basic functions of human personality fails, malfunction will set in, and its mental condition will start regressing toward the vegetative state.

110

Vegetative State. This is a mental state which is void of cognition: a condition where the ego state is unable to function: the ultimate catatonic condition. Only rarely will a human personality regress to this state. Usually, when such a regression gets under way, personality adjustments will fall into place as compensations, thus halting the regression. You can find good accounts of such compensations in books on identical twin studies.

111

The Confirming Effect of Inducted and Deducted Generalizations. Inducted generalizations are derived through the assessment of specific cases where the Law of Cause and Effect is the deciding factor of change. Deducted reasoning in the assessment of specific cases is derived from the broadest generalization, or universal. When a person inducts and deducts with valid ideas about the same subject, he or she finds a confirming effect between inducted and deducted generalizations when they meet along the valid line of reason. This line of reason is what this study refers to as the Vector of Reason: it builds during valid reasoning (self-actualization); it stays in the individual's Reality as a residual which lends guidance in the formulation of decisions and ideals; it is present in all reasoning human minds; it is the Christ which Jesus of Nazareth acknowledged within him and all men; and it is the way to the Fold of Reality and prodigious happiness in eternal life.

112

This should not be construed as an assault against Immanuel Kant in any manner. My mind always settles upon the idea that if he had been preceded by Charles Darwin, Charles S. Peirce, William James, Sigmund Freud, John Dewey, and Albert Einstein, his would have been a "hard act" for this study to follow. In fact, it seems certain that he would have already covered the intellectual ground which you and I are operating on here. For example, he used the term "a priori" to indicate an earlier cause of an existing effect. If he were writing today, he would be casting the same meaning with the word "genetic," and expand in thought so as to connect its meaning with that found in all of the other concrete sciences which are with us today--the Law of Cause and Effect.

113

Bear in mind that the actual self is part of Actuality, and receives need information from the id and sense data from the senses; but the Real self is part of Reality, and receives values reporting prior experience. When the Real self projects itself upon the actual self, the phenomenal self is created. And whenever the values of the actual self and the Real self are reconciled, the phenomenal self will be located at the A-R Interface, ego state harmony will prevail, and the experiencing of valid reasoning will occur. This is the most detailed explanation of valid reasoning one can give without going into the biophysics of it all, and that explanation still lies ahead of us.

Also bear in mind that all of the information which arrives at the actual self is coming from places that are part of Actuality. This includes information which comes from books, radio, television, human mouths, and seemingly an infinite number of other sources. The fact is that all of the information which is brought from the Reality of one personality to the actual self of another personality is conveyed by such perceivable objects as written and verbal word symbols; and as far as the receiving ego state is concerned, it has become part of Actuality. Therefore, if your view of a human personality is one that sees the individual as standing alone in the human and Natural worlds, it might be more right than wrong. And I say it this way because of the rare possibility that direct value crossover (telepathy) between human Realities may have occurred in the past, and may continue to occur in the future. But here again is something that concrete science must confirm, one way or the other.

114

In this study, Jesus of Nazareth is viewed as being a mortal. In recognition of this, in this book, you would read that Jesus of Nazareth was himself a pragmatist. But this study also recognizes the real existence of Christ; therefore, in this book, you might also read that Jesus Christ is Himself a pragmatist...indicating the linkage between Jesus and God and eternal life.

115

Earlier, in the last chapter, I mentioned the Staff which has guided me in writing this book. I know full well that I am not a genius, nor am I something divine. I am a mortal whose average intelligence has been aided by my use of the Staff. Now let me explain the Staff further. In this study, it is being called the Vector of Reason. It is what becomes realized when my mind --that is to say, my mind's ego state--refines its self-actualization down to the point of complete harmony between Actuality and Reality. When this occurs, I get a slight wetting in my eyes, and this lets me know that I am on the right intellectual track and at a valid new horizon.

Certainly I am not unique in using the Vector of Reason; for although it is demonstrated in my case, it is also demonstrable in each of the five and one-half billion living human beings on earth. The lesson here is that the Vector of Reason is a dynamic factor in all human personalities, but many of us fail to level with truth enough for it to be unveiled and become realized through a faint tearing of the eyes.

A true Christian is one who has come to realize that Jesus of Nazareth had Actuality and Reality so perfectly balanced that he could experience the existence of Christ within him, and in doing this, he became Jesus Christ. What you who are true Christians will be doing for the remainder of this chapter is to, in insight, move yourself to the realization that the Vector of Reason just mentioned, the Staff which I referred to in the last chapter, and the Christ which has become the central ideal in Christianity are different words for the same meaning. The Vector of Reason is the Staff and the Way of living which has been religiously acknowledged as Christ.

You may now see how a true Christian is a God-oriented pragmatist. But if it is still not clear, then consider what the situation would be if there were four boys at the swimming pool. Three of them stood at the side, pondering over what it would feel like to be in the water. However, not stopping to ponder, the fourth boy jumped in clothes and all, and called back, "I can feel it in my eyes." This may give you an idea of what the situation is for the true Christians and concrete scientists who are at the pool of life. They have jumped in and become God-oriented pragmatists who are experiencing self-actualization. As they experience the veracity of the A-R Interface, a slight wetting occurs, and they call back, "I can feel it in my eyes."

116

The Need for an Ego State Harmony Study. Tearing effect will no doubt be focused upon in future scientific studies, because it tends to signal an abrupt alteration in the pattern of harmony between Actuality and Reality in the ego state. This alteration appears on at least three levels. One level is where body injury is reported by the central nervous system and effects both a biological adjustment in order to retain homeostasis and a psychological adjustment in order to restore harmony between Actuality and Reality in the ego state. A second level is where discord between relating Realities, as in lover quarrels, causes the pattern of harmony to become altered in the ego state. And a third level is where the pattern of harmony in the ego state becomes altered when, in an intellectual pursuit, the individual's self-conception changes each time a new valid horizon is reached--this being attributable to the manner in which a normally behaving phenomenal self will, as a product of mortality, always identify with the actual self. One of the results in these three levels of experience is most often seen as a triggering of tears in the eyes.

A new study, whose task would be to bring all three of the functional approaches into construct with all four of the structural approaches and focus on the alteration and consistency of ego state harmony, would provide some graphic understanding of exactly how human personality operates, as the next paragraph tends to indicate.

If you view the first level of alteration from the Gestalt Approach, you will see that the ontogenetic need for survival has been met by a negative Gestalt consisting of pain and tears. If you view the second alteration from the Behavioral Approach, you will see where an element of environment--in this case, our subject's lover--has gained significance in an interpersonal relationship, and in so-doing, become a provider of negative reinforcement in a conflict situation which plays out with an alteration of the subject's ego state harmony. And if you view the third alteration from the Humanistic Approach, you will see where the achievement of a new intellectual horizon has provided the subject with a new foundation from which to derive human values--the result being that the ego state harmony has been altered just enough to send a signal to the biological formatting (the thalamic area and cerebral cortex) and trigger a slight release of tears.

Conceivably, all three of these levels of alteration of the pattern of harmony could be found in psychotic personalities as well. But that would be the subject of some other study, where the focus would be on personalities whose practical bearing had become lost to disorder.

117
Messiah: English, Messiah; Latin, Messias; Greek, Messias; Hebrew, Mashiach.

118
Christ: English, Christ; Latin, Christus; Greek, Christos; Hebrew, Mashiach.

119
Jesus: English, Jesus; Latin, Jesus; Greek, Iesous; Hebrew, Yeshua.

120
The Vector of Reason is used here as a descriptive term: it is describing the condition that exists whenever the phenomenal self is located at the A-R Interface and achieving perfect agreement between Actuality and Reality: it is a vector in that it is a line extending to and from Almighty God and the Greater Reality when the real value of time--tictoc time-- is taken in to account.

121
Reaction Formation. Reaction formation is one of the psycho-

logical defenses. A typical example of it is when a person's love for another person or thing reverses in quality and comes out in a display of hate, or dislike...a completely opposite reaction.

One case that I worked with as a high school counselor was when teachers reported drastic behavior changes in one of the students. Let us call him Dan. After calling Dan in and interviewing him, it became clear that he returned from summer vacation with a strong dislike for his history teacher, Mrs. Smith. Upon further inquiry, I learned that Dan's father died during the summer and Mrs. Smith's husband also died at that time. I checked into the history of Dan's past relationship with Mrs. Smith and found that she was his favorite teacher. It was then that it became clear: Dan was suffering from a reaction formation. The remedy was to have him repeat, I hate Mrs. Smith quickly until told to stop. He did, and after about four times, the word "hate" changed to "like," and the reaction formation disappeared.

122

You are reminded that in this section I will be building a Reality construct. It will be a reconstruction of the framework of my personal Affective Reality. This must be emphasized because I may be telling you some things about my Reality that simply do not "jive" with what you find in yours. What should be known are the similarities and differences between the parts of my Affective Reality and yours. We request information you may have concerning your Reality. This information would become part of a basis for conducting future Reality analysis studies. Also, we would like to know about any professional literature and understandings that you might have on this subject. Be assured that your name will not be published without proper release and that you would receive a copy of the report.

Please send information to:

> Reality Analysis
> Merriconn Guidance, Inc.
> P.O. Box 2713
> Conroe, Texas 77305-2713

123
How to Get Out of This World Alive from a Technical Viewpoint.

We are now at a place in this study where the question of how to get out of this world alive can be at least partially answered from the technical point of view. While writing this book, I tried to make the text a place where I could relate directly with the personality of the reader, and in so-doing, avoid some technical discussion. What many readers gain from reading the text of this book should help them understand the answer to this survival question without going into the nuts-and-bolts discussion which we are about to have here.

Most of the strands of reason in the following discussion derive from the Psychoanalytical, Phenomenological, and Existential Approaches to human personality. You should find that they add meaningful substance to your eclectic display.

In case the moment of death for a human individual's carcass comes while his or her phenomenal self is identified with the actual self--which is the case for all minds operating in the normal range of behavior--the phenomenal self will experience death as well. What we are going to explore here is the possibility that the phenomenal self can also identify with the Real self, and thereby escape death.

The explanation begins early in the first year of infantile development, when the first issue of self appears. This first issue of self has become known as the omnipotent self, because it just doesn't know when to stop owning things; that is to say, it assumes that all perceivable objects reported by sense data are part of that self. Throughout childhood, the omnipotent self becomes "frosted" with self-realizations--first with those occurring during the puppet master episode, where the child learns to distinguish between his or her body parts and things in the environment. Then comes the time when the ego-state appears to have taken effect, when biological formatting in the thalamus and cerebral cortex begins to record such motor skills as those found in language and dexterity, and when the actual self assumes control of the voluntary nervous system, or to say it another way, when the actual self takes the reins from the puppet master. You will want to keep these things in mind as we continue on through the following paragraphs.

There in the first year of infantile development, the ego-state begins to play a hand in decision-making. This is when the actual self--now holding the reins to the biological format-- takes its place on the Actuality side of the ego-state.

This is also when self-realization first occurs, when the phenomenal self emerges with its "I-feeling," and when newly created ideas begin to flow (introject) into the Reality medium. After a few days or weeks, the introjected ideas have become a polarized group of ideas, and begin to send attitudinal impulses back to the Reality side of the ego-state; and it is there that the point guard of Reality emerges--what has long been called the superego, and what is being referred to here as the Real self. Here again is some setting that you may want to bear in mind as we move along.

It was said above that the time comes when the ego-state appears to have taken effect. I said "appears" because that is what many generally think--that the ego-state appears to have taken effect when verbalized ideas are first created. But although that may be getting close to the truth, it is not exactly correct. The exact truth is that the ego-state emerges when the individual first experiences the feeling of "I," and that might be as early as the omnipotent stage--certainly no later than the end of the puppet master episode. The contention here is that the "I" feeling begins during the omnipotent stage, and has become a dynamic personality factor when the puppet master episode begins. Whichever the case may be, the ego-state is operable before two postnatal months of life have gone by.

You many recall that in Chapter Two the term "founding value" was used, and that its exact definition was deferred to a later point in this book. We have reached that point, and may now say that the founding value for the entire value system in all human personalities is omnipotence. Omnipotence in personality development is the feeling of ownership that a human child realizes during the first issue of self-conception; it is the feeling of owning everything that the senses can perceive; and even though it becomes "frosted" over with values that arrive through subsequent experience, it is the founding value which stands implicitly in the center of all human value systems.

This brings us to some considerations that should be made if we are to fully realize the answer to the survival question, How to get out of this world alive. These are:

1. *Psychoanalysis and Affective Realism.* Psychoanalysis and Affective Realism cover the same intellectual ground; they adhere to the same Laws of Nature and principles of concrete science; and they scrutinize the same population of living humans. The only difference between them is that Actuality and Reality are deemed to be the same thing in Psychoanalysis and different things in Affective Realism.

This is much like the case of two ladies. They went to the store and bought two sheets. Lady A opened her sheet, ran it through the washer, and hung it up to dry. Lady P did the same. Later, when they went out to gather the sheets, they were surprised to find that Lady A's sheet was twice the size of Lady P's. Come to find out that Lady P did not recognize the fact that her sheet had two halves whose congruence led her to ignore the fact that they were different. We find such similarity between Actuality and Reality.

2. *The Founding Human Value.* Granting the possibility that some or all humans develop a degree of prenatal self, let us draw the line at the instant of vaginal delivery and start consid-

ering the development of self at that point.

At or not long after delivery, the child's senses begin reporting a growing measure of the external world, the feeling of omnipotence takes place, and the first issue of self, the omnipotent self, comes in to effect. During this first issue of a child's self, the id begins to reflect organismic need, the sense data bring word of significant objects in the environment (usually the mother and/or father), and the fledgling expressions of want and relief are nothing more than cries and sighs. What happens as this and subsequent stages of actual development unfold is well-documented in Psychoanalytical literature. This study is in complete agreement with that, for as far as it goes. What this study picks up on is that part of human personality which Psychoanalysis has had difficulty structuring in theory and refers to as the unconscious. In Affective Realism, that "unconscious" is found to be Reality.

This is where things stand today. Psychoanalysts believe that omnipotence is realized as one of the earliest ideations of self-conception; its essence is captured and fixed in the development of ideas of omnipotence; and those ideas are passed into affect--presumably in the thalamus and/or the cerebral cortex. Affective Realists believe the same until the matter of affect is reached, but they find that ideas do not pass into actual affect and become stored with the biological formatting; rather, they find ideas to pass through the Real self and become the building-blocks in the individual's Reality. What it amounts to is that psychoanalysts tend to view all human faculties and values as being part of the Actuality medium. Affective realists, on the other hand, can agree that the human biological faculties lie in the Actuality medium, but insist that all real human values lie in the Reality medium. And being one of the first, if not the first, building block to introject into an infant's Reality, the omnipotence idea is viewed here as being the founding value in all human personalities. An idea is a human value consisting of real substance...something which concrete science has yet to explain.

3. *Projection of Self.* One of the basic facts about humanity is that once a human value is introjected into the individual's Reality, it will be there forever. This is because, outside of Almighty God, there is nothing that can destroy it. One can downplay a certain value, in which case, it will be ushered to one side of his or her Reality and out of the field of play; one can emphasize a certain value, and make it a vital factor in achieving his or her "I" feeling; but one can never himself or herself get rid of a human value once it has become introjected into Reality.

Advanced human societies are particularly adept at keeping the omnipotence value "alive" and right in the midst of mental activity. In reading books, we project our selves; in watching television, we project our selves; and in seemingly an infinite number of other ways, we do the same. What makes us able to do this is that other humans--namely family members and peers and people at work and school--have conditioned us to keep the omnipotence value "alive" and right in the midst of our mental activity. This act of keeping the omnipotence value viable as an unreasoned justification for projecting the self to any thing or event that sense data may report is, I surmise, the one human achievement that enabled our forerunners to climb down from the tree, take refuge in the caves, and progress to where we are today. Or allow me to say this another way. Any human on earth today, who has lost the ability to project his self or her self, had better take refuge in a safe place, even the caves, and perhaps make retreat to the trees. And I say this, not in jest, but with an eye on the probability that that which brought humanity to a peak will in absence mark the trail of human decline. Here in this study we are viewing projection of self as a vital factor in getting out of this world alive. However, it becomes a vital factor to be viewed in many other studies as well: for instance, in the study of group belonging, as in the family, religious and political, and tertiary institutions (eg, a fire brigade); and in such interpersonal relations as those found in marriage, bisexual, and homosexual encounters.

A further importance of the connection between omnipotence and the projection of self is to be found in the matter of spontaneity. One might think that the projection of self is a spontaneous behavior. But that is not correct. The truth is that there is a cause and effect relationship between one's decision to project self and the value system in his or her Reality. This discussion which we have been having on omnipotence should be some indication of that. What we must all be mindful of is the fact that every element of a human personality is the effect of a cause. And although we may not know the causes of some of the effects that we view, for example, the "I feeling," just wait a while, and concrete science will arrive with answers.

4. *Identification.* Recall the action (light bulb) ego-state model which we discussed in the last chapter. We began discussing it in psychoanalytical terms, calling one electrode the "id" and the other electrode the "superego." Then it became evident that before we could discuss the action model in terms of Affective Realism we would have to make changes that would distinguish between Actuality and Reality. So the name of one electrode was changed from "id" to "actual self" and the name of the other electrode was changed from "superego" to "Real self." What it amounted to was that Psychoanalysis was making the superego a part of Actuality, and what we had to do was change its name from "superego" to "Real self" in order to acknowledge it as part of Reality.

What this study is proposing is that the actual self is little more than a "vegetable." Along with organismic need, sense data, and libidinal impulses, the actual self may be visited by occasional intuitive and instinctive impulses, but by and large, Nature has placed it in the thalamus as the matured puppet master ready to play, though not conduct, such human performances as writing and speaking and song and dance and the manipulation of meaningful symbols. In Actuality, the actual self of an eighth grade student in an advanced nation is an instrument that can receive and transmit virtually all of the intellectual values that a human has generated and stored in his or her Reality. Thus you may agree that the actual self is the point guard of the biological format.

This study is also proposing that the Real self is the "I," not only of an individual human personality, but of the Reality whose interplay with Actuality accounts for that unique personality. In other words, the Real self is the point guard of an individual's personal Reality; it is the stream of human attitude which Sigmund Freud first noted and called the superego; it is the "mouth" through which newly created ideas are introjected into Reality; and it is the one component of Reality which we so far know to have sufficient electromotive force (EMF) to be able to project itself and affective data across the A-R Interface and onto the actual self.

And the final proposal here is that this is exactly what happens. The Real self projects itself across the A-R Interface and onto the actual self, thus bringing in to effect a psychological situation that can best be described by the existential term "desine," which means "ending there." While this close association between the actual self and the projected Real self is occurring under conscious conditions, the phenomenal self appears. When this close association is disrupted, as when the actual self enters the resting mode which we think of as sleep, the phenomenal self will disappear.

What we should not overlook is that the projection of the Real self upon the actual self first occurred after there had been an accumulation of enough real substance human values (ideas) to provide a polarization that would send attitudinal impulses to the conscious state. When these impulses protruded into the conscious state, they became the first issue of the Real self, and the ego-state was born. The earliest projection of the Real self occurs near the beginning of infancy.

The position taken in this study is that once the first projection of Real self is made, the "I" emerges as the master of the individual's Reality, and the phenomenal self emerges with its "I feeling" and becomes the master of his or her counterpart (carcass) in Actuality--what we naively think of as being "me." Under normal conditions, the projected Real self and the phenomenal self remain in place during consciousness until the carcass dies.

This brings us to the matter of identification. You will note that throughout the normal life of an individual, his or her Real self and actual self are not only held together by the Real self projection, but they are both sharing values that have to do with Actuality; for example, they share the same values that relate to the child's physical size, shape, ability, and feelings of need and pleasure; they also share values which relate to cultural objects, for instance, to the parents, toys, words, word inflections, rituals, songs, and family manners. All this makes for a close-knit teamwork between the value system in an individual's Reality and the biological format in his or her actual body. Hence you may see how, in most human societies, an individual's personality is bent toward Actuality. In other words, all mortal personalities, including such components as the phenomenal and Real selves, tend to be identified with Actuality. What this means is that insofar as the phenomenal self is identified with the actual self and carcass in general, it will experience death right along with them, when it occurs.

5. *A Closer View of the Phenomenal Self.* Back during the Victorian Era, Sigmund Freud recognized the center of human cognition and called it the "ego." Medical science began using this term, and to this day, members of Psychoanalysis have made it the word symbol for the cognitive component of the ego state--the other two components being the id and the superego. Here again, as in the case of the superego, this study is in agreement with Psychoanalysis for as far as it goes. However, a differing of view arises when it comes to saying what medium the ego is a part of. Psychoanalysts hold that the ego is wholly in Actuality, but affective realists see it as being partly in Actuality and partly in Reality. Moreover, psychoanalysts view the "unconscious world" as being something that is wholly a part of Actuality, while affective realists view it as a completely different medium and call it Reality. To accommodate these views of affective realists, the term "phenomenal self" has been taken from the Phenomenological Approach and used to sug-

gest a phenomenon whose essence involves a transcendence from both the Actuality and Reality mediums.

In definitive terms, the phenomenal self is the exact location of the interplay of human values between Actuality and Reality. In other words, the phenomenal self is that point in the A-R Interface where the above-named interplay occurs; it is the point where the two point guards, the actual self and the Real self, are in closest proximity; it is a functional part of the conscious state; and when all of these factors are in place at the same time, the process of self-realization begins to manufacture ideas, the "I feeling" (nominative case) and the "me feeling" (objective case) emerge, and the phenomenal self becomes a condition wherein actual self-images or Real self-images are generated--depending upon which side of the Interface self-realization is occurring.

We have already noted how in everyday life people tend to identify with their actual selves. Now, in the light of what has just been said, we may say that another way of explaining such identification is that those people are conducting their processes of self-realization on the actual self side of the A-R Interface; hence they see themselves as being a part of Actuality. And of course when death comes to the actual bodies (the carcasses) of these people, it will come to their phenomenal selves as well. But now let us take an even closer look at the phenomenal self.

The actual self is a "thing" in the sense that it consists of emotional reactions and nervous energy; and the Real self is a "thing" in the sense that it consists of values with real substance (ideas) and psychic energy. However, the phenomenal self is not a "thing"; rather, it is a condition within which "things" interact; and in the human phenomenal self, there are two things interacting--the actual self and the Real self.

We have already discussed one interaction which takes place in the phenomenal self: that is when the Real self projects itself upon the actual self. When this happens, the "I" of Reality is virtually transplanted upon the actual self, and has become fixed in a position where it can continue to project itself, only this time it can do it upon objects reported by both sensory and affective impulses. In this regard, I ask that you recall the founding value, omnipotence, and its functional importance in making all of these projections seem to end in Actuality.

This apparent ability to project into environment is also a widely misunderstood factor in the maturation process. It becomes misunderstood because the projection of the "I" upon environmental objects is so frequently a routine behavior, and becomes so well-represented by the biological format, that one tends to get the idea that the format is making some or all of the human self-realizations happen. Subsequently, the full role of the phenomenal self is often overlooked.

6. *Retroprojection.* Most human beings have been cultured to believe that self-conception can only occur on the Actuality side of the A-R Interface. Human societies have reinforced this belief by emphasizing such things as make up, hairdo, clothing, and physical attribute. This is the way that most human minds operate today: they are working on the assumption that human self-realization can only occur when the mind is experiencing consciousness and the phenomenal self is on the Actuality side of the A-R Interface. This has made our mentality a situation where we project our "I's" of Reality into both sense and affective data, but because we are deluded to think that Actuality and Reality are both on the same side of the A-R Interface, our projections into sense data provide us with the desire feeling of "being there," while our projections into affective data (Reality) yield only experiences in imagination and the recalling of data. But this is only part of what a human personality is capable of doing.

What a human personality is also capable of doing is to let the phenomenal self straddle the A-R Interface. However, in normal range behavior, there is only one way that this can be done, and that is for the "I" of Reality to project itself from its fixed position on the actual self, cross through the A-R Interface, and land upon the Real self. This action is what we will be calling retroprojection.

Retroprojection is the process wherein the fixed projection of the "I" of Reality upon the actual self elects to make a return projection to and upon the Real self...a matter of flip-flopping, if you will. The result of this action is that the two parts of the phenomenal self, the actual and Real selves, are equipped to interplay any and all sensory and affective data through the A-R Interface with strings of ideas which we tend to think of as strands of reason. This psychological process brings the Actuality and Reality sides of the ego-state together in an action which provides for the highest degree of reason and makes the ego-state itself become a phenomenal self which commands both sides of the A-R Interface at the same time. When this occurs, the ego-state becomes a balanced phenomenal self whose behavior we refer to as self-actualization--the highest level of mentality that is attainable by mortal man. Yet many human personalities have been having difficulty in reaching this level of self-actualization, and settle for mere projection into sensory and affective data from the actual self location. Why is that?

The main reason why we humans have difficulty reaching the level of self-actualization is that we suffer from the most colossal myth of all, and that is that we cling to the belief that Actuality and Reality are the same thing. This has put us in a mental position where we have a hard time getting our intellectual "feet wet" on the Reality side of the A-R Interface. And in using the term "intellectual," I am suggesting the gathering of knowledge about demonstrable causes and irrefutable facts, as opposed to fiction, fable, and other nonbeing values.

Up to this day, the best that the majority of humans have been able to do along the line of self-actualization has been to construct real things and/or conditions which reflect and build upon their counterparts in Actuality. In essence, what is happening is that we are introjecting intellectual data into our Realities and calling the whole gathering of data a "construct." One way of explaining a construct is to liken it to a building, where, if bricks were the building blocks of the building, then ideas would be the building blocks of the construct; if sections of laid brick were the walls of the building, then concepts would be the walls of the construct; and if the finished brick production would be called a building, then the finished ideational production would be called a construct, or to be more exact, a Reality construct.

Using the terms, "colossal myth" and "construct," we can pretty much tell what the intellectual world has been doing throughout the Ancient and Western Civilizations. In its adherence to the colossal mythical sameness between Actuality and Reality, and in its subsequent need of relying on Reality constructs as Reality bases from which to reason, the intellectual world has been able to carry on some degree of self-actualization. The problem has been that, while the members of the intellectual world have been using their self-actualizations effectively in producing human progress and revealing the makings of the Universe, they have had little understanding of how the human mind works in making such intellectuality happen; and aside from saying that these important (Reality) constructs lie somewhere in the unconscious, they have had little concrete information to give on the subject.

We could continue on in this examination of intellectuality, but other than to note how the presence of Reality constructs is evidence that retroprojection has taken place and may very well be the result of education and/or guidance, the matter might be better pursued in other studies. Our concern here is not so much what has happened in man's intellectual past, but what will happen in his intellectual future.

7. The Three Modes of Self-Realization

The Unimodal Phenomenal Self. In this study, when we use the term, "self-realization," we are referring to the mental process wherein the "I-feeling" is being experienced. In previous discussion, we considered how this mental process gives rise to the holistic (whole body) feeling of self when the "I" of Reality is projecting from its fixed position on the actual self. This leads to experiences where one feels that his or her entire body is "I" (nominative case) or "me" (objective case) for as long as the founding value of omnipotence is in force. Furthermore, it also leads to out-of-body (desine) experiences with those things and conditions that sense and affective data report, and again, for as long as the founding value is in force. When a human personality generates this kind of self-realization, its manifestation is referred to here as being a unimodal phenomenal self. Taking attitudinal influence from their personal Realities (superego), but with little or no consideration for consequence and implication of decisions to act, this is the mode which most people use in everyday living; hence it may also be thought of as the everyday mode.

The Bimodal Phenomenal Self. Recall the colossal myth, which is where one clings to the belief that Actuality and Reality are the same thing. When a human personality holds to this colossal myth and uses the mental process of generating an "I-feeling" to develop Reality constructs, then a bimodal phenomenal self may be said to exist. What makes this happen is that the "I" of Reality elects to retroproject back onto the Real self and make it possible for the ego state to pass ideas back and forth through the A-R Interface. Through this action, the mechanics for reasoning are set into motion, and intellectual behavior is the result. Because the bimodal phenomenal self is used so extensively in intellectual activities, for example, in formal education and the professions, it may also be referred to as the intellectual, or work, mode; although it joins the unimodal phenomenal self on the Actuality side of the A-R Interface, and unthinkingly skews itself toward Actuality and the assumption that Actuality is all there is to human existence.

The Trimodal Phenomenal Self. Any human personality that has been able to achieve the bimodal phenomenal self can, in the twinkle of a eye, achieve the trimodal phenomenal self. All it has to do is challenge the colossal myth and let Actuality and Reality be the separate things that they are. When this happens, the "I-feeling" will be free to emerge on the Reality side of the

A-R Interface and provide the sensation of being in Reality, just as it has been doing in Actuality. In this action, the entire ego-state becomes the trimodal phenomenal self; and because intellectual weight, or validity, can be realized from both the actual and real sides of an idea, the highest level of reason, self-actualization, can be attained. Thus because the trimodal phenomenal self is the seat of self-actualization, it may also be referred to as the mode of wisdom.

The trimodal phenomenal self has been one of the most difficult achievements for mankind to reach. This is primarily due to our tendency to develop a tenacious relationship between what we think Actuality to be and what we think Reality to be. What happened was that the closer one could bring his or her Table of Reason (point of view) to the point of self-actualization, where perceptions of Actuality and their counterparts in Reality (conceptions) enjoy the same valid causes and effects, the more tenacious this relationship would become, and the more convincing it would seem that Actuality is all that there is to human existence. Could it be that this tenacity has become the blinder which kept mankind upon the road to human destiny, allowing so much revelation through intellectual construct, yet letting Reality remain the undiscovered goal which we have been religiously and intellectually looking for? Could it be that our's is a case where he who is best qualified to understand a fact is least likely to know it? And could it be that Jesus of Nazareth anticipated this day and time, when men and women would have gathered enough irrefutable factual information to challenge the colossal myth, arrive at the mode of wisdom, and realize that human destiny is already upon them?

8. *A Word of Caution.* What we have just been describing, in our discussion of bimodal and trimodal self-realization, is retro-projection which occurs in personalities that are performing in the normal range of mental behavior. It is normal retroprojection because it involves projection between an individual's actual self and his or her Real self when only one well-organized "I" of Reality is involved. In rare instances, however, real

selves contain disturbed or multiple "I's" of Reality. This is usually due to the individual's need to reconcile his or her Reality with discordant segments of the outer milieu: it is found in cases of multiple personality and psychotic withdrawal--the latter often weakening and, in extremely rare instances, destroying the original projection of the "I" of Reality upon the actual self, thus placing the subject into the catatonic or even the vegetative state of mind. As a word of CAUTION to those readers who are reading this subsection for other than professional reasons, for example, to learn how to jump out of Actuality and into Reality, let me suggest that you visit a psychiatrist or clinical psychologist and have it explained how you may be setting yourself up for such mental disorders as those that were just mentioned. The rule of inquiry which this study adheres to is that one can safely explore the workings of the human mind for as long as all interaction between Actuality and Reality is done through the projection of the Real self, or to be more precise, through the projection of the one "I" of Reality which is found in each normal range human personality.

9. *Identifications by the Trimodal Self.* One way of telling when and if you are operating with a trimodal phenomenal self is to see if you are identified with both the Actuality and the Reality mediums at or near the same time. This would indicate that your phenomenal self is straddling the A-R Interface, and that you are prepared to project yourself into either medium at or near the same time. There are three main ways of verifying that these identifications have been made. One way is to check for mobility, a second way is to see if you have clear view of the Fold of Reality, and the third way is to see if your eclectic display is coexisting with your carcass. And here, let me say that I dislike using the word "carcass" just as much as you may dislike hearing me use it. But the fact is that your carcass is going to die, while your eclectic display is affording you some view of your real body in the making for eternal life.

10. *Mobility of the "I" of Reality.* We have already discussed

the desine effect, where one gets the feeling of being there. This is when one projects his or her "I" feeling to things, events, and/or conditions in Actuality. Now we are finding that when that person achieves the trimodal self, he or she can realize the same desine effect while projecting into Reality. Moreover, because that person has retroprojected back onto the Real self, his or her projected "I" of Reality can jump aboard the original "I" of Reality and, as with a speedboat, go anywhere in that personal Reality. What we are becoming aware of is that while the human carcass is the "speedboat" in Actuality, the original "I" of Reality is the "speedboat" in Reality. This gives some indication of what future studies may prove to be true--that the human "I," or "me," is the nucleus of that person's Reality.

11. *A Case of Retroprojection.* The contention in this study is that vast numbers of humans have carried on the process of retroprojection, and vast numbers will continue to carry it on. But saying that is as far as this study can go without becoming involved in the matter of individual and group differences--a subject for other studies. What will be presented here is the case history of one retroprojection, my own.

In the summer of 1993, this study had progressed to the point where I became so much convinced of the difference between Actuality and Reality that my "I" of Reality carried out the process of retroprojection. When this first occurred, a flash of light appeared, and then came a vivid view of my personal Reality. The first images were of the rolling hills of New Hampshire, where I had spent much of my childhood. After admiring the view for a few minutes, I turned my mind to other things. Then during the days that followed, I attempted to experience that same flash of light again, but it failed to reappear. Nevertheless, though less vivid, my personal Affective Reality was still in view. That was the time when I began to write this book.

During the rest of 1993 and most of 1994, I reasoned on the assumption that I was viewing Reality with my animal vision, just as I view Actuality; but eventually it became evident that the real images I was viewing were appearing in my frontal lobes, and had little or nothing to do with my animal senses.

What I came to find out was that when I was using my bimodal phenomenal self, real images were being picked up through projection and brought into view on the Actuality side of the A-R Interface--in my frontal lobes. But when I was using my trimodal phenomenal self, real images were being picked up through retroprojection and brought into view (seemingly) in the same manner that perceptions are brought to mind. I can't say that these images were showing in my frontal lobes, because I was viewing into Reality at the time. On the other hand, I can't say that my perceived images were showing in my frontal lobes, because I was viewing into Actuality at the time. What I can say is that when I make use of retroprojection, it's like sitting on a fence and being able to look both ways.

End of Technical

124

Value. A value is the quality in any object that one's self has thought worthy of introjection. A value is the character in an actual or real thing which arrives at the ego state through perception and/or recall, and registers that thing as being worthy of introjection and reconstruction in Reality through the creation of ideas, concepts, and constructs. Values are found in material objects and human reasonings, and are referred to by such terms as ideal, principle, design, capacity, goal, size, color, age, good, bad, demonstrable, and valid.

125

Field of View. My field of view is what my phenomenal self scans into. In this case, I elected to take the broadest possible view. But as with a television set, I could have elected to project my self to any program (prior experience) that I have recorded in my Reality. The only things that would have gotten in the way would be the psychological defenses that took effect over the years. In such cases, a desired program might be made hazy, or even blocked out. But I have managed to erase most if not all of those defenses.

126

Any value that I find to be a possible nonbeing value is treated as a nonbeing value, and remains in the nonbeing grouping until it can be shown to belong with the being values. This is the way concrete scientists and true Christians behave: they accept nothing as a being value unless it can be demonstrated or shown to have practical bearing. But of course, if the shortage of concrete scientists is any indication, most Americans do not impose this restriction upon themselves, and let the "possibles" pass as being values.

127

Actual Values. These are material objects that can be perceived by our senses, for example, a table, a cow, or a boat. An actual human value is one component of a human carcass--meaning that Jill's right arm is one of her actual human values, and Jack's right arm is one of his actual human values. However, this does not mean that Jill's right arm would be one of Jack's actual human values.... That would be a case where Jill's right arm became one of Jack's actual social values.

Real Values. These are human values that are not material, for example, ideas, concepts, constructs, and attitudes that stimulate the feelings of belonging, love, and hate.

Future studies of actual human values and actual social values, and the conflicts which arise from their interaction with real human values, should provide clear understandings of such deviations as narcissism, infidelity, and homosexuality.

128

Foundational Real Values. Foundational real values are the ideas, concepts, and constructs that provide the basic structure of a mortal Reality. They are foundational, not only because they add dimension to the structure of a mortal Reality, but they give rise to at least two secondary types of real value. One of these secondary types includes those values that can best be expressed through verbal and/or artistic displays, for example, principles, ideals, and goals. These are referred to as *core values*. The other type is referred to as *action values*: it includes nonverbal displays where the ego state is involved in causing such things as the wink of an eye, a smile, a frown, or a meaningful gesture.

129

Human life is not the only thing at stake here. I am willing to stand before others and state unequivocally that human life begins at the moment of fertilization. Any man or woman who knows as much about prenatal development as I do is aware of this fact, and that includes every zoologist, physician, nurse, and biology teacher on earth. If anyone with such knowledge allows himself or herself to commit, or conspire to commit, a human abortion, he or she is guilty of first degree murder; and not even the Supreme Court or a member of Congress or the president himself can stand on valid intellectual ground and rule otherwise. But while such murderous acts disturb me, my aim in writing this book is to go beyond such acts and explain how a human Reality is only as strong as its foundational values can make it; and the misconception of human prenatal development has become established in the Realities of about one-half of the American adult population. Is this a symptom of a human society in the early stages of collapse? Or is the presence of debatable issues merely serving as "itches"--to let us know that something needs to be taken care of before the situation gets worse?

Consider this implication. When the state executes a human being, it is merely killing that person's carcass: it is not touching his or her Reality--which will go on to live for eternity. But what about the doctor who commits an abortion? In that case, he or she is killing the person's carcass, but it was done before a Reality could begin to develop. This puts that doctor's

Reality in the role of God; for he or she prevented a human Reality from occurring in a Natural manner...a situation which in the Grand Scheme of Things may be tantamount to murder.

130

The moment of fertilization can also be reached outside the mother's womb, as in an in vitro setting, and placed back into her or some other woman's womb. We have not yet advanced to the point where we can develop in vitro babies all the way up to the time of Natural delivery.

131

Intelligence is defined as being the capacity to know, or understand, through reason. One of the most effective ways of increasing this capacity is to replace nonbeing values (invalid ideas, concepts, and constructs) with being values (valid ideas, concepts, and constructs) in the accumulation of foundational real values. This replacement of values is done at the advancing foundation of an issue--a situation where the issue develops increased validity in the present, while leaving newly found invalid ideas to lie dormant in the past. This is the way being issues develop, while nonbeing issues build upon the gathering of misconceived (invalid) ideas.

132

In doing this, we were using the incidence of effect dimension of our personal Realities. This allows us to stop our projections of self and consider just one physical realm (now recorded in affect), or, we can let the realms merge as in motion pictures-- in which case, we can have the framings occur anywhere within a range extending from around thirty per second down to zero.

133

Tictoc time may also be a dimension of Realities found in other animals, but I have heard of no conclusive evidence to indicate one way or the other. However, there appears to be evidence of time as a history of events in other animals, as may be found in the migratory habits of birds and fishes.

134

Realms. In normal range behavior, the physical realms generated on the actual self side of the A-R Interface will be met by their real counterparts (affective realms) at the Interface. If the physical and affective realms don't "jive," then the phenomenal self is faced with confusion and probably a goofed up play. But if they "jive," then the chances of a successful play are increased. This shows how important experience is in competitive events.

135

Life Style. Those who have been staying with the Behavioral Approach altogether may want to consider the possibility that behavioral reinforcement need not stop at the carcass, but can be carried right on in to the client's Reality and deal with the system of issues that is promoting an unacceptable mode of behavior.

136

Primary and secondary education are *fundamental issues.* They may have been resolved with graduation ceremonies, but their implication in training one's biological format was enough to keep their values tied to the present activity of that format. Moreover, some people will accept their graduation as a fact of life, but keep the education issue in process and go on to become such things as college students, professional students, and teachers. In such cases fundamental issues will have become main issues. In advanced societies, the education issues are vital elements of the social fabric--no matter if they have been resolved or are still ongoing. And we should remind ourselves that social fabric exists only in the Realities of that society's members.

This discussion could be continued on to explain the dynamic aspects of group and interpersonal relationships, for example, sexual attractions, the feelings of belonging, and the setting of goals and objectives.

137

Master Issue. Every human has a master issue. A master issue is the all-encompassing flow of reason in a human Reality. The most common master issues are those where the flow of reason moves toward Almighty God. All of the remaining master issues have been or are moving toward something other than God--be it the devil, a snake, the unknown, or some other imagined thing to aim for.

Secondary Issue. A normal human Reality will have one master issue and possibly two or more secondary issues. A secondary issue is a component of a master issue where the flow of reason is following one course, or mode of reason. For example, those of us who are pursuing God both as Christians and as concrete scientists will possess two main issues that aim toward God, and because they both aim toward God, they become secondary issues which lie within the one master issue. Our concrete science secondary issues are pursuing God in the central mode of reason, and our Christian secondary issues are pursuing God in faith and acceptance that Jesus Christ is the Way to God. These secondary issues break down into hierarchies of supporting issues which range down to the reasoned behaviors of everyday life.

138

A derelict nonbeing issue is one that has been found to contain possible misconceptions and/or invalid information. It is removed from ongoing status and remains in the Nonbeing League or Being League, available as a source of information, but not to be recalled to ongoing status.

139

This study's main illustration of a nonbeing issue is the matter of abortion. At one time, I believed in a woman's right to abort her child. But after researching the biological aspects of fetal development, it became clear that the child is not born at the time of delivery, but at the time of fertilization. Subsequently, I have removed abortion as one of my ongoing issues and let it become a derelict nonbeing issue in my Being League--a Being League issue invalidated. No longer does it compete for billing in my system of ongoing issues. It is in my judgement a criminal act which I can only act assertively against.

140

During the past four decades of my life, I have been working through many of the myths and suspect notions (fine issues) in my Reality. In addition, I have been more ready to reject the obtuse notions that some people have been thrusting upon my senses. This has meant that, over the past four decades, my system of ongoing issues became more and more a part of my Being League, and my nonbeing issues became less and less present as ongoing issues. The result was that my Being League of values has been growing, while my Nonbeing League has been dwindling into the past.

141

Components of an Issue. Human issues are flows of reason which emerge in response to existing goals or problems. They have three main components. The first component is the foundation of the issue; the second is its flow of reason; and the third is its resolution, or ending.

142

The terms "concrete science" and "Christian" are symbols for specific meanings in the English language. These same meanings may be expressed by different word symbols in other languages.

143

Some invalid (nonbeing) ideas and concepts will exist in all Being League issues. What we are implying here is that Being League issues are on the right track, but may still have some nonbeing values to purge from the system.

144

Valid Point of View. One who is operating with a valid point of view is following issues that display exact agreement between their constituent ideas and concepts and their counterparts (respective things and happenings) in Actuality.

When a concrete scientist reveals an irrefutable fact about Actuality, he or she is displaying the valid point of view. And when Christians make a decision for Jesus Christ, He and God will have become real entities in their lives. Here again is a display of the valid point of view.

145

Archimedes revealed a number of Aristotle's invalid conclusions concerning Actuality.

146

Advancing Foundation. One way of conceptualizing the foundation of an issue is to view it as being located at the top of the issue, in or near tictoc time and the present. If this turns out to be the case, then the "I" of Reality, the goal of the issue in use, its flow of reason, and its foundation would all exist at or near the present, and only the introjected ideas would trail into the past as a history of events to support the foundation. Whether this is a valid way of viewing an ongoing issue remains to be seen.

147

Invalid Point of View. In this case, Aristotle might have noted a fly larva (maggot) at the bottom of the garbage pail and reasoned that it too was a product of the pail, but of a different species of the Insecta Class. His view of the maggot would therefore be invalid.

148

However, Aristotle's deductive science was quite successful in bringing such things as logic and syllogistic reasoning (mediating between opposing premises) to ancient, medieval, and modern cultures. What seems to have misled him in the study of Actuality was his belief that God is the first cause of each unit of matter in Nature. He failed to conceive of development as a matter of cause and earlier causes...with God being the earliest (or First) Cause.

149

Prenatal and neonatal development become the beginning, or foundation of the human issue which also flowers into Reality.

150

Self-serving Issue. A self-serving issue is one that distorts a valid fact in order to promote an interest of the self. In this case, the distortion was of the fact that all humans have a right to exist, but the mother and her supporters distorted this valid fact and made it an apparent fact that the child is in her body, hence disposable.

151

Or consider the national debt issue. It was a valid issue while it was being used to help us prevail in World War II and in the Cold War against communism. But then it became involved in the matter of robbing Peter to pay Paul, for example, raising the debt so that carcasses, whose Realities lack self-reliance, can be sustained. In effect, this became a matter of taxing the self-reliant as a means of sustaining those who lack self reliance...robbing Peter to pay Paul.

We should not overlook the facts that self-reliance has been one of the major features of American character; that it fell a bit during the great depression of the 1930's, but was regained during World War II; and that the federal income tax, which was begun in 1912, has increasingly become the means of sustaining those who lack self-reliance.

152

The Normative Approach. This is used to established norms concerning the occurrence of things and/or events.

153

This study uses the snag and hang-up concept to differentiate between abnormal and normal-range human behavior. One way of explaining this concept is to imagine a man fishing near the bank. Say that he casts the bait so as to have it become tangled in a tree limb. If he can free the bait from the tanglement on his own, then his problem is a snag; but if he has to have someone come out from shore and free the bait from the tanglement, then his problem is a hang-up. In differentiating between abnormal and normal-range human behavior, it might be said that normal-range behavioral problems are snags and abnormal behavioral problems are hang-ups.

154

The contention in this study is that my phenomenal self "captures" the image of my Nonbeing League and displays it in my field of view, thus allowing the League to remain in a fixed position. This "capturing" can be a view of the entire League or of particular constituent issues and specific events. This is all done as a function of the "I" of Reality.

155

Invalid values. These are invalid ideas, concepts, issues, and constructs.

156

Incidence of Effect. The incidence of effect is the point at which the time line intersects the being-nonbeing continuum. Along with time, being, and nonbeing, this is one of the internal dimensions which pinpoint the exact location of ideas within a human Reality.

157

Here, projection seems to be going into sense data, but it is actually being made into the physical and/or affective realms that are being created during the moment of cognition. This is because cognition is the time when real values are given to sense data.

158

Targeted Real Values. These include affective realms, ideas, concepts, constructs, and issues.

159

Concerning Medical Aid. After my one encounter with my pit of nonbeing, I found that my ego state could hardly operate, my phenomenal self became confused, and my biological format was becoming dazed and unable to effect motor responses. To remedy things, I immediately turned my thinking to other subjects, and within about five minutes my ego state and biological format were functioning normally.

What had happened was that my phenomenal self innocently picked up information form my pit of nonbeing, for example, the image of men with giant eyes instead of heads, and fed it into my ego state. But I (my "I" of Reality) couldn't find an ongoing being issue that would accept such nonsense, and all of my nonbeing issues had been closed for decades. This meant that I had to accept that nonsense as a foundation of a new issue or reject it. I obtusely accepted (introjected) that nonsense into my Reality. The result was that while my ego state and biological format got through the ordeal in good shape, I had bad dreams for almost a week...until I could replace the invalid ideas in that nonsense issue's foundation with valid ideas and let the issue pass with time away from ongoing status and remain a deflated untruth in my history of events. The lesson to me is that I must be more astute in rejecting nonsense information from my Reality; for after all, I could have avoided those six nights of bad dreams...by just staying away from that pit of nonbeing.

160

The "I" of Personality. This is your "I" of Reality expressing itself. It is what one experiences when he or she says "I"; generally, it is reflecting upon some problem or successful matter in the issue which it is geared to at the time. When a personal counselor hears a client say "It," it generally indicates that he or she is referring to the issue which is in gear with the ego state at that moment. "I" and "It" will often be alluding to the same issue. But when a client says "me" or "my," the indication is that he or she is referring to some part of the carcass or to a significant other.

161

The nature of the ego mind set has been very well explained by Freud and the psychoanalysts who came after him. Their explanation rested in an ego state model which had organismic need impulses (id) coming in from one side and affective need impulses (superego) coming in from the other side. When the two different impulses meet and clash, the personality experiences a negative emotional response, as with rejection and/or anxiety. But if the two different impulses accommodate each other, the personality experiences the positive emotional response which we refer to as cognition--where the accommodation is accompanied by deliberation, a flowing of reason, and a rising of ego strength. The result is that ideas begin to develop, self-conception follows, and the ego mind set falls into place to make everything perceived (Actuality) seem real.

This is the mind set which holds Reality to be a synonym for Actuality. Subsequently, it follows that those affective impulses which enter the ego state as superego have rootings in Actuality, along with the id impulses. Thus emerged a general mind set that viewed all perceptual and recalled values as being part of Actuality. For example, I am hearing myself say it now, and I am sure that next year I will recall what I said; because tissues in my brain will hold it ready to be remembered. Such is a typical view of the ego mind set.

162

The Phenomenal Self Mind Set is the outlook which people have toward life in general when they have discarded the colossal myth (that Actuality and Reality are the same). We call it the phenomenal self mind set because it results from the joining of real and actual values in creating the phenomenal self. In other words, it is the view one gets when the actual values of the ego are eclectically joined with real values and cause the ego to sublimate and transcend into becoming the holistic (whole) body--an example of the phenomenal self in action. This is rendered possible by the founding value of Reality, which is the idea of omnipotence, e.g. everything I see is me.

What it all comes down to is that the human being has two essences. One essence is his or her actual existence--what is referred to here as the carcass; and the other essence is his or her real existence--what is referred to here as the nucleus, or "eye," or "I," of his or her Reality. The paradox is that the two essences coexist so completely that the more one achieves the intellectual capacity for telling them apart the less inclined he or she will be to do it. The tact used in this study is to help the reader gather enough intellectual values in construct to prompt him or her to try projecting into it, see the real essence, the real Reality, and thereby slay the colossal myth. What was for so long thought to be the unconscious would then become what it is--Reality.

The irony to be found in studying the two general mind sets is that they both make use of the same psychological mechanics. However, one, the ego mind set, has become blinded from seeing the possessor's real existence; while the other, the phenomenal self mind set, allows the possessor to witness his or her real existence. It all boils down to the individual's ongoing issue of life. Does it contain the colossal myth value? Or has it been slain, and now lies dormant in the possessor's history of events... one more nonbeing value put to rest?

163

Studio Quality. This term is used here to indicate precise detail in form, color, and line...an exceptionally clear view.

164

The ego mind set makes fertile ground not only for dreaming, but for the practice of hypnosis and such nonbeing ploys as psychic counseling, trances, and mystic religions. The position taken here is that until such ploys can be shown to have concrete foundation, they must be regarded as whimsical nonsense and gaming with the unknown.

165

Signifying a lower overview of human personality.

166

I was astonished to find that I had managed to slay the colossal myth and at the same time keep the ego mind set. Perhaps further study will show that mind set is not a function of Reality, but of the biological format.

167

The wherewithal of our computer and electronics experts is rapidly approaching that stage of readiness.

168

Time Line. One of the seven dimensions of Reality.

169

This was a secondary issue within my main issue of concrete science.

170

One part that can move with time is the advancing foundation of an issue. This is the part of an ongoing issue which lies closest to the Real self when the ego state is carrying on cognition. When misconceptions are purged from this advancing foundation, it tends to inch closer to the Fold of Reality. The result is that when this purging continues over a long period of time, the entire issue appears to skew toward the Fold--meaning that the skewing effect is caused by the advancing foundation's movement toward the Fold, while the rest of the issue remains in a fixed position. I wish that I could give more information about the size and shape of the advancing foundation, but because it lies so close to the present, neither of my projection processes (projection of self and retroprojection) can bring it into view.

Scanning my Being League, I find that some of my issues are occasionally skewing toward my Fold, few if any are skewing away from my Fold, and the rest are maintaining the same incidence of effect (same position in Reality). What this tells me about my personality is that I have a pretty steady outlook on life, a tendency to resist nonbeing issues, and some readiness to move toward my Fold. The net assessment of my personality is that I am a pretty good guy, but certainly no angel.

171

Stand Right There. My meaning in saying "stand right there" is that I retroprojected right up to that issue as it rested near to the Fold and could witness its coalescence with the Fold. The explanation which I give to this is that my retroprojecting "I" of Reality was sending information back to my phenomenal self, which then presented that information to the actual self, as is done with id and sense data impulses, and fed into the process of cognition. The result was that I got to remember this coalescence experience--which is now stored in my Fold. I wouldn't want to bet on the validity of this explanation, but it may be helpful for others to know that this is what appears to have happened.

172

Christian Fold. We have covered this matter already; but let me remind you that this book is written in English, and in English, "Christ" is a word symbol which is used to reflect upon the divine redeemer. Other words in other languages may be used to reflect upon the same thing. What it amounts to is that the word is insignificant: the meaning behind it is everything.

173

The click of death will come to every human carcass. Its Natural coming is understandably preferred; but failure to act against the colossal myth has brought mankind to this day of reckoning: either we get rid of the myth and go on to live the good life in truth, or, if current trends are any indication, have our carcasses perish before their time. As for whether the click will be a general happening for all people on earth, neither you nor I can say. But notwithstanding the fact that our's is a loving and just God, He may very well be prepared to say that enough is enough.

Nor should anyone come later and say that we realists were not explicit enough in calling mankind to the Fold, and that he or she would have acted differently had the message been more compelling. But anyone can see the storm clouds coming, that now is the time to "gather hay", and that the decision to act is his or hers to make, now.

Let no one be deceived. Now is the time to come to the Fold.

174

You are reminded that this book considers only being values. In this study, "good" values are being values and "bad" values are nonbeing values. Nonbeing values are subjects for other studies in Affective Realism. However, we should be cognizant of the fact that the real vehicle of one's life is the Reality which he or she built since early childhood. It includes the nucleus, or "I", of Reality and every bit of real substance (ideas) that was ever introjected into it. Some of the real substance is completely valid and coalesces to form the Fold of the person's Reality. Some of the real substance is partially composed of invalid ideas, but exists in a God-oriented master issues. This is the substance which gathers to become the Being League of values. And some of the real substance is partially or totally composed of invalid ideas, and exists in issues that are not God-oriented. This is the substance which gathers to become the Nonbeing League of values.

All this means that the human carcass is like a motorcycle sidecar. It is not needed when the time comes for the real vehicle of life to operate in the Greater Reality on its own. For those of us who have gathered enough intellect and/or acceptance of Truth, the balance has swung, and we see ourselves as the Realities that we are. But this is where the caution light goes on. It does not mean that we break free from our carcasses, our "sidecars," during mortal life. If we were to do that, our carcasses would end up as "vegetables" in a psychosis ward. What it amounts to is that the members of each mind-set must cherish their carcasses throughout mortal life; for although it becomes evident that the carcass is expendable in eternal life, its biological format is our tie with the world of Actuality and the Realities of others; hence it is essential that we strive to maintain homeostasis in our carcasses and balance in our ego states.

175

Self-service. Self-service is a subject for a nonbeing study; however, we should consider it here...just enough to know that it has nothing to do with Being League values. Being League values are all geared to the Real Almighty God; they include all of the values one employs while serving the needs of other people; they include all of the values one employs while promoting human progress; they include all of the values one uses in service to God; and they include all of the values that one gathers while doing these services, for example, the joys and satisfactions in owning a nice home, in advancing intellectually, and in having fellowship with others. All other real human values may be nonbeing values; if so, the one thing they will have in common is that they involve self-service.

What is meant by the term "self-service" is that it involves the way one gathers actual and real values in effort to elevate his or her status among others and/or in fantasy. It is found in those human minds that center upon their needs and identity within a group or fantasy rather than upon the needs and identity of the group or interpersonal relationship itself. Such values usually lie in the Nonbeing League of values.

176

Being mortally least may be eternally most.

177

Our Answers. The answers provided in this book are certainly not what should be presented to school children, or for that matter, anyone who is not working at the college level. Most of its substance must be reworked and presented in terms that the general public can understand. I wrote this book at a more profound level because that was where I had to work in order to erase the misconceptions that were getting in the way. This is where you (the reader) come in. The chances are that you have more scholastic ability than that which exists in my average mind. You must reshape this information and get it out to all nations in words that every child can understand. Please feel free to quote any part of this book, but not more than one page at a time, except by permission.

178

What is the Fold of Reality? In the event that the meaning of the term "Fold of Reality" is unclear to you, it might be helpful if you were to think of the Fold as being nothing more than common sense. Children begin to gather their common sense during infancy and continue to build it throughout life. It generally becomes the home base for crucial decision-making during the course of everyday living. Or to say this another way, common sense is that part of a human Reality which contains completely valid ideas, and can best react to sensory and organismic stimuli when it has been previously entered into teamwork with the biological format. During adolescent and adult life, this common sense grows according to the behaviors one elects to do, for example, a boy who elects to play football or a man who has achieved proficiency at his work.

Common sense goes much further than such things as athletic and work abilities. It also becomes heavily involved when we deal with intellectual values--those which are used in our educational, social, and religious endeavors. One thing that happened in American society was that while most of the citizens were operating within a God-oriented master issue, they allowed their secondary issues to become contaminated with misconceptions. The misconceptions of human birth which we have been alluding to is one example. The work of Sinclair Lewis in destroying many of the political and economic myths during the first half of this century is another example. And perhaps the best known religious misconception are those that have surrounded the matter of human creation. If this is a matter of concern to you, then you may want to consult the unpublished New Testament Scriptures. The compilers of the King James version of the Bible seem to have chosen New Testament Scriptures that smoothed out any conflict between Moses and Jesus on the matter of human creation. If you consult the unpublished New Testament Scriptures, you may find Jesus to have been more explicit. Or, if you check the rear dictionary in many of the modern Bibles, you will find this matter concerning creation already discussed.

The bottom line in this discussion is that most people on earth hold misconceptions concerning human existence. This has caused Being Leagues to bulge and gatherings of common sense to lie without growth. The reason for this is that human issues and ideas which are created with misconception can never become elements of common sense. The Fold of a humans' Reality is the measure of his or her common sense--which can go on to become common among all humans on earth and be in alignment with God and the Fold of the Greater Reality. Bringing valid issues from the Being League to the Fold is the universal way to erase most psychological and social conflicts on earth.

179

If 350 years earlier Aristotle had used inductive reason as the method of science, the intellect of the people in the Holy Land could very well have been what existed in America at the end of World War II. Consider the implications.

180

Many if not most of the problem ideas that professional counselors arrive at are caused by the founding value--the idea of
omnipotence. Children are often inclined to take responsibility
for events that they witnessed but were not actually involved in;
for example, when mother fell down the stairs, or when the cat
caught the mouse. This feeling of responsibility becomes captured in the form of a problem idea and it will remain as a misconception until it is discovered and rendered invalid. Getting
rid of these misconceptions is the most important thing one can
do to validate his or her issues and thereby move closer to the
Fold. It is when a person is able to work at his or her Fold of
Reality that the colossal myth is most easily destroyed.

181

Moses. Bear in mind that back in the fifteenth century B.C., the
followers of Moses knew very little about Actuality. This left
them to consider human existence in terms of the Realities they
were creating. This is what Moses was doing. He was addressing the interactions that existed between human Realities in one
of the most desolate places on earth. The fact that the Holy
Land was such a place gave Moses the opportunity to teach in
terms of real values--foremost of which were the values relating to our Real Almighty God.

182

The Mother Load of Reason. The Fold of a human Reality contains valid ideas that are or are capable of becoming common to
all humans on earth. When viewed collectively, all of the mortal Folds on earth join the Fold of the Greater Reality in becoming the Mother Load of Reason. One of the most gratifying
understandings is found in the fact that the closer one gets to his
or her Fold the more obvious the Mother Load of Reason
becomes, and the more evident our Real Almighty God and
Greater Reality stand before us. For as long as increasing num-

bers can be moving toward their Folds, I will be a meliorist.

183

Come to the Fold. This phrase carries some important connotations. Three of these connotations have to do with behaviors that maintain human progress. When a human is in the process of moving to the Fold, he or she will automatically demonstrate increasing degrees of three behaviors. They are: self-reliance, personal responsibility, and morality.

To those of you who do not fully comprehend these connotations and the overall message in this book, I urge you to keep the faith, do good, live love, and think truth; otherwise, you may be left behind.

184

Empedocles (455?-395 B.C.), a Greek physicist, was a contemporary of Socrates (469-399 B.C.). There is some indication that Empedocles conceived the earliest roots of evolutionary theory; and there is some speculation that Socrates may have picked these roots up and passed them along to Plato and Aristotle. Notwithstanding this possibility, Aristotle brought the concept of evolution into full view in the ancient Greek and Roman intellectual world. This concept was revived during the Modern Era and made more reasonable by investigations in concrete science.

185

Whether the Anti-Universe is or is not the Greater Reality is something that future work in concrete science will determine. Whichever way it turns out, humanity will have progressed to a better understanding of its relationship to the Greater Reality and the Grand Scheme of Things in the Universe.

As each mortal moves toward his or her Fold and joins the Fold of the Greater Reality, the more obvious the Mother Load of Reason becomes and the more evident our Real Almighty God is, creating a better world for all.

References

Cajori, Florian. A History of Physics. "In Its Elementary Branches, Including the Evolution of Physical Laboratories." New York: The Macmillan Company, 1899.

Ducan, John Charles. Astronomy. "A Textbook." New York and London: Harper & Brothers Publishers, 1946.

Eby, Frederick. The Development of Modern Education. New York: Prentice-Hall, Inc., 1952.

Funk & Wagnalls Company. New Standard Dictionary of the English Language. New York and London: Funk and Wagnalls Company, 1913.

Funk & Wagnalls Corporation. <u>World Almanac and Book of Facts 1994</u>. Mahwah, New Jersey: World Almanac Books, 1993.

Gray, Henry. <u>Anatomy of the Human Body</u>. Philadelphia: Lea & Febiger, 1966.

Haines, C. Grove and Walsh, Warren B. <u>The Development of Western Civilization</u>. New York: Henry Holt and Company, 1941.

Hayes, Carlton J. and Moon, Parker Thomas. <u>Ancient and Medieval History</u>. New York: The Macmillan Company, 1929.

Holmes, Oliver. <u>Human Neurophysiology</u>. London, Glasgow, New York, Tokyo, Melbourne and Madras: Chapman & Hall, 1993.

Leet, L. Don and Judson, Sheldon. <u>Physical Geology</u>. Englewood Cliffs, New Jersey: Prentice-Hall, Inc., 1958.

Lide, David R., Editor in Chief. <u>Handbook of Chemistry and Physics</u>. "72nd Edition, 1991-1992." Boca Raton, Ann Arbor, and Boston: The Chemical Rubber Publishing Company, 1983.

Merriam-Webster Inc. <u>Webster's Third New International Dictionary of the English Language</u>. "Unabridged." Springfield, Massachusetts: Merriam-Webster Inc., 1986.

Ruch, Theodore C. and Patton, Harry D. <u>Physiology and Biophysics</u>. Philadelphia and London: W.B. Saunders Company, 1965.

Russell, Bertrand. <u>The ABC of Relativity</u>. London: George Allen & Unwin Ltd., 1958.

Struthers, Parke H. Human Frontiers. Nelson, New
    Hampshire: Merriconn Press, 1951.

--------. Your Face and Mine. Nelson, New Hampshire:
    Merriconn Press, 1952.

Swanson, Carl P. Cytology and Cytogenetics. Englewood
    Cliffs, New Jersey: Prentice-Hall, Inc., 1957.

Watson, Robert I. Psychology of the Child. New York: John
    Wiley & Sons, Inc., 1959.

Wiedersheim, R. Translation edited by G.B. Howes, F.L.S.
    The Structure of Man. "An Index to His Past History."
    London: Macmillan and Co., 1895.

Winchester, A.M. Genetics. "A Survey of the Principles of
    Heredity." Boston: Houghton Mifflin Company, 1951.

Index

Abraham, **32**, 63
Abnormal behavior, 138
Abnormal human behavior, 167,
    253
Abortion, 58, 62, 151, 152, 164,
    247, 250
Absolute velocity, **82**, 199
A case of retroprojection, 244
Action model of the ego state, 107,
    108, 123, 212
Action values, **247**
Actual and apparent human bodies,
    54
Actual human values, 150, **246**
Actual self, 105, **112**, 113, 122-124,
    128, 141, 153, 157, 170, 175,
    218, 219, 223, 224, 226, 229,
    230, 234-239, 240, 242, 243,
    249, 259
Actual social values, 246

Actual time, 81, **83**, 84, 156, 157
Actual truth, 11, 30, 52, 60, 65,
    116, 164
Actual values, **150**, 182, 183, 217,
    246, 257
Actuality, 26, 42, 43, 50, 56, 58,
    62,68, 70, 71, 73-75, 78, 79,
    80, 81, 83-85, 89-92, 100,
    106,112,115-117, 120-130,
    132, 133, 140-142, 146, 149,
    150, 153-157, 162-166, 169,
    170, 172-175, 179-181, 184,
    186, 192, 199, 200, 210, 215,
    219, 220, 223-227, 230-232,
    234-245, 251, 253, 256, 261,
    264
Actuality and Reality, 26, 75, 83-
    85, 89, 90, 106, 112, 115-117,
    120, 123-125, 127, 128, 140,
    142, 150, 154, 165, 169, 173,

175, 179-181, 184, 192, 199,
219, 225-227, 231, 234, 237,
238, 239-241, 243, 244, 256
Actuality-Reality Interface, 42, **84**
Advancing foundation, 163, **248**,
252, 259
Affect, 14, 53, 68, **87**, 98, 111, 114,
189, 206, 213, 214, 218, 232
Affective emotional reactions, 95,
96, **98**, 202, 206, 210
Affective Realism, 10, 11, 14, 17,
18, **69**-74, 82, 88, 94, 106,
115, 143, 178, 180, 183, **197**,
231, 232, 234, 260
Affective Realism: Goal, Premises,
and objectives, 74
Affective realist, 72, 73, 83, 106,
115, 126, 132, 147, 232, 236
Affective Reality, **71**, 72, 74, 88,
89, 133, 147, 197, 200, 228,
244
Affective realm, 127, **157**, 159,
249, 254, 255
Almighty God and Christ are real,
63, 145
An Allegory, 34
Ancestral past, 105, 203, 207
Apparent truth, 163
Aquinas, Thomas, **13**
A-R Interface, **84**, 85, 90, 92, 112,
116, 117, 120-122, 124, 125,
132, 155-157, 162, 164, 166,
170-172, 174, 175, 184, 185,
205, 210, 216, 219, 220, 224,
225, 227, 235, 237-239, 241,
243, 244, 245, 249
Archimedes, **191**, 252
Aristotelian deductions, 12, 190
Aristotle, **11**-14, 18, 21, 22, 25-29,
42, 44, 45, 52, 63, 69, 119,
163-165, 190-192, 194, 252,
263, 265
Aristotle's science, 191

Aristotle's work, 12, 27, 42
Army of scholars, 22-25
Assertive component of Reality,
166
A word of caution, 171, 242
Axiom for genetic engineering, **54**

Bacon, Francis, **12**, 14, 24, 45, 172,
192, 193
Behavioral Approach, 76, 94, 137,
138, 203, 209, 217, 226, 249
Being experience, **149**, 150, 240
Being League, 49, 58, 62, 63, 65,
149, 150, 152, 155, 156, 160,
163, 166-168, 171, 175-179,
183, 250, 251, 254, 259, 260,
261, 263
Being least may be most, 182
Being values, 62, 69, 79, 81, 84,
89, 110, 117, 124, **149**-152,
167, 168, 175, 183, 189, 199,
216, 239, 246, 248, 251, 260,
261
Being values and nonbeing values,
182, 260
Berne, Eric, **15**
Bimodal phenomenal self, **241**, 244
Biological format, 87, 95, 113, **126**,
153, 158, 167, 200, 221, 227,
230, 232, 235, 236, 238, 249,
255, 258, 261, 262
Biophysical Approach, 74, 76, 88,
96, 115, 202, 210
Biophysical Approach to human
personality, 74, **88**, 111, 113
Biophysical Factors in Human
Personality, 94
Birth and delivery, 101, **208**
Birth myth, 60
Blood relationships, 60
Blood sugar, 101, **208**

Call to the Fold, 178, 180

Call to the Fold of Reality, 18, 19, 180

Capsular theory, **50**-52, 54, 152, 195

Carcass, 130-133, 146, 147, 150, 153, 154, 156, 158, 165-167, 186, 200, 218, 219, 221, 229, 235-237, 243, 244, 246, 247, 249, 253, 257, 259, 260, 261

Cathect, 108, 113, 213

Cell theory, 51, 195

Central mode of reason, **142**-144, 162, 250

Cerebral cortex, 94, 96, 102, 103, 112, 121, 200, 203, 204, 206, 208, 210, 221, 227, 230, 232

Children of God, 63, 146

Christ, 9, 19, 25, 63, 64, 89, 119, 124, 127, 133, 136, 137, 142-144, 179, 182, 184, 187, 220, 223-225, 227, 259

Christian Doctrine, 139

Cicero, **162**

Coalescence of issues, 176, 177, **183**, 185, 259

Coexisting Universes, 89

Cognition, 14, 81, **86-88, 98**-100, **110**, 123, 128, 158, 159, 173, 174, 193, 202, 206, 220, 222, 236, 254, 256, 258, 259

Cognition involves ongoing issues, 158, 159

Cognitive arena, 85, **86**-87, 97, 98, 111, 204, 208

Cognitive emotional reactions, **98**, 99, 103, 105, 126, 159, 210

Cognitive experiences, 157, 158

Cognitive system, 22, 193

Colossal myth, **26**, 154, 165, 166, 169, 170, 173, 174, 178-180, 184, 185, 187, 239, 242, 256-258, 260, 264

Colossal myth axiom, 154

Come to the Fold, 187, 260, 265

Comenius, John Amos, **24**, 193

Comforter, or Holy Ghost, 187

Comparative Realism, **167**

Components of an issue, **251**

Components of the ego state, 107

Conception, 52, **68**, 69, 78, 88, 112, 117, 124, 127, 133, 139, 149-152, 154, 194, 196, 199, 212, 218, 226, 231, 232, 238, 256

Concrete sciences, **11**, 64, 73, 117, 158, 218, 223

Conscious, **86**, 87, 95, 98, 133, 178, 193, 210, 235

Conscious level, 86, 87, 94, 95, 98, 99, 102, 202-204, 206

Conscious state, 95, 100, 102-105, 117, 123, 128, 132, 201, 202, 208, 210, 211, 219, 235, 237

Control center, 96, 219

Core values, **247**

Cursory effect, 176

Danger zones, 169-172

Darwin, Charles R., **51**, 52, 140, 190, 191, 223

Demonstrable cause, 13, 16, 125, 133, 138, 139, 142, 144, 151, 162, 187

Deductive reason, 12, 13, 26, 30, 32, 88, 163, 165, 166, **190**, 192, 252

Desine, 235, 238, 241, 243, 244

Dewey, John, **140**, 223

Descartes, Rene, **23**, 218

Dimensions of my Reality, 148

DNA and RNA, 53

Dogmatic science, 72

Dual mind sets, 174, 258

Eclectic display, **16**, 17, 77, 115, 137, 138, 140, 142, 144, 197, **220**, 221, 229, 243

Eclectic view, **16**, 17, 94, 111, 115, **217**

Ego, 14, 85-**87**, 97, 98, 100, 106-110, 112, 113, 121, 123, 173, 193, 207, 209, 210-214, 236, 256, 257

Ego mind-set, **172**-174, 178-182, 185, **256**-258

Ego state, 15, 71, 87, 102, **106**-117, 121-128, 132, 133, 138,147-149, 151, 157-159, 162, 166, 169, 175, 185, 202, 205, 210-212, 215, 219, 220, 222, 224-226, 230, 231, 234-236, 238, 239, 242, 245, 247, 255, 256, 258, 261

Ego state harmony, 142, 224, 226, 227

Ego state tenacity, 124, 125, 145

Einstein, Albert, 69, **81**, 82, 92, 223

Emergence of self, 100, 104, 112, 207, 219, 230, 235

Emotion, **88**, 99, 110, 201

Emotional feelings, 110, 216

Emotional reactions, 94-96, 98-100, 102, 103, 105, 126, 158, 159, 202-204, 206, 207, 210, 237

Erasmus, Desiderius, 45, **194**

Essence of human personality, 120

Eternal life, 39, 127, 131, 134, 141, 158, 178, 223, 224, 243, 250, 261

Evolution, **52**

Evolving Natural world, 12

Existential Approach, 16, 57, 76, 115, 117, 119, 137, 201, 203, 210, 229, 235

External world inroads in the human body, 56

"Eye" of Reality, **132**, 133, 147, 160, 220

Feelings-to-Act Table, 15

Feral children, 93, 201

Fertilization, 52, 54, 59, 153, 215, 247, 248, 250

Fertilization and embryonic development, 59

Field of view, 149, 150, 152, 155, 166-168, 176, **245**, 254

First paradoxical understanding, 78

First things first, 126, 127

First verbal expression of need, 102

Flow of Reason, 45, 151, 152, 155, 157, 159, 161, 165, 172, 250-252, 256

Fold of Reality, 18, 19, 46, **85**, 89, 131, 132, 136, 170, 172, **175**-180, 182-184, 186, 221, 223, 243, 258, **262**, 264

Formation of the ego state, 107

Foundational values, 73, 149-**151**, 154, **246**-248

Founding value, 72-74, **77**, 78, 128, 154, 170, **197**, 198, 219, 231, 232, 238, 241, 257, 264

Four-approach overview of the ego state, 115

Free association of words, 186

Freud, Anna, **212**

Freud, Sigmund, **15**, 86, 87, 101, 107, 109, 114, 173, 185, 186, 202, 212, 213, 223, 235, 236, 256

Froebel, Friedrich, **145**

Front line trench of science, **10**-12, 17

Functional approaches, 16, 17, **137**, 138, 222, 226

Functional mental health problems, 107, 212

Fundamental issues, 249

Galen, Claudius, **192**

Gargantua, **23**

Generalization, 135, 136, 162, 220,

222, 223

General mind sets, **172**-174, 256, 257

Ego mind set, 172-174, 178-182, 185, 256-258

Phenomenal self mind set, 172-174, 180-183, 185, 256, 257

Genetic engineering, 54

Gestalt Approach, 43, 76, 137, 138, 203, 209, 218, 226

Gestalt experience, 110, 111, **216**, 222

God is Real, 74, 145

God-oriented pragmatist, 139, 142, 225

Greater Reality, 39, 72, **89**, 132, 144-146, 162, 179, 183, 227, 260, 263, 264, 265

Hippocrates, **191**

Holy Roman Empire, **22**, 195

Homeostasis, 88, 95, 96, 201, 226, 261

Homosexuality, 198, 212, 233, 246

Hooke, Robert, **51**

How to get out of this world alive, 10, 69, 133, 229, 231

Human Affect, 53

Human culture of Actuality, 153

Human culture of Reality, 153

Human metamorphosis, 118

Human personality, 14-19, 22, 24, 31, 43, 46, 64, 70, 74-77, 85, 87, 88, 94, 96, 97, 106, 108, 112, 115, **117**, 120, 122-128, 135, 137-140, 157, 169, 173, 177, 183, 185-187, 192-194, 197, 201-203, 206, 207, 209, 211, 213, 215-218, 220, 222, 224-226, 229, 231, 232, 234, 235, 238, 239, 241, 243, 258

Humanism, 21, 26, 42, 43, 45
    birth of, 23

definition of, **24**

religious form, 23

roots of, 24

secular form, 24

the Humanistic Movement, 24

Humanistic Approach, 17, 23, 76, 137, 138, 201, 203, 209, 227

Humanistic movement, 24, 192

Hypnosis, 87, 185, 258

Hypothalamus, 87, 95-97, 102, 103, 111, 121, 203, 208

Id, 14, 22, 85, **86-88**, 96-100, 102, 106-113, 116, 121-124,129, 202, 203, 206, 207, 211-213, 218, 223, 232, 234, 236, 256, 259

Ideas, 12-14, 22, 23, 27, 31, 32, 34, 42, **68**, 83, 98, 100, 105, 112, 114, 115, 118, 120, 123, 128, 138, 139, 141, 142, 149, 150, 151, 155-159, 163, 165-167, 170, 171, 174, 176, 178, 186, 189, 190, 192, 193, 196-198, 207, 210, 219, 223, 230, 232, 235, 237, 239, 241, 245, 246, 248, 251, 252, 254-256, 260, 262-264

Id-superego conflict, 108

Identification, 212, 234, 236, 237

Identifications by the trimodal phenomenal self, 243

Imaginary visit with Joe, 101

Incidence of effect, 70, 148, 168, 197, 248, **254**, 259

Inducted generalizations, 162

Induction, 13, 136

Inductive reason, 12, 14, 30, 31, 42, 43, 45, 46, **88**, 119, 151, 163, 165, **190**, 263

Inductive Sciences, 32, 46, 118, **218**

Infantile stages of development,

101
Instinct, 100, **206**, 234
Intellectual, 9, 11, 12, 14, 16, 18,
    22, 28, 33, 45, 52, 64, 69, 70,
    73-75, 83, 85, **87-89**, 99, 107,
    109, 120, 133, 137, 139-143,
    146, 148, 154, 169, 175, 179,
    184, 192, 193, 198, 210, 213,
    215, 223, 225-227, 231, 234,
    239-242, 247, 257, 262, 265
Intelligence defined, 154, **248**
Introjection, 109, 110, 112, 213,
    214, 245
Intuition, 86, 97, **99**, 205, 207, 219
Intuitive emotional aptitude impuls-
    es, 105
Intuitive emotional reaction, 102,
    103, 206
Intuitive need impulses, 100
Invalid Foundational idea, 158,
    163, **165**
Invalid point of view, 163-165, 252
Invalid values, 168, 169, **254**
"I" of Personality, 147, 151, 172,
    219, **255**
"I" of Reality, 163, 166, 172, 176,
    200, 220, 237-244, 252, 254,
    255, 259, 260
Isolated self, 79
Issues, 158, **159**
    A Cornerstone Issue, 160
    Categories of human issues,
        153
    Debatable issue, 151, **152**
    Derelict nonbeing issues, 160,
        250, 251
    Issue length, 158
    Issues lie in fixed positions,
        155
    Main issues, 158
    Master issue, 158, 160, 162,
        163, 165, 167, 168, **250**,
        260, 263

Secondary Issue, 158, 160,
    162, 163, **250**, 258, 263
Supporting Issue, **250**
Valid issues compliment each
    other, 185
Valid issues--what are they,
    151

James, William, **139**, 140, 223
Jesus, 12, 14, 144, 186, 187, 224,
    227, 263
Jesus Christ, 19, 25, 136, 144, 162,
    182, 184, 187, 224, 225, 250,
    252
Jesus of Nazareth, 14, 43, 52, 63,
    69, 77, 141, 144, 158, 186,
    187, 223-225, 242

Kant, Immanuel, **140**, 223
Knowledge, 13, 14, 18, 22, 25, 31,
    32, 51, 63, 72, 75, 86, 118,
    125, 137, 140, 163, 181, 223,
    225, 234, 239, 247

Laminated tissues, 97
Libido, **99**, 107, 108
Living ego state specimen, 121, 123
Love, 26, 102, 104, 147, 153, 182,
    183, **209**, 214, 215, 226, 228,
    246, 265
Low intellect, 184, 263
Luther, Martin, **25**, 26, 42, 192, 194
Lutheran Church, 23, 42

Magnetic moment, 90, 200
Main objective of this book, 44, 62,
    67, 196
Master issue, 158, 160, 162, 163,
    165, 167, 168, **250**, 260, 263
Mechanics in science, 191
Medical Aid, 172, 255
Medieval Church, 12, 13
Medulla, 97, 203

Mendel, Gregor, **52**
Messiah, 144, 227
Metamorphosis, 29, 30, 92, 118
Mind-set and group differences, 174
Mind-set grading, 181
Misconception, 26, 57, 60, 149, 151, 152, 154, 155, 158, 163, 165, 177, 179, 184, 186, 187, 198, 247, 250, 258, 262-264
Mobility of the "I" of Reality, 243
Modes of self-realization, 240
Mode of wisdom, 242
Mohammed, **187**
Montaigne, Michael, **24**, 193
Mood swing, 95
Mortal Domain, 47, **48**, 49
Moses, 69, **186**, 187, 263, 264
Mother load of reason, 187, 264
Moving to the Fold, 184, 185, 262, 263, 265
Myths and dogmas, 17-19, 46

Nationalistic movement, 192
Natural world, 12
Nature, 25, 42, 43, 52, 54, 61, 62, 73-75, **80**, 82, 83, 87, 91, 92, 96, 100, 102, 116, 118, 119, 124-126, 130, 140, 190, 191, 198, 199, 215, 234, 253
New Learning, The, 24, 25
    Back-looking humanists, 25, 42
    Front-looking humanists, 25, 42
Nonaffective emotional reaction, 95, 96, **98**, 126, 158, 204
Nonbeing experience, **149**, 150
Nonbeing issue, 160, 164, 248, 250, 251, 255, 259
Nonbeing League, 49, 58, 62, 63, 65, 150, 156, 160, 166-168, 171, 176, 178, 183, 250, 251,
254, 260, 261
Nonbeing values, 69, 79, 81, 84, 89, 110, 117, 124, **149**-151, 167, 168, 175, 183, 199, **216**, 239, 248, 251, 260, 261
Normal range behavior, 107, 109, 138, 222, 229, 238, 242, 249
Normative approach, 167, 253
No straight lines in Nature, 82
Note to ego mind-setters, 180
Nucleus, or eye, of Reality, 160, 166

Omnipotence, **78**, 112, 114, **128**, 154, 170, 198, 208, 219, 230-234, 238, 241, 257, 264
One play of a football game, 157, 248
Ongoing issues, 158-160, 172, 251, 252, 257, 258
Ontogenetic need impulses, **99**, 100, 211
Organic mental health problems, 212
Organismic, **14**, 95, 122, 123, 232, 234, 256, 262
Our answers, 184, 262

Paradoxical understanding, 11, 43, 44, 71, 78, 92, **190**
Peirce, Charles S., **139**, 140, 223
Perception, **67**, 68, 70, 78, 86, 100, 117, 124, 153, 173, 218, 220, 242, 245
Personality formatting, 125, 126
Phenomenal self, 101, 104, **105**, 113, **114**, 117, 122, 123, 127, 128, 130, 131, 133, 147, 148, 158, 166-174, 201, 218-220, 222, 224, 226, 227, 229, 230, 235-243, 245, 249, 254-257, 259
Phenomenal self mind-set, 180-183,

185

Phenomenological Approach, 16, 76, 113, 114, 115, 137, 201, 202, 210, 217, 229, 236

Phenomenology, 211, 217

Phylogenetic need impulses, **99**, 100

Physical Realm, 75, **81**, 127, **157**, 170, 171, 248, 249

Pit of nonbeing, 170, **171**, 255

Plato, **11**, 13, 14, 21, 22, 28, 34, 41, 43, 63, 69, 77, 119, 165, 187, 192, 264

Plato-Aristotle influences, 13

Population explosion, 47, 48, 54

Pragmatic reason, **139**, 141

Projection, 68, 109, 110, 112, 113, 159, 169, 170, 213-215, 238, 239, 242, 243, 245, 254, 259

Projection of self, **68**-70, 112, 113, 123, 147, **170**, 171, 173, 233-236, 243, 259

Proprioceptor, 95, 202

Protestant Reformation, 24, **25**

Protrusion of Reality, 105, 123

Psychic energy, 86, 97, 99, 100, 105, **205**, 207, 211, 237

Psychoanalysis, 14-16, 43, 106, 107, 109, 115, 173, 211, 231, 232, 234, 236

Psychoanalytic model, 106, 211

Psychoanalytic Approach, 14, 15, 76, 96, 111, 113, 115, 202

Psychological defenses, **109**, 110, 200, 213, 216, 222, 227, 228, 245

Puppet master episode, **103**, 104, 112, 230

Quantum theory, 81, 82

Rabelais, Francois, **22**

Ramus, Peter, **25**-27, 192

Reaction formation, 102, 147, 227, 228

Realism, 13, 45, 167

Reality, 13, 33, 34, 42, 44, 48, 68, 73, 74, 75, 78, 80, **81**, 83-85, 89-92, 100, 105, 116, 117, 120, 122-135, 137, 141-187, 192, 197-203, 210, 215, 218-264

Reality analysis, 146, 147, 176, 178, 221, 228

Reality configuration, 168

Reality construct, **68**, **70**-72, 78-80, 84, 87, 89, 136, 137, 183, 187, 199, 200, 215, 216, 228, 240

Reality recapitulation, **145**

Real Human body, 91, 133

Real human values, 150, 183, 232, 246, 261

Real philosophy, 10

Real self, 105, 122-124, 128, 133, 141, 157, 166, 170, 186, 200, 218-220, 223, 224, 229, 230, 232, 234-239, 242-244, 258

Real time, **83**, 84, 156

Real time line, 159

Real values, 117, 170, 182, 183, 217, **246**, 254, 255, 257, 261, 264

Real value range, 175

Reason, 13, 14, 28, 32-34, 39, 41, 44, 45, 52, 60, 63, 64, 66, 68-71, 74, 75, 81, 83, 87, **88**, 91, 98-100, 102, 105, 108-111, 114, 119, 135, 139-144, 150-155, 157, 159, 161-163, 172, 184, 186, 197, 206-208, 211, 212, 223, 229, 239, 240, 242, 248, 250-252, 256

RED LIGHT, 110, 216

Relationship between actual time and real time, 156

Religious mode of reason, **143**

Renaissance, 24, 25, 192

Resolution of debatable issues, 153
Reticular formation, 97, 203, 206, 207
Retroprojection of self, **170**, 171-173, 176, 238
Rogerian Psychotherapy, 14, 15
Rogers, Carl, **15**
Romanticism, **52**
Rousseau, Jean Jacques, **24**, 52, 69, 140, 145, 193
Russell, Bertrand, **82**, 83, 198

Safeguards in Reality analysis, 147
Scholasticism, 13, **21**-23, 25, 26, 194, 195
Schleiden, Jocob M., 51, **195**
Schwann, Theodore A., 51, **195**
Scientific procedure, 12
Secondary issue, 158, 160, 162, 163, 250, 258, 263
Secondary values, **246**, 247
Secular mode of reason, **142**
Self-actualization, 23, **69**, 79, 89, 108, 109, 117, 141, 172, 193, 213, 222, 223, 225, 239, 240, 242
Self-realization, 69, 100, 105, 183, 230, 237, 238, 240-242
Self-service, 77, 183, **261**
Self-serving issue, 165, **253**
Seven approaches to human personality, 16, 17, 75, 76
Six essential tools, 67
Snag, 185, **254**
Snag and hang-ups, **254**
Socrates, **27**, 62, 69, 72, 191
Spinal cord reflex, 95, 158
Spontaneous behavior, 149, 155, 234
Staff, 70, 224, 225
Static model of the ego state, **106**, 107, 212
Stereoscopic view, 127, 128, 218

Structural approaches, 16, 137, 138, 220, 226
Studio quality, 173, **257**
Style of living, 158, 208, 249
Subatomic particles, 90
Subconscious, **86**, 87, 95, 97, 98, 158, 201, 202, 204, 206
Summary of intellectual progress, 140
Superego, 14, 22, 71, 85-**87**, 95, 97, 99, 100, 103, 105-108, 110-114, 116, 117, 121-124, 132, 185, 206-208, 210-213, 230, 234-236, 241, 256
Super Collider, 90, 122
Supreme Being, **11**, 12, 33, 34, 191
Syllogism, 12

Table of Reason, 135, **136**, 141, 143, 242
Targeted real values, 170, **255**
Teleology, 73, **198**
Thalamic Area, 68, 84, 85, 87, 96-98, 103, 107, 111, 125, 126, 202, 203, 227
Thalamus, **85**-87, 95-98, 102, 103, 111, 121-123, 125, 162, 175, 200, 203, 206, 207, 210, 221, 230, 232, 234
Thales, Miletus, **27**
The Snowplow, 128-132
The Trail of Reason, 17, 46, 65, 69, 71, 73, 77, 114, 203
The "unconscious" is Reality, 232, 236
Thirty Years' War, 23
This book is a central undertaking, 64, 195
Three-approach overview of the ego state, 113, 116
Three jobs to do, 19, 178, 180
Three modes of reason, 142
Tictoc time, **84**, 117, **156**, 157, 227,

248, 252
Time as a property of motion, 82
Tip the scale, 137, 220
Tools for Reality exploration, 169
Tools for the Climb, 67, 75, 196
Transactional analysis, 14, 15
Transcendence of self, 113, 114
Transcendence of values, 96, 133
Trimodal phenomenal self, **241-**
243, 245
True Christians and Concrete
Scientists, 9, 18, 19, 65, 142,
162, 164, 225, 251
True Christians are God-oriented
pragmatists, 139, 142, 225
Two-approach overview of the ego
state, 111
Two kinds of human values, 150,
246

Unconscious, **86**, 95, 98, 111, 113,
114, 123, 174, 185, 186, 198,
206, 232, 236, 240, 257
Unconscious state, **87**, 113
Unimodal phenomenal self, 240,
241
Use of the Reality construct, 136

Valid point of view, 162-167, **252**
Valid reasoning, 119, 124, 140, 141,
223, 224
Values, 50, 57, 63, 85, 87, 91, 97,
100, 116, 140, 143, 149, 157,
168, 182, 183, 195, 198, 223,
224, 232, 236, 237, **245**, 247,
248, 256, 260, 261
Human, 117, 120, 138, 142,
150, 152, 227, 235, 237,
246
New, 96
(see Actual Values, Being
Values, Nonbeing, Values,
Real Values)

Value range scale, 176
Vector of Reason, 10, 85, 136, 137,
141, 143, 144, 172, 175, 177,
180, 187, **223**, 225, **227**
Vegetative state, 138, 147, 222, 243
Vegetable, 234, 261
Viewing from the Existential
approach, 117
Viewing the actual human body, 91
Viewing the ego state through
affective Realism, 115
Viewing the real human body, 91
Virchow, Rudolf, **51**
Vives, Juan Luis, **45**, 69

Western Civilization, 12, 13, 22, 44,
50, 51, 54, 63, 64, 69, 105,
108, 119, 182, 184, 194, 240
What is the phenomenal self?, 128
What is the Table of Reason?, 135
Word of caution, 171, 242, 243
Working ego state model, 175, 258

Yeshua, 144, 227

Notes

Notes

Notes

Notes

Notes

Notes

Notes